Teach Yourself®

Essential German Grammar

Jenny Russ

For UK order enquiries: please contact Bookpoint Ltd,
130 Milton Park, Abingdon, Oxon, OX14 4SB.
Telephone: +44 (0) 1235 827720. Fax: +44 (0) 1235 400454.
Lines are open 09.00–17.00, Monday to Saturday, with a 24-hour
message answering service. Details about our titles and how to
order are available at www.teachyourself.com

For USA order enquiries: please contact McGraw-Hill Customer
Services, PO Box 545, Blacklick, OH 43004-0545, USA.
Telephone: 1-800-722-4726. Fax: 1-614-755-5645.

For Canada order enquiries: please contact McGraw-Hill
Ryerson Ltd, 300 Water St, Whitby, Ontario, L1N 9B6, Canada.
Telephone: 905 430 5000. Fax: 905 430 5020.

Long renowned as the authoritative source for self-guided
learning – with more than 50 million copies sold worldwide –
the *Teach Yourself* series includes over 500 titles in the fields of
languages, crafts, hobbies, business, computing and education.

British Library Cataloguing in Publication Data: a catalogue record
for this title is available from the British Library.

Library of Congress Catalog Card Number: on file.

First published in UK 1998 by Hodder Education, 338 Euston
Road, London, NW1 3BH, as Teach Yourself German Grammar.

First published in US 1998 by The McGraw-Hill Companies, Inc.,
as Teach Yourself German Grammar.

This edition published 2010.

The *Teach Yourself* name is a registered trade mark of
Hachette UK.

Copyright 1998, 2003, 2010 Jenny Russ

Typeset by MPS Limited, A Macmillan Company.

Printed in Great Britain for Hodder Education, a division of
Hachette UK, 338 Euston Road, London, NW1 3BH.

The publisher has used its best endeavours to ensure that the URLs
for external websites referred to in this book are correct and active
at the time of going to press. However, the publisher and the
author have no responsibility for the websites and can make no
guarantee that a site will remain live or that the content will remain
relevant, decent or appropriate.

Hachette UK's policy is to use papers that are natural, renewable
and recyclable products and made from wood grown in sustainable
forests. The logging and manufacturing processes are expected to
conform to the environmental regulations of the country of origin.

Impression number   10 9 8 7 6 5 4 3 2

Year   2014 2013 2012 2011

Meet the author

I didn't have a clue about the language when I started to learn German at school, aged 12, but was blessed with an inspiring teacher who introduced me to the grammar in bite-size pieces and soon infected me with his enthusiasm. I found I could understand each new detail and discovered how satisfying it was to learn the rules, apply them and produce accurate German.

I then studied German at university, which involved spending a semester at Kiel University on the Baltic coast. There I met a fellow student of the German language, four years later we were married and we have shared a passion for German ever since. I trained as a language teacher and spent more than 30 years teaching the German language, literature and culture at every level and to every age group. Perhaps my biggest challenge was teaching my two sons A-level German, but the older one is now a German teacher himself and is married to a German teacher! I also wrote a book on German customs and festivals and became an examiner of both written and oral German for several UK examination boards.

I still love the German language and try to listen to it daily on satellite TV and visit the country two or three times every year, armed with a notebook to record new vocabulary.

Acknowledgements
I should like to record my grateful thanks to Ginny Catmur for being such a patient and pleasant editor, always available with immediate answers to my queries. I also want to thank my two sons, Jamie and Thomas, and my daughter-in-law, Kate, for their very helpful suggestions, and Thomas for his photograph. I owe the biggest debt to my husband, Charles, for his constant support, plying me with good food and good examples in equal measure.

Finally, I dedicate this book to the memory of my late mother, who used to battle with German grammar.

Jenny Russ

Contents

indisputably belong to the past from the narrator's point of view • Turn direct into reported speech • Describe states or actions which occurred before some past event • Describe a past event or activity in writing

Only got a minute?

More than 90 million people speak German as their mother tongue and another 20 million are thought to have learned it, or to be learning it, as a second language. It is a very satisfying language to learn as it obeys its own rules, which can easily be learned and applied.

At first sight there are several similarities between English and German vocabulary, for example **die Mutter** (*the mother*), **der Vater** (*the father*), **die Hand** (*the hand*), **der Finger** (*the finger*). This is because German is a sister language to English, as well as to Dutch, the Scandinavian languages and the now defunct Gothic. All these languages descend from a common Germanic parent language, known by linguists as Proto-Germanic.

But in contrast to English, German has more variations in its grammatical forms. German has three genders (**der**, **die**, **das**), whereas English has none. (The English definite article *the* covers everything.) German also has four cases: nominative, accusative, dative, genitive. (English has only remnants of a case system in words such as *who/whom*, *he/him*, *she/her*.) All nouns start with capital letters in German, and the rules for word order are much stricter in German than in English. German also uses two signs that are unfamiliar to English speakers: the β (**Eszett**), which is pronounced as a voiceless *s* as in English *six* or *so*; and the umlaut sign (¨), which is sometimes found above the vowels **a**, **o** and **u** and changes their pronunciation.

Please don't worry: our study of German grammar will never be pure theory! It is taught in context as the key to unlocking the living language, to enable us to communicate with business partners, to make new friends and, of course, to enjoy exploring beautiful Germany, Austria and Switzerland.

5 Only got five minutes?

The German language

German is spoken not only in Germany, Austria and Switzerland but also in many far-flung areas of the world in probably 40 different countries. It is the official language in Germany, Austria and two-thirds of Switzerland, and is spoken in Liechtenstein and Luxembourg. It is also spoken by the Vatican Swiss Guard, who are responsible for the Pope's safety. There are many German-speaking communities throughout the world, for example in South Tyrol (Italy), Alsace-Lorraine (France), the eastern part of Belgium, the southern area of Denmark close to the North German border, in Russia, Southern and Central America, North America and Namibia.

The past

If you are a historian, you may well enjoy looking into how German came to be spoken in so many countries. Pennsylvania Dutch is an interesting example: in this case, *Dutch* stands for **Deutsch** and is a German dialect (most probably from Rhineland-Palatinate) which was taken across the Atlantic by settlers in the 17th century in their search for freedom to practise their religion. It can still be heard within communities such as the Amish and Mennonites in North America.

Similarly, it is thought that the existence of German-speaking communities in present-day Kazakhstan dates back to the settlement in the 18th century of German peasant farmers, who were brought over to the south of Russia by Catherine the Great, herself a German.

The present

Given how widely German is spoken, it is not surprising that there are very many variations in the way it is spoken, not only in different countries but also within Germany itself. The standard German pronunciation is based on North German usage because it is generally perceived to reflect the spelling more closely. When the standard language is spoken with a regional variation, this is known as an accent. If the regional variations also affect the grammatical structure and vocabulary, we call it a dialect, but these dialects are rarely written. Some dialects are very different from the standard language but speakers of **Schweizerdeutsch** (*Swiss German*) in Switzerland, for example, are normally able to switch into the standard language as required.

Regional colour

In the same way as there are different regional words for a bread roll in English, such as *bap*, *cob* and *stottie*, you will notice that there are some regional differences in vocabulary within Germany, chiefly between the north and south of the country. Perhaps the most important difference is that *Saturday* is known as **Sonnabend** in the north of Germany, whereas in the south it is **Samstag**. Here are some other examples you may well come across:

English	North German	South German
bread roll	das Brötchen	die Semmel
butcher	der Schlachter	der Metzger
red cabbage	der Rotkohl	das Rotkraut
chimney	der Schornstein	der Rauchfang, der Kamin
to look	gucken	schauen
to sweep	fegen	kehren

The gender of nouns can also occasionally vary regionally, for example the German for *yogurt* can be **der Joghurt** or **das Joghurt**. In fact, you might even hear **die Joghurt** in colloquial speech! And occasionally the plural can differ regionally: the singular form **der Wagen** (*the car*) becomes plural **die Wagen** (*the cars*) in the north, but the plural form **die Wägen** can be heard in the south.

There are also a few grammatical differences between the north and south, for example the verbs **sitzen** (*to sit*), **liegen** (*to lie*) and **stehen** (*to stand*) form their perfect tense with the auxiliary verb **haben** (*to have*) in the north, whereas in the south it is formed with the verb **sein** (*to be*). This difference is particularly significant in the south, where the phrase **Ich habe gesessen** suggests *I have been in prison* rather than *I have been sitting!*

The living language

Being a living language, German has regularly changed over the ages and continues to change. As we will learn in this book, the genitive case is less frequently used nowadays to express possession than it once was. The genitive is now often replaced by a preposition such as **von**, for example **Das neue Auto meines Onkels ist riesengroß** (*My uncle's new car is huge*) is now more commonly expressed as **Das neue Auto von meinem Onkel ist riesengroß**. These changes affect the grammar to a lesser extent than the vocabulary, but the impact on the latter has been enormous.

Recent historical and social influences

The vocabulary of any language is subject to change either as a result of internal developments or under foreign influences. During the 40 years when there were two German states (1949–89), it was thought that some differences would probably develop between the language of the former German Democratic Republic (GDR, East Germany) and that of the Federal Republic of Germany (FRG,

West Germany). But after unification in 1990 this proved not to be the case, largely because much of the political vocabulary of the former GDR disappeared.

Over the years, many foreign words have been assimilated into German, so much so that few would still recognize their foreign origin. No one who visits Germany today can fail to notice the huge amount of English and American words in regular use. They are found in the language of the media, advertising, fast food, computing, technology, telecommunications, commerce, sport, transport, pop culture and in **Jugendsprache** (*the language of youth*). You will have no difficulty in recognizing **chatten, downloaden, jetten, managen, mixen, relaxen, toasten** or even **Ich muss meinen Computer neu booten** and **Die Software ist gecrasht**. Such use of English words in German has met with varied responses. Some consider it to be cool or broad-minded, others regard it as lazy or a corruption of the German language. The new term **Denglisch** (from **Deutsch** and **Englisch**) is a half-humorous, half-critical blend to describe this mixture of German and English. Unlike France, Germany has never used legislation in an attempt to maintain the purity of its language.

The future starts here

I hope you can already see that when we study a language we are dealing with a living, ever-changing, dynamic means of communication, but the grammar which undergirds the language changes at a much, much slower rate than the vocabulary. The grammar provides you with the structure or framework into which you can slot all manner of vocabulary and so deal with many different situations. Once you have mastered the grammatical rules, you can start to speak and write with confidence.

So as we start to work through this book, let's move into the future together – or as many a German strapline reads: **Zusammen in die Zukunft.**

10 Only got ten minutes?

Why learn another language?

Throughout my career as a language teacher, I have always been interested in the reasons why people want to study a second or foreign language. Some schoolchildren have little choice in the matter and so do not give it very much thought. But adult learners almost always have definite reasons for making a conscious decision to get to grips with a language. So I was particularly fascinated by the reasons that adults gave for signing up to learn German at a night class after a full day at work. Some of the various reasons I was given were:

▶ they had a German-speaking partner
▶ their parents or grandparents had been native German speakers
▶ they had a German son-in-law or daughter-in-law and wanted to be able to communicate with grandchildren
▶ they loved walking in the Black Forest or Switzerland
▶ to be able to understand the text of Schubert's **Lieder** or the libretti of operas
▶ they had made German friends whom they wanted to visit
▶ to set themselves a personal challenge to keep their grey cells working
▶ to be able to read German academic papers in their particular discipline, whether it be history, maths, chemistry, theology or landscape gardening
▶ their local company had been taken over by a German firm
▶ to be able to entertain business contacts.

One night-class student elaborated on the last reason by explaining how he always took the German team out for a meal on the final evening of his visits to the company headquarters in Germany. He told me how the whole group were very happy to speak English with him during the meal, but how terribly embarrassed he always felt when he had to rely on one of them to ask for the bill in German so that he could pay it!

Many of these adult learners had started to learn the language at school but had given up before acquiring a good foundation. Some had decided that a foreign language was more difficult than other subjects and so opted for something they found easier and gave up German at the first opportunity. Later in life they came to regret this.

SO WHY DO WE MAKE SUCH A BIG DEAL OUT OF LANGUAGE LEARNING?

Have you ever realized that language is the only discipline which uses itself to explain itself? This might sound a bit abstract but let's think about it for a moment. We use language to describe the intricacies of physics, nutrition, football, anatomy or absolutely any subject we enjoy talking about. When children first start school, they are already fluent in their mother tongue and are often confident little chatterboxes. Professor David Crystal describes how young children then

> **have to learn a new range of linguistic skills – reading, writing and spelling. And they find themselves having to talk about what they are doing, which requires that they learn a special technical vocabulary – 'a language for talking about language', or metalanguage.**
>
> David Crystal The Cambridge Encyclopedia of Language
> (Cambridge: Cambridge University Press, 1987), p. 248

Remember what a rude shock it was to have to learn spellings, practise reading and writing, etc. when you first went to school. In addition to achieving basic oral proficiency, you face much the same challenge as the schoolchild when you start to learn a new language, but this book is designed to guide you through it as easily as possible. When I use the term 'grammar', I mean it in the sense of a subdivision of this special language to describe language, what David Crystal calls a 'metalanguage'. Metalanguage also refers to other specialisms such as phonology, syntax and semantics – but don't worry, we won't be dealing with these in this book, only grammar!

WHY IS GERMAN SOMETIMES PERCEIVED AS BEING DIFFICULT TO LEARN?

In my mind, the answer to this question lies both within the language itself and in the way it is taught.

Firstly, there are many more possible variations in the German language than in English and these have to be understood and learned in order to use the language effectively. And in order to understand when these variations are used, we have to use old-fashioned grammatical terms (and these are part of the metalanguage mentioned above). This is nothing to be frightened about! On the contrary, I have always found that students feel a great sense of relief when they know how to identify a particular grammatical term, for example the direct object of a sentence, and know both what it is called and how to use it. In this book, I never shy away from using the appropriate grammatical term but I do always explain both what it means and how to use it. At the back of the book you will find the Glossary, where short explanations of the most frequently used terms are to be found. You may well like to keep a bookmark in this page!

Secondly, fashions in the style of language teaching have come and gone over the course of my learning and teaching life. When I was young, for instance, accuracy of grammar was considered much more important than ability to communicate naturally in the foreign language. This led to the fear, hopefully unfounded, that it could be possible for a university student to graduate with a good degree in a foreign language and yet be unable to go into a bank in the foreign country and set up an account.

The pendulum then swung towards the other extreme with the advent of language courses which had as their goal natural communication in the foreign language, which would be understood by a sympathetic native speaker. Understanding of the grammar of the language was not considered to be vital.

The theory behind this approach was that as babies and small children we learn to speak our mother tongue by natural immersion in the language, not by analysing the language according to grammatical structures. So it was assumed that this same approach should work for learning a second, foreign language. But there are major differences between the learning experiences of babies and schoolchildren:

▶ Babies are only working with their inborn language learning ability, but schoolchildren always have their own mother tongue as their reference point.
▶ Babies hear their mother tongue all the time, but schoolchildren hear the new foreign language for only four or five hours a week.
▶ Babies are naturally inquisitive and uninhibited, but schoolchildren often start to learn a foreign language at precisely the time when they feel self-conscious about making new sounds.
▶ Babies mostly learn in a one-to-one situation with a native speaker of the language, but schoolchildren usually learn in a class of up to 30 pupils, often taught by teachers who have learned the foreign language as their second language.

One of the problems with this communicative approach was that students would learn set structures and areas of vocabulary for a given context (for example at the post office or reserving a room in a youth hostel), but they found it difficult to manipulate the language for use in other contexts because they had little or no understanding of the grammar. Unkind critics of this approach were heard to call it 'ice-cream French' or 'beer-garden German'. In the UK, a chasm developed between such teaching material for GCSE and the more grammar-based expectations of the A-level syllabus. Many regard this as one of the main reasons for the sharp drop in numbers of students at A-level and thus the reduction in numbers of foreign language students at UK universities.

An added difficulty was that, for some time, formal grammar was not taught even within the English curriculum in UK schools, so schoolchildren started to learn a foreign language with no concept of what a noun, verb or clause was. Fortunately, grammar is now being taught once again to young children in their English lessons, and modern methods of foreign language teaching require competence in the four skills of writing, reading, oral communication and listening comprehension.

SO WHAT DO WE ALREADY KNOW ABOUT GRAMMAR?

Did you know that the word 'grammar' is connected to the word 'glamour'? Or that the book in which the grammar of a language was explained was also known as 'a grammar'? Or that a 'grammar school' was originally a school in which Latin and Greek were taught? Or that most of the grammatical terms we still use (for example 'verb', 'adverb', 'case', 'object') come from Greek or Latin?

WHAT EXACTLY DO WE MEAN BY GRAMMAR?

My favourite definition of grammar is one of the simplest:

the art of the right use of language by grammatical rules.
Chambers 20th Century Dictionary (Edinburgh: Chambers, 1983), s.v. 'grammar'

It's now time to look at the idea of language in more detail and more specifically at the role of grammar within it. Language does not simply consist of a list of words, but has a number of recurring sentence patterns into which words can be slotted to give meaning to the sentences. In the most general sense, these recurring patterns form the grammar of the language. Once we've learned these patterns, we can begin to use the language with confidence in many different situations.

German is sometimes said to 'have a lot of grammar' in the sense that nouns, verbs and adjectives have many more different forms

than in English. German word order is also more restricted.
Let's look at some of these different forms with reference to
nouns and verbs.

A QUICK TASTER OF GERMAN GRAMMAR

The singular noun in German can have one of three genders. This is
shown in a dictionary by using the definite articles **der** (masculine),
die (feminine) or **das** (neuter). These three definite articles all
change to **die** when used in the plural. The singular noun itself also
normally changes to show the plural form, for example:

Singular	Plural	English meaning
der Mann	**die Männer**	*the man/the men*
die Frau	**die Frauen**	*the woman/the women*
das Kind	**die Kinder**	*the child/the children*

We can also increase the information about the noun by
adding a verb, such as *is* or *are*, and an adjective, such as *old*,
kind or *noisy*:

Singular	English meaning	Plural	English meaning
Der Mann ist alt.	*The man is old.*	**Die Männer sind alt.**	*The men are old.*
Die Frau ist lieb.	*The woman is kind.*	**Die Frauen sind lieb.**	*The women are kind.*
Das Kind ist laut.	*The child is noisy.*	**Die Kinder sind laut.**	*The children are noisy.*

You will soon discover that the adjective can also be placed before
the noun, for example *the old man, the kind woman, the noisy child*.
In Unit 15, you will learn that special endings must be added to
adjectives when they appear before the noun.

In the above examples, we used the verb forms **ist** (*is*) and **sind**
(*are*), both of which come from the verb **sein** (*to be*). This verb
is used very often and is easy to understand, but you are advised

to learn all its various forms because it is irregular and does not fit into any regular pattern: see Unit 1. You will find the forms of other irregular verbs in the verb list in Section 10.7 of the Reference grammar near the back of this book.

The verb in the above examples was preceded by a noun, but it is very often preceded by a pronoun (*I*, *you*, *he*, *she*, *it*, *we*, *they*). The important point to note is that we have only one pronoun for *you* in English, but German has three:

▶ If you are talking to a friend, a relative, a child or an animal, you use the familiar singular pronoun **du** (*you*).
▶ If you are addressing two or more friends, relatives, children or animals, you use the plural pronoun **ihr** (*you*).
▶ If you are talking to one or more people whom you do not know well, for example your doctor or a ticket collector, you use the polite pronoun **Sie** (*you*). This pronoun is used in both the singular and the plural, i.e. for one or many people whom you might be addressing.

So let's look at the full form of the present tense of a typical regular verb such as **kochen** (*to cook*). You will notice that there are three possible ways of expressing the present tense in English, whereas there is only one way in German:

ich koche	*I cook, I am cooking, I do cook*
du kochst	*you cook, you are cooking, you do cook*
er kocht	*he cooks, etc.*
sie kocht	*she cooks, etc.*
es kocht	*it cooks, etc.*
wir kochen	*we cook, etc.*
ihr kocht	*you cook, etc.*
Sie kochen	*you cook, etc.*
sie kochen	*they cook, etc.*

You will notice that the verb form changes depending on which pronoun is being used. You will learn all the details in Unit 5.

You can give more information about the verb by using an adverb, for example *well*, *slowly*: **sie kocht gut** (*she cooks well*).

The major difference between English and German is that German uses the case system to show the different functions of the nouns in a sentence. There are four cases in German: the nominative, the accusative, the dative and the genitive. You will find these fully illustrated in Units 3, 4 and 12 and further explained in Section 6 of the Reference grammar near the back of this book.

As you work through the book, you will also realize that there are stricter rules for word order in the German sentence than in English. In a normal sentence, the verb is the second 'idea', but some conjunctions (words which join phrases or clauses) such as **weil** (*because*) and **obwohl** (*although*) send the verb to the end of the clause. All will be revealed as you work through the book ...

WHAT IS SPECIAL ABOUT THE APPROACH TO GRAMMAR IN THIS BOOK?

In this book, we will be using a dual approach to our study of German, both *functional* and *grammatical* in the traditional sense. In each unit, we will look at a particular language function, for example how to talk about habitual actions, how to give directions and instructions, how to describe people, places and things, or how to report what was said and asked. Each of these functions requires the use of a particular grammatical structure, so each unit then continues with a summary of the grammar required. For example:

Function	Grammatical structure
How to talk about habitual actions	Reflexive verbs
How to give directions and instructions	The imperative mood
How to describe people, places and things	Adjectival endings
How to report what was said and asked	The subjunctive mood

The specific part of grammar which is under the spotlight in any given unit is then illustrated in a section called 'In context'. This is followed by some exercises, where you have the opportunity to practise the grammar you have just learned; you will find the answers for these exercises near the back of the book. Finally, you are given a list of ten key learning points from the unit.

While you are working through the units, you are encouraged to consult the Glossary at the back of the book to make sure that you understand what is meant by each particular grammatical term. You may find it helpful to cross-check what you are learning in the units by consulting the formal Reference grammar, which provides a fuller picture of each grammar point. You will also find some suggestions about websites and reading materials which will help you take your studies further.

Please don't be discouraged when you make mistakes. Just keep practising. Never forget that Germans occasionally make the odd 'mistake' in their own language, and remember that the pursuit of correct grammar is not an end in itself. It is always a means of achieving effective and accurate communication.

AND FINALLY ...

If I were ever asked in an interview for the weekend press 'Who would you most like to sit next to on a long-haul flight?', my answer would be Mark Twain. I would dearly love to take him to task for all the things he wrote about the German language and show him the error of his thinking! You can easily look up what he actually said, but please work through this book first! Then I hope you will agree with me that the German language is most satisfying to learn and opens up all manner of life-enhancing possibilities.

Introduction

This book is intended as a reference guide for those who, with or without the help of a teacher, wish to study the essentials of German grammar. It presupposes a modest familiarity with the language such as one might achieve by regular visits to the country or attendance at a beginners' evening class.

A particular feature of the book is the two-fold approach to the language, linking the communicative skills to the learning of grammar. The Functional grammar consists of 21 units illustrating the various uses to which the language can be put – for example giving instructions or talking about the recent past. The more traditional Reference grammar deals with grammatical structures, such as the imperative or the perfect tense. A few points not covered in the Functional grammar are to be found in the Reference grammar.

The beginner will find that all terms are explained in the Glossary at the back of the book, all structures are illustrated and all examples are translated into English. The more advanced student will be able to progress at a faster pace, either by working through any or all of the units in the Functional grammar as necessary, or by starting at any given point in the Reference grammar and cross-referencing to the relevant Functional section, whenever illustration or further practice is required.

The first page of each unit in the Functional grammar gives details of the language uses and grammatical structures covered in the unit. This means that each unit can be approached from either the functional or the structural perspective. Additionally, the provision of exercises at the end of each unit allows students to test their understanding of the material covered. The final item 'Ten things to remember' acts as an aide-memoire to consolidate learning. Coupled with a regular 15 minutes per day of learning grammar and vocabulary items, the student should quickly establish firm linguistic foundations.

How to use this book

The Glossary is at the back of the book for easy reference whenever the explanation of a term is required.

Each of the 21 units in the Functional grammar consists of the following five sections:

1 Grammar summary
2 In context
3 Taking it further
4 Practice
5 Ten things to remember

The following procedure is suggested for working through each unit: first, read through the bullet points at the beginning of the unit. You can then go on to read the brief explanation and some examples of the language you will encounter in this unit. English translations are given throughout to aid your understanding.

After you have worked through the examples and translations, you should be ready to move on to the 'Grammar summary' section. Read through this carefully, checking that you understand all the explanations and examples. See if you can work out further examples of your own, if necessary referring back to the beginning of the unit or to the Reference grammar, to check that you understand the link between the particular usage of the language and the grammatical structure.

Now you will be in a position to study the passages in 'In context', which illustrate how examples of such usage and structures are used in a realistic situation. Read through each passage, referring to the 'Grammar summary' or 'Quick vocab' as necessary. The serious student will want to keep his or her own vocabulary book, noting not only new words and their meanings but also each gender and plural. If possible, try to learn a few of these systematically each day.

When you are confident that you understand the language and can handle the structures covered, you can move on to the next section, 'Taking it further'. The aim of this section is to expand on the material covered and deal with allied areas.

Finally, there is the opportunity for you to test yourself by attempting the exercises in the 'Practice' section, followed by 'Ten things to remember' to help you in your learning.

Those students who already have some knowledge of the language may choose to start with the Reference grammar and then cross-refer to the relevant examples in the Functional grammar.

I have taken the conscious decision to simplify the description of verbs, for simplicity's sake, referring merely to regular and irregular verbs. A comprehensive verb list is to be found in Section 10.7 of the Reference grammar.

1

Asking for and giving personal information

In this unit you will learn how to
- *Say who you are*
- *State your nationality*
- *Say where you are from*
- *Say what your occupation is*
- *Give similar information about other people*
- *Ask for personal information about other people*

Language points
- *Subject pronouns*
- *Sein in the present tense*
- *Gender of nouns (nominative case)*
- *Plural of nouns*
- *Nouns and adjectives indicating nationality*
- *Ask questions (interrogative sentences)*
- *Negative sentences*

To ask for and give personal information you will need the German equivalent of words like *I*, *you*, *he*, *she*, etc. These are known as pronouns. You will also need a verb. This shows an action or state, for example *I cook*, *you buy*, *he is*, etc. In this unit we will learn the verb **sein**, which means *to be*.

SAYING WHO YOU ARE

Ich bin Hans Schmidt.   *I'm Hans Schmidt. (male)*
Ich bin Inge Schneider.   *I'm Inge Schneider. (female)*

STATING YOUR NATIONALITY

Ich bin Deutscher.   *I'm German. (male)*
Ich bin Deutsche.   *I'm German. (female)*

Insight

Every noun in German begins with a capital letter, e.g.
der Mann (*the man*), **die Frau** (*the woman*), **das Kind**
(*the child*). You will notice that the endings are different
in the two examples above, the **-er** referring to a male
German, the **-e** to a female. These are both examples of
so-called adjectival nouns. For more details see Reference
grammar 5.2.

SAYING WHAT YOUR OCCUPATION IS

Ich bin Arzt.   *I'm a doctor. (male)*
Ich bin Ärztin.   *I'm a doctor. (female)*

Insight

You will again notice the different endings in the two
examples above. Here, the endings denote the difference
between male and female professions. Sometimes we
make the same distinction in English, e.g. *the actor* (**der
Schauspieler**), *the actress* (**die Schauspielerin**), *the waiter*
(**der Kellner**), *the waitress* (**die Kellnerin**).

The sign (¨) is known as an umlaut and can occur only above
the vowels **a, o** and **u**. The addition of the umlaut alters the
pronunciation.

SAYING WHERE YOU COME FROM

Ich bin aus Berlin.	*I'm from Berlin.*
Ich bin aus Deutschland.	*I'm from Germany.*

GIVING INFORMATION ABOUT OTHER PEOPLE

Er ist Lehrer.	*He's a teacher.*
Sie ist Lehrerin.	*She's a teacher.*

Insight

In English, we say: *I am **a** doctor, He is **a** teacher.* In German, you normally say the equivalent of: *I am doctor, He is teacher.*

But if you want to describe the person in more detail using an adjective, you do use the article (*a, an, the*):

Ich bin ein alter Arzt.	*I am an old doctor.*
Sie is eine gute Lehrerin.	*She is a good teacher.*

Er ist Schweizer.	*He is Swiss.*
Sie ist aus Zürich.	*She's from Zurich.*

ASKING FOR PERSONAL INFORMATION ABOUT OTHER PEOPLE

a) in a formal or polite way, using the polite pronoun **Sie**:

Sind Sie Deutscher?	*Are you German? (male)*
Sind Sie Architekt?	*Are you an architect? (male)*

Insight

If you do not know the adult or adults to whom you are speaking, always use the polite **Sie** (*you* – singular or plural) with the plural form of the verb. This particular **Sie** is always written with a capital letter. None of the other pronouns (**ich, du, er, sie, es,** etc.) requires a capital unless at the beginning of a sentence.

b) familiarly, using the pronoun **du**:

Bist du Österreicherin?	*Are you Austrian? (female)*
Bist du aus Wien?	*Are you from Vienna?*

Insight

The pronoun **du** (*you*) is used when addressing one person you know well, a child or an animal. Never use **du** when addressing your doctor, a lawyer, a shop assistant, etc. The Germans tend to be more formal when talking to colleagues and professionals, so to be on the safe side, always use **Sie** in these situations until you are invited to use **du**.

Apparently, some people in Germany have even been fined for addressing the police as **du**! In church services, however, God is always addressed as **du**.

Grammar summary

SUBJECT PRONOUNS

To say *I*, *you*, *he*, *she*, etc. in German (as you would for the subject of the verb, i.e. the person or thing performing the action of the verb: *I* speak, *you* learn, *she* likes), we use the following set of words:

Singular		Plural	
ich	*I*	**wir**	*we*
du	*you* (familiar)	**ihr**	*you* (familiar)
Sie	*you* (polite)	**Sie**	*you* (polite)
er	*he*	**sie**	*they*
sie	*she*		
es	*it*		

FAMILIAR AND POLITE FORMS OF ADDRESS

▶ As we noticed above, German uses familiar and polite forms of address. In general, the familiar forms (**du** and **ihr**) are used when addressing a child or children, members of one's family, a close friend (or friends), an animal (or animals) or God (in prayer and worship).

▶ You will remember that the polite form **Sie** is used when addressing one or more person(s) whom you do not know or do not know well. In other words, the same form is used for both the singular and the plural polite form. The polite **Sie** is the only subject pronoun which is always written with a capital letter.

SEIN (TO BE) IN THE PRESENT TENSE

The verb **sein** is frequently used in German when giving personal information such as nationality or your occupation, and often for your place of origin and name. Here is the full form of **sein** in the present tense together with the appropriate subject pronouns:

Singular		Plural	
ich bin	*I am*	**wir sind**	*we are*
du bist	*you are* (familiar)	**ihr seid**	*you are* (familiar)
Sie sind	*you are* (polite)	**Sie sind**	*you are* (polite sing. or plural)
er ist	*he is*	**sie sind**	*they are*
sie ist	*she is*		
es ist	*it is*		

> **Insight**
> It is worth learning the whole of this verb **sein**. Later on, you will find that it is also used to form parts of the past tense.

Do not confuse the infinitive of the verb **sein** with the possessive adjective **sein**, which means *his* or *its*:

Sein Haus ist in Köln.   *His house is in Cologne.*

GENDER OF NOUNS

(Reference grammar 2.1)

A noun is a word for a person, a thing, a place, or even an idea. Apart from personal names, such as *Wilhelm* or *Berlin*, it can be preceded by either *the* or *a/an*, for example *the* dog, *the* post office, *a* carrot, *an* egg. For full details of nouns, see Reference grammar 2.

Insight

You will soon discover that a noun can also be preceded by the following:

▶ **kein/keine** *(not a)*
  Da ist kein Parkplatz.   *That is not a car park.*

▶ **mein/meine** *(my)*, **dein/deine** *(your)*, **sein/seine** *(his/its)*
  Dein Auto ist toll.   *Your car is super.*

▶ **dieser/diese/dieses** *(this)*, **jener/jene/jenes** *(that)*
  Dieser Lastkraftwagen   *This lorry is from Bulgaria.*
  kommt aus Bulgarien.

▶ **welcher?/welche?/welches?** *(which?)*
  Welches Buch suchen Sie?   *Which book are you looking for?*

All nouns in German begin with a capital letter and are masculine, feminine or neuter. Their gender is shown by the use of the definite article: **der** for masculine, **die** for feminine, or **das** for neuter, preceding the noun; but in dictionaries or coursebooks, gender is sometimes shown by *m.*, *f.* or *nt.* This form is known as the nominative case and is used after the verb **sein** and for the subject of the sentence.

Insight

Do try to learn the gender with each new word. In some contexts, the **der**, **die** or **das** which you find in the dictionary will change and it is very important to know what the original gender is.

Occasionally the same word can have a totally different meaning, depending on its gender:

der Gehalt	*the content*	**das Gehalt**	*the salary*
der See	*the lake*	**die See**	*the sea*
das Steuer	*the steering wheel*	**die Steuer**	*the tax*
der Tor	*the fool*	**das Tor**	*the goal/gate*

Der, **die** and **das** are translated as *the* in English. If you wish to say *a/an* instead of *the*, then the indefinite article **ein** (for both masculine and neuter) and **eine** (for feminine) is used. As in English, the indefinite article is not needed when stating one's nationality; but unlike English, it is also not required when stating one's profession.

Gender of nouns indicating nationality and profession

Nouns which refer to people, such as those indicating nationality, profession or occupation, often show the masculine or feminine form in the noun itself, for example by adding a feminine ending such as **-in**:

Er ist Engländer.	*He is English.*
Sie ist Engländerin.	*She is English.*
Er ist Kellner.	*He is a waiter.*
Sie ist Kellnerin.	*She is a waitress.*

For the sake of political correctness and brevity, the following form with an internal capital letter I is sometimes found in some areas of journalism: **LehrerIn**, **SchülerIn**. This form stands for **der Lehrer** and **die Lehrerin**, **der Schüler** and **die Schülerin**. It is not recognized as an official spelling.

In nouns of nationality where the masculine form ends in **-e**, the final **-e** is replaced by **-in** in the feminine form:

Jens ist Däne.	*Jens ist Danish. (male)*
Jytte ist Dänin.	*Jytte is Danish. (female)*
Jozef ist Pole.	*Jozef is Polish. (male)*
Franya ist Polin.	*Franya is Polish. (female)*

NB There are a few exceptions to the above, for example the German words **Arzt** (*doctor*), **Franzose** (*Frenchman*) and **Koch** (*cook*). In these cases not only is **-in** added, but the vowel preceding the ending is changed by adding the umlaut sign (¨), e.g. **a → ä, o → ö, u → ü**, as in **Ärztin, Französin, Köchin**. An umlaut can be put on the letters **a, o** or **u** (**ä, ö, ü**), and this alters the pronunciation (Reference grammar 1.2).

Er ist Koch.	*He is a cook.*
Sie ist Köchin.	*She is a cook.*

PLURAL OF NOUNS

(Reference grammar 2.3)

As in English, most nouns in German can have singular and plural forms. In English, most nouns form their plural by adding *-s* or *-es*, but there are a few exceptions such as *ox → oxen, mouse → mice*, etc.

Unfortunately, the formation of the plural in German is not so simple as in English, and it is always worth checking in a dictionary, where the plural is given in brackets after the noun, e.g. (**-e**), (**-**), (**-n** or **-nen**), (¨), (¨**-er**), or (¨**-e**). The dash in these brackets represents the singular stem of the noun and the additional information is the plural ending; (¨) indicates an added umlaut. The plural (¨**-er**) is chiefly used with neuter nouns, but **der Mann** (*man*) has the plural **Männer**.

der Ingenieur (-e)

Hans ist Ingenieur.	*Hans is an engineer.*
Hans und Otto sind Ingenieure.	*Hans and Otto are engineers.*

NB In a mixed group of people the masculine form is used.

der Mechaniker (-)

Klaus ist Mechaniker.	*Klaus is a mechanic.*
Klaus und Ilse sind Mechaniker.	*Klaus and Ilse are mechanics.*

die Krankenschwester (-n)

Inge ist Krankenschwester.	*Inge is a nurse.*
Inge und Beate sind Krankenschwestern.	*Inge and Beate are nurses.*

die Studentin (-nen)

Karin ist Studentin in München.	*Karin is a student in Munich.*
Karin und Dagmar sind Studentinnen in München.	*Karin and Dagmar are students in Munich.*

der Vater (̈-)

Johann ist Vater.	*Johann is a father.*
Johann und Reinhard sind Väter.	*Johann and Reinhard are fathers.*

(The ä is pronounced almost like *ay* in English *say*.)

der Arzt (̈-e)

Helmut ist Arzt.	*Helmut is a doctor.*
Helmut und Norbert sind Ärzte.	*Helmut and Norbert are doctors.*

A few words denoting nationality or a profession form their plurals in German by adding -s, e.g. **der Israeli(s), der Pakistani(s)**:

David ist Israeli.	*David is an Israeli.*
David und Menachem sind Israelis.	*David and Menachem are Israelis.*

Akram und Mumtaz sind Pakistanis.	*Akram and Mumtaz are Pakistanis.*

> **Insight**
>
> Curiously, there are several nouns which are found only in the singular form in German but which are used in the plural in English, e.g. **die Brille** (*the reading glasses*, *spectacles*), **die Hose** (*the trousers*), **die Schere** (*the scissors*).

ASKING QUESTIONS (INTERROGATIVE SENTENCES)

It is possible to form questions in German in several ways:

▶ Reversing the order subject–verb (i.e. by starting the sentence with the verb):

Sind Sie Amerikaner?	*Are you American?*
Bist du Schotte?	*Are you Scottish?*

This form is normally answered with **ja** (*yes*) or **nein** (*no*).

▶ Using a special question word, known as an interrogative. Most of the German question words (interrogatives) begin with **w**, the most common being:

wie?	*how?*
Wie ist das Klima in Ägypten?	*What is the climate like in Egypt?*
wo?	*where?*
Wo ist Namibia, bitte?	*Where is Namibia, please?*
was?	*what?*
Was ist die Hauptstadt von Bulgarien?	*What is the capital of Bulgaria?*
wann?	*when?*
Wann ist der Nationaltag in der Schweiz?	*When is Switzerland's National Day? (literally 'When is the National Day in Switzerland?')*
warum?	*why?*
Warum sind Sie in Ulm?	*Why are you in Ulm?*

▶ In informal speech, one can form a question simply by making a statement followed by a phrase or word such as **nicht wahr?** (literally *not true?*) or **oder?** (literally *'or?'*), or, in Southern Germany and Switzerland, **gell** or **gelt?** (*right?*) and making one's voice rise at the end of the sentence. The words **oder?** and **gelt?** are colloquial, and **gell/gelt** is not usually written. In English, these are rendered by the so-called tag questions where the pronoun of the sentence is repeated in a question:

Sie sind Schwede, *nicht wahr?*	*You're Swedish, aren't you?*
Sie ist katholisch, *oder?*	*She's Catholic, isn't she?*
Ihr seid evangelisch, *gell?*	*You're Protestant, aren't you?*

Insight

The expression **gell?** (or **gelt?**) is a regional tag question which is translated as *isn't it?, aren't you?* etc. It comes from the verb **gelten** (*to be valid, to be in force*). **Gell** literally means something like *Let it be* or (colloquial English) *Right?*, as in **Na, du machst jetzt dein eigenes Bett, gell?** (*Now, you'll make your own bed, right?*).

NEGATIVE SENTENCES

If you want to negate the verb in a sentence, you use the word **nicht** (*not*):

Ich bin nicht aus Russland.	*I am not from Russia.*
Er ist nicht Amerikaner.	*He is not American.*

If you want to negate the noun, i.e. say *not a/no* in a sentence, you use **kein** or one of its forms:

Er ist kein Deutscher.	*He is not a German.*
Sie ist keine Mutter.	*She is not a mother.*
Es ist kein Geschenk.	*It's not a present.*

In context

Study these conversations between people who have just met and are getting to know each other. The first exchange is formal, using the polite pronoun **Sie**, and the second is informal, using **du**.

A) Professor	Sind Sie Spanierin?	
Professorin	Ja, ich bin Spanierin, und Sie?	
Professor	Ich bin Türke. Ich bin aus Ankara.	
Professorin	Ich bin aus Madrid.	

Spanierin *Spaniard (female)*
Türke *Turk (male)*

Insight

You will notice the symbol **ß** below. It is known as **Eszett** (because in old German it was written **sz**) or as 'sharps'. It is pronounced like the **s** in English words such as *sun* and *song*. It only occurs after long vowels and diphthongs. (A diphthong is when two vowels come together, as in the English words *house*, *rain*, etc.).

B) Schüler	Grüß dich! Wie heißt du?	
Schülerin	Ich heiße Heidi, und du?	
Schüler	Ich heiße Karl Schmidt. Kommst du aus Köln?	
Schülerin	Nein, ich komme nicht aus Köln. Ich komme aus Bonn.	

der Schüler *schoolboy*
Grüß dich! *(chiefly South German) Hello!*
die Schülerin *schoolgirl*
ich heiße *I am called*
Kommst du ...? *Do you come ...?*
aus Köln *from Cologne*

Look at this piece of writing which gives personal information:

Ich heiße Andreas Bauer. Ich bin Deutscher. Ich komme aus Kiel und ich bin Medizinstudent.

Taking it further

ASKING SOMEONE'S NAME IN A FORMAL WAY

Wie heißen Sie? *What is your name?* (literally 'How are you called?')

Ich heiße Inge. *I am (called) Inge.*

SAYING WHAT YOUR OCCUPATION IS

When giving your occupation or profession, German does not use the equivalent of the English word *a*, as in *I'm a student*:

Ich bin Student. *I am a student.*
Er ist Dirigent. *He is a conductor (of an orchestra).*

The exception to this is when you want to use an adjective before the noun:

Ich bin *ein armer* **Student.** *I am a poor student.*
Er ist *ein berühmter* **Dirigent.** *He is a famous conductor.*

SAYING WHERE YOU COME FROM

You can use either the appropriate form of the verb **sein** (*to be*) or **kommen** (*to come*):

Ich *bin* **aus Indien.** *I come from India.*
Woher *kommst* **du?** *Where do you come from?*
Er *ist* **aus Japan.** *He comes from Japan.*
Woher *kommen* **Sie?** *Where do you come from?*

TRANSLATING 'WHERE' INTO GERMAN

In the old days, the words *whither* and *whence* were common in English to express the idea of *Where are you going to?* and *Where have you come from?* Nowadays, they are considered old-fashioned and we tend to use the word *where* (sometimes with a preposition) to convey both of these ideas, as well as the static idea of where something is to be found.

In German, the following distinctions are made:

wo? (*where?*) is used to express the static idea, as in:

Wo wohnen Sie?	*Where do you live?*
Wo ist Ihr Auto?	*Where is your car?*

woher? (*where ... from? whence?*)

Woher kommst du?	*Where do you come from?*

wohin? (*where ... to? whither?*)

Wohin fahren sie?	*Where are they going to?*

Insight

Sometimes, in colloquial language, you will find **wohin** and **woher** written or spoken separately:

Wo kommst du her?	*Where do you come from?*
Wo fahren sie hin?	*Where are they travelling to?*

INFORMATION ABOUT STATUS, RELIGION OR POLITICAL AFFILIATION

Ich bin der Chef hier!	*I'm the boss here!*
Er ist Oberleutnant.	*He is a first lieutenant.*
Sind Sie evangelisch?	*Are you Protestant?*
Ist sie Feministin?	*Is she a feminist?*

INFORMATION ABOUT MARITAL STATUS

Sind Sie verheiratet oder ledig?   *Are you married or single?*
Ich bin geschieden.   *I am divorced.*

Practice

EXERCISE A

Read through the questions and answers below and link the most appropriate answer to each question:

Fragen (*questions*)

1 Ist er aus Zürich?
2 Bist du Studentin?
3 Ist Marie Polin?
4 Sind Sie katholisch?
5 Wie heißen Sie?
6 Woher kommen Sie?
7 Bist du verheiratet?
8 Seid ihr aus Dänemark?
9 Ist Fritz Student in Halle?
10 Sie sind kein Deutscher, oder?

Antworten (*answers*)

A Ich komme aus Indien.
B Nein, ich bin evangelisch.
C Nein, ich bin Österreicher.
D Nein, er ist aus Basel.
E Ja, wir sind Dänen.
F Ich heiße Otto Braun.
G Nein, ich bin Lehrerin.
H Nein, er ist Student in Erfurt.
I Nein, ich bin geschieden.
J Nein, sie ist Französin.

EXERCISE B

Fill in gaps 1–5 using one each of the following words:

> • wohin? *where (to)?* • wo? *where?* • woher? *where from?*
> • wie? *how?* • warum? *why?*

1 __ wohnen Sie?
2 __ ist das Klima in Südafrika?
3 __ kommst du?
4 __ fahren Sie?
5 __ sind Sie in Ulm?

Ten things to remember

1 Every noun in German starts with a capital letter.

2 There are three genders for singular nouns in German: **der, die** and **das**.

3 Sometimes the ending of the noun varies, to show the gender of the nationality or profession referred to.

4 The plural of nouns is formed in several different ways. Be sure to check each plural form, preferably in a dictionary, before you use it.

5 Some nouns which are singular in German are plural in English.

6 The formal pronoun **Sie** (*you*) is used to address one or more persons whom you do not know well.

7 The familiar pronoun **du** (*you*) is used only for friends, children and animals.

8 The English word *where* can be translated in three different ways in German: **wo, wohin** and **woher**.

9 The symbol ß is pronounced as **ss**.

10 The sign (¨) is known as an Umlaut and can occur only above the vowels **a, o** and **u**. The addition of the umlaut alters the pronunciation.

2

Introducing and identifying people, places and things

In this unit you will learn how to
- *Introduce yourself and other people*
- *Greet people when being introduced*
- *Say goodbye*
- *Identify people, places and things*
- *Ask questions in order to identify people, places and things*
- *Talk on the telephone*
- *Write letters*
- *Pass on greetings*

Language points
- *The verb* wissen
- *The verb* kennen
- *The demonstratives* dieser *and* jener
- *The interrogative* welcher

INTRODUCING YOURSELF

Insight

In Germany, business relationships are generally more formal than in English-speaking countries. When being introduced, expect to be greeted with a handshake. When introducing yourself, give your name as you shake hands. Titles and surnames are very frequently used when addressing others:

Guten Morgen, Herr Doktor Schmidt.	*Good morning, Dr Schmidt.*
Grüß Gott, Frau Professor Wiesinger.	*Hello, Professor Wiesinger.*

In Unit 1, we learned that one can introduce oneself simply by saying:

Ich heiße Eva Rohweder.	*I am called Eva Rohweder.*

There are many other ways of introducing yourself, for example:

Darf ich mich vorstellen?	*May I introduce myself?*
Mein Name ist Eva Rohweder.	*My name is Eva Rohweder.*
Mein Vorname ist Eva.	*My first name is Eva.*
Mein Nachname ist Rohweder.	*My surname is Rohweder.*
Ich bin die Sekretärin von Dr. Müller.	*I am Dr Müller's secretary.*
Ich bin Christiane Frenz, geb. (geborene) Pflegge.	*I am Christiane Frenz, née Pflegge.*

Less formal ways of introducing yourself:

Ich bin (der) Henning.	*I'm Henning.*
Ich bin (die) Beate.	*I'm Beate.*

Insight

In colloquial speech, the definite article can be used with names, but it should never be written:

Der Klaus ist schon da.	*Klaus is already here.*

Ich bin die Freundin von Arno.	*I'm Arno's girlfriend. (literally 'I'm the girlfriend of Arno.')*

INTRODUCING OTHER PEOPLE

Das (hier) ist mein Mann.	*This is my husband.*
Das ist meine Frau.	*This is my wife.*
Das sind meine Kinder.	*These are my children.*
Kennen Sie schon Frau Lieske?	*Do you already know Mrs Lieske?*

Kennen Sie sich schon?	*Do you already know each other?*
Ich möchte Ihnen Fräulein König vorstellen.	*I should like to introduce Miss König (to you).*
Darf ich (Ihnen) meinen Mann vorstellen?	*May I introduce my husband (to you)?*

GREETING PEOPLE WHEN BEING INTRODUCED

Guten Morgen, Herr Tobias!	*Good morning, Mr Tobias!*
Guten Tag, Frau Honig!	*Hello, Mrs Honig!*
Grüß dich, Klaus!	*Hi, Klaus! Hello there, Klaus!*
Guten Abend!	*Good evening!*

REGIONAL VARIATIONS

Grüß Gott! is used widely in southern Germany and Austria as a
greeting at any time of the day, or simply as *Hello!*

Grüezi! (singular) or **Grüezi mitenand!** (plural) is used in
Switzerland as a greeting at any time of the day, or as an informal
Hello! or *Hi!* This is not found in writing.

Servus! is used in Austria and southern Germany for both *Hello!*
and *Goodbye!*

Moin! Moin! is the North German equivalent of **Morgen!** and is
heard throughout the day in parts of northern Germany.

Guten Appetit! Bon appetit! are said at the beginning of a meal.

Mahlzeit! (meal) is an informal greeting used around mealtimes, meaning *Enjoy your meal!*

Guten Morgen allerseits! *Good morning to you all!* (literally 'on all sides')

Insight

When entering a hotel dining room, a doctor's surgery, etc. in Germany, it is customary to issue a general greeting to everyone present. Similarly, a farewell is also offered to everyone, sometimes followed by **Einen schönen Tag!** (*Have a good day!*) or **Einen schönen Sonntag!** (*Have a good Sunday!*).

FORMAL FAREWELLS

Auf Wiedersehen!	*Goodbye!* (Looking forward to seeing you again!)
Auf Wiederschauen!	*Goodbye!* (used in southern Germany and Austria)
Gute Nacht!	*Goodnight!* (used only late at night)
Auf Wiederhören!	*Goodbye!* (Looking forward to hearing you again! – when speaking on the telephone)

SAYING GOODBYE

There are many ways of saying goodbye to friends:

Tschüss!	*Bye! Cheerio!* (colloquial)
Tschau! Ciao!	*Bye! Cheerio!*
Ade! (*stressed on the* e)	*Farewell!* (in the south-west of Germany)
Servus!	*Hello!* or *Goodbye!* (particularly in southern Germany and Austria)

The following phrases use the preposition **bis** (*until*):

Bis bald!	*See you soon!*
Bis morgen!	*See you tomorrow!*
Bis Donnerstag!	*See you on Thursday!*

QUESTIONS TO IDENTIFY PEOPLE, PLACES AND THINGS

(Wie ist Ihr) Vorname?	*What is your first name?*
Wie ist Ihr Nachname?	*What is your surname?*
Wie ist Ihr Mädchenname?	*What is your maiden name?*

Insight

You might be surprised to discover that the gender of the German word for *girl* is neuter: **das Mädchen**. This is because it is actually the diminutive form of the old-fashioned word **die Magd** (*the maid*). The addition of the diminutive suffix **-chen** makes the noun neuter.

Similarly, **das Häuschen** (*the cottage*) is the diminutive form of **das Haus** (*the house*), and **das Brötchen** (*the bread roll*) is the diminutive form of **das Brot** (*the bread*).

A second, less frequently used diminutive suffix is **-lein**, which you come across in **das Fräulein** (*the young lady, Miss*), which comes from **die Frau** (*the woman*).

Wie heißen Sie mit Vornamen und Nachnamen?	*What is your first name and surname?*
Sind Sie Frau Müller? Ja, das bin ich.	*Are you Frau Müller? Yes, I am.*
Wer ist der Herr da?	*Who is the gentleman there?*
Wie heißt er? Ich weiß nicht.	*What's he called? I don't know.*
Welcher Herr ist der Chirurg? Der Herr da.	*Which gentleman is the surgeon? The gentleman there.*
Welche Dame kommt aus Finnland? Die Dame dort drüben.	*Which lady comes from Finland? The lady over there.*

QUESTIONS AND ANSWERS TO IDENTIFY PLACES

Was ist der nächste Halt, bitte? Odeonsplatz.	*What is the next stop, please? Odeon Square.*

Was ist die Hauptstadt von Ägypten? Kairo.	*What is the capital of Egypt? Cairo.*
Was ist unser Ziel heute? Königswinter am Rhein.	*What is our destination today? Königswinter on the Rhine.*

IDENTIFYING THINGS, USING **WELCHER?** (WHICH?)

Welches Buch ist sein neuestes? Das da.	*Which book is his latest? That one there.*
Welche Gruppen spielen heute Abend? Die eine aus Berlin und die andere aus Cottbus.	*Which (music) groups are playing this evening? (The) one from Berlin and (the) one from Cottbus.*
Welches Hemd ist reduziert? Das rote.	*Which shirt is reduced? The red one.*

IDENTIFYING THINGS USING **WAS?**

Was ist der Grund für diesen Streik? Zu wenig Lohn.	*What is the reason for this strike? Too little pay.*
Was ist das? Das ist eine Art Obst aus Südafrika.	*What is that? That's a (sort of) fruit from South Africa.*
Was ist das Problem? Der Motor ist defekt.	*What is the problem? The engine is broken.*

THE USE OF **DIESER** (THIS) TO IDENTIFY THINGS

Dieser Kaffee aus Kenia ist sehr stark.	*This coffee from Kenya is very strong.*
Diese Farbe ist viel zu grell.	*This colour is much too garish.*
Dieses Buch ist wirklich spannend.	*This book is really exciting.*
Diese Filme sind nicht für Kinder.	*These films are not for children.*

Grammar summary

*THE VERBS **WISSEN** AND **KENNEN** (TO KNOW)*

> ## Insight
> There are two German verbs which can be translated as
> *to know*: **wissen** and **kennen**.

▶ **Wissen** means 'to know intellectually, conceptually or
factually', possibly denoting knowledge gained by studying
or learning:

Ich weiß die Lösung des Rätsels. *I know the solution to the puzzle.*

▶ **Kennen** means 'to be acquainted with', 'to know a person or
place':

Ich kenne deinen Vater.	*I know your father.*
Er kennt München gut.	*He knows Munich well.*

Wissen has the following forms in the present tense:

Singular		Plural	
ich weiß	*I know, I do know*	**wir wissen**	*we know*
du weißt	*you know*	**ihr wisst**	*you know*
Sie wissen	*you know* (polite)	**Sie wissen**	*you know* (polite)
er weiß	*he knows*	**sie wissen**	*they know*
sie weiß	*she knows*		
es weiß	*it knows*		

Examples:

Wissen Sie, wie er heißt?	*Do you know what he is called?*
Ich weiß nicht.	*I don't know.*
Weißt du schon das Neueste?	*Do you know the latest?*

Kennen is an example of a regular verb, and the full form in the present tense is as follows:

Singular		Plural	
ich kenne	I know, I do know, I am acquainted with	**wir kennen**	we know
du kennst	you know	**ihr kennt**	you know
Sie kennen	you know (polite)	**Sie kennen**	you know (polite)
er kennt	he knows	**sie kennen**	they know
sie kennt	she knows		
es kennt	it knows		

Examples:

Kennen Sie einander?	*Do you know each other?*
Ja, wir kennen uns gut.	*We know each other well.*

Insight

▸ The noun from the verb **wissen** is **das Wissen,** meaning knowledge in the general sense of 'the sum of knowledge'. **Die Wissenschaft** means *science*, and **die Sprachwissenschaft** means *linguistics*.

▸ The noun from the verb **kennen** is **die Kenntnis,** meaning knowledge in the sense of 'personal (humanly limited) knowledge', often of a particular field, e.g. **Seine Sprachkenntnisse sind gut** (His knowledge of the language is good).

*THE DEMONSTRATIVE **DIESER** (THIS) AND THE INTERROGATIVE **WELCHER?** (WHICH?)*

You will notice that the demonstrative **dieser** and the interrogative **welcher?** end almost in the same way as the definite article **der.**

Look at the following chart, which compares the three words in the nominative case:

Masculine	Feminine	Neuter	Plural
the:			
der	**die**	**das**	**die**
this/these:			
dieser	**diese**	**dieses**	**diese**
which?:			
welcher?	**welche?**	**welches?**	**welche?**

Jener (*that*) has the same endings as **dieser,** and tends to be used in more literary contexts.

In context

Study the following brief encounters. The first exchange is formal, the second is familiar.

A) Herr Fuchs	Guten Tag, Pastor Fischer! Darf ich Ihnen meine Frau vorstellen? Sie ist Sprachtherapeutin.
Pastor Fischer	Guten Tag, Frau Fuchs. Es freut mich, Sie kennen zu lernen. Meine Frau ist auch Sprachtherapeutin!
Frau Fuchs	Guten Tag, Pastor Fischer. Ich freue mich auch. Wie geht es Ihnen?
Pastor Fischer	Sehr gut, danke. Und Ihnen?
Frau Fuchs	Auch gut, danke. Wo ist Ihre Frau?
Pastor Fischer	Das ist die Dame in Schwarz da drüben.
Frau Fuchs	Ach, wie schön! Und wer ist die Dame neben ihr?
Pastor Fischer	Ich weiß nicht. Ich kenne sie nicht.

Insight

Did you notice the word **schön** in the conversation above? It is an adjective which means *nice, pleasant, beautiful* or *handsome*. Be careful not to confuse it with the adverb of time **schon,** which means *already*.

B) Christel	Grüß dich, Willi!
Willi	Grüß dich, Christel! Wie geht's dir?
Christel	Furchtbar. Ich bin müde. Und dir?
Willi	Mir geht's prima, danke! Hier ist meine Freundin, Anita.
Christel	Ach, grüß Gott, Anita. Bis bald!

Taking it further

BEGINNING AND ENDING A LETTER

Look at the following examples of the formulae used to start and finish formal letters:

Sehr geehrte Damen und Herren   *Dear Sir or Madam*

NB In German the plural form is used, the equivalent of
'*Very honoured Ladies and Gentlemen*'.

Sehr geehrter Herr Debus   *Dear Mr Debus*
Sehr geehrte Frau Wagner   *Dear Mrs (or Ms) Wagner*

NB Fräulein is used only to address the young.

Mit freundlichen Grüßen   *Yours sincerely, Yours faithfully*
Mit bestem Gruß   *With best wishes*

NB You may find that in more formal situations the form
Hochachtungsvoll is used for *Yours faithfully* but this tends to be
used less frequently nowadays.

Formulae to start informal letters:

Lieber Hanno   *Dear Hanno*
Liebe Karin   *Dear Karin*
Liebe Familie Lange   *Dear Lange family*
Ihr Lieben!   *Dear all* (literally '*You dears*')

Finishing an informal letter:

Mit herzlichen Grüßen   *With best wishes*
Viele liebe Grüße   *Many good wishes*
Alles Gute   *All the best*

Practice

EXERCISE A

Look at the following snippets and link up one from each column
to form a greeting.

1 Grüß	**A** Wiederhören
2 Guten	**B** grüßen
3 Darf ich meine Sekretärin	**C** Willkommen
4 Auf	**D** mitenand
5 Einen schönen Gruß	**E** vorstellen
6 Ich soll von Mutti	**F** Tag, Herr Müller
7 Es freut mich,	**G** bald
8 Herzlich	**H** an Ihre Frau
9 Bis	**I** dich, Inge
10 Grüezi	**J** Sie kennen zu lernen

EXERCISE B

Insert the appropriate verb form from the box below into each of gaps 1–10:

> • bist • kenne • sind • heißt • bin • ist • heiße
> • kommen • kennen • wissen

1 Ich __ die Frau von Karl.
2 Mein Vorname __ Hans.
3 Ich __ Dr. Schleiffenbaum gut.
4 __ du Studentin, Christel?
5 __ Sie, wie er heißt?
6 __ Sie einander?
7 Wir __ aus Wien.
8 Wie __ du?
9 Ich __ Max Schulz.
10 Dorothea und Waltraud __ Krankenschwestern.

EXERCISE C

Using the chart on **dieser** (*this*) and **welcher?** (*which?*) in this unit's Grammar summary, supply the correct form **Welcher?/Welche?/Welches** or **Dieser/Diese/Dieses** for each of the following gaps:

1 __ Zahn tut weh? (der Zahn   Which tooth hurts?
 the tooth)
 __ Zahn tut weh.   This tooth hurts.

2 __ Auto ist reduziert? (das Auto   Which car is reduced?
   the car)
   __ Auto ist reduziert.
3 __ Dame ist Doktor Brauns   Which lady is Dr Brown's
   Sekretärin? (die Dame *the lady*)   secretary?
   __ Dame ist Doktor Brauns
   Sekretärin.
4 __ Maschine ist defekt?   Which machine is broken?
   (die Maschine *the machine*)
   __ Maschine ist defekt.
5 __ Student kommt aus Japan?   Which student comes from
   (der Student *the student*)   Japan?
   __ Student kommt aus Japan.

Ten things to remember

1 In Germany, business relationships are generally formal and use the polite form **Sie** (*you*) and titles.

2 The form of address **Frau** (*Mrs*) is widely used, irrespective of whether the person is married or not.

3 It is normal to issue a general greeting on entering a hotel dining room, doctor's surgery, etc.

4 **Auf Wiederhören** is used to say *goodbye* on the telephone.

5 **Welcher?, welche?** and **welches?** (*which?*) are interrogatives (used in questions) and change their form in the same way as the definite article (**der, die, das**).

6 **Dieser, diese** and **dieses** (*this/these*) are demonstratives and change their form in the same way as the definite article.

7 The irregular verb **wissen** means 'to know intellectually, conceptually or factually'. The first person singular is **ich weiß** (*I know*).

8 **Die Wissenschaft** means *science*; **die Sprachwissenschaft** means *linguistics*.

9 The regular verb **kennen** means '*to be acquainted with*', '*to know*'.

10 **Die Kenntnis** means 'personal knowledge', often of a particular field, e.g. **meine Sprachkenntnisse** (*my knowledge of the language*).

3

Expressing existence and availability

In this unit you will learn how to
- *Ask if something exists or is available*
- *State that something exists or is available*
- *Ask and answer questions regarding quantity*

Language points
- **Sein**
- **Existieren**
- **Es gibt**
- **Bestehen**
- **Haben**
- *Indefinite articles in the accusative case*
- *More words used to ask a question (interrogatives)*
- **Wer?**
- **Wie viel?**
- **Wie viele?**
- **Was?**
- **Wo?**
- *Compound nouns*

Insight

You will remember from Unit 1 that you can form a question in several ways. Immediately below are some examples of questions which are formed by starting the sentence with the verb.

To ask if something exists, you either use the appropriate question form of the verb **sein** (see Unit 1).

Ist hier eine Steckdose?	*Is there an electric socket here?*
Ist hier ein Hotel?	*Is there a hotel here?*

or use **gibt es?**, the German equivalent of the English expression *is there?* or *are there?* **Es gibt** can be used for both the singular and plural forms.

Gibt es ein Hotel in Ohlsdorf?	*Is there a hotel in Ohlsdorf?*
Gibt es Restaurants in der Nähe?	*Are there (any) restaurants nearby?*
Es gibt einen gotischen Dom in Köln, oder?	*There's a Gothic cathedral in Cologne, isn't there?*

··

Insight

Es gibt, or the question form **gibt es?**, is a very useful phrase in German, similar to the French phrase '*il y a*'.

You will notice in the last example above that the article **ein** changes to **einen** after **es gibt** whenever you are using a masculine noun, e.g.

Gibt es einen Gott?	*Does God exist? (literally 'Is there a God?')*
Gibt es einen guten Arzt in Einfeld?	*Is there a good doctor in Einfeld?*
Es gibt einen guten Kinderarzt und einen Augenarzt aber keinen Hausarzt.	*There's a good paediatrician and an eye specialist but not a family doctor.*

Contrast these with the following example, which uses a feminine noun, **die Toilette**:

Gibt es eine Toilette hier in der Nähe?	*Is there a toilet near here?*

(Contd)

> Or with the old pop song, which uses a neuter noun, **das Bier**:
>
> **Es gibt kein Bier auf Hawaii.**   *There's no beer in Hawaii.*
>
> For fuller details, see this unit's Grammar summary.

Es gibt keine Hotels in Wellingdorf, nicht wahr?
There aren't any hotels in Wellingdorf, are there?

STATING SOMETHING EXISTS USING **SEIN** AND **EXISTIEREN**

To reply to questions about existence, you can use the appropriate form of either **sein** or **existieren**:

Ein Arzt ist schon da.	*A doctor is already there.*
Ein Elektriker ist hier.	*An electrician is here.*
Ein Testament existiert wohl.	*A will does presumably exist.*
Kein Frauengesetz existiert dort.	*There's no women's law in existence there.*

STATING THAT SOMETHING EXISTS USING **ES GIBT**

Es gibt einen Fernsehraum.	*There's a TV lounge.*
Es gibt eine Garage.	*There's a garage.*
Es gibt ein Tischtenniszimmer.	*There's a table-tennis room.*

STATING EXISTENCE USING THE VERB **BESTEHEN** (TO EXIST)

Die Universität zu Kiel besteht schon seit 1665.	*The University in Kiel has been in existence since 1665.*
Es besteht die Hoffnung, dass er noch lebt.	*There is hope that he is still alive.*

STATING LACK OF AVAILABILITY USING **ES GIBT**

Es gibt can be used in the same way with the negative form, as follows:

Es gibt keinen Parkplatz.	*There isn't a car park.*
Es gibt keine Sonnenterrasse.	*There's not a (no) sun terrace.*

Es gibt kein Restaurant.	There isn't a restaurant.
Es gibt keine Doppelzimmer.	There aren't any double rooms.

ASKING ABOUT AVAILABILITY USING THE VERB **HABEN**

Insight

You will come across the verb **haben** (*to have*) very frequently. It is an irregular verb and is worth learning in full because (as you will soon discover) it is also used to form some past tenses.

You will also see that the masculine article changes its form after the verb **haben**:

Hast du einen Bleistift da?   *Have you got a pencil (there)?*

For a full explanation, see this unit's Grammar summary.

Haben Sie ein Zimmer frei?	Have you a room (free)?
Hast du ein Taschentuch, bitte?	Have you got a handkerchief, please?
Hat das Hotel eine Sauna?	Does the hotel have a sauna?
Hat das Zimmer einen Balkon?	Has the room got a balcony?
Hat er ein Telefon?	Has he got a telephone?

STATING AVAILABILITY USING THE VERB **HABEN**

Ja, ich habe ein Zimmer frei.	Yes, I do have a room available (free).
Er hat den Flugschein.	He has the air ticket.
Wir haben einen Tisch frei.	We have a table available (free).
Die Schule hat zwei Tennisplätze.	The school has two tennis courts.

STATING LACK OF AVAILABILITY USING **HABEN**

Similarly, **haben** can be used to show the lack of availability:

Das Gasthaus hat keinen Parkplatz.	The guesthouse has no car park.
Die Wohnung hat kein Bad.	The flat has no bathroom.

Ich habe heute keine Zeit.	I've no time today.
Wir haben keine Tische frei.	We haven't any tables free.

ENQUIRING ABOUT AVAILABILITY USING **GIBT ES?**

Gibt es keinen Parkplatz?	Isn't there a car park?
Gibt es eine Apotheke in der Nähe?	Is there a chemist's round here?
Gibt es da keine Toiletten?	Aren't there any toilets there?
Gibt es noch Fisch?	Is there any fish? (literally 'Is there still fish?')

Insight

In Swiss High German and in parts of south-west Germany, you will hear the phrase **hat es?** or **es hat** in place of **gibt es?** or **es gibt,** for example:

Hat es noch Wein? Nein, es hat nur noch Bier. *Is there still (some) wine? No, there is only beer.*

QUESTIONS AND ANSWERS ABOUT EXISTENCE AND AVAILABILITY USING **WER?** (WHO?), **WIE VIEL?** (HOW MUCH?), **WIE VIELE?** (HOW MANY?), **WAS?** (WHAT?) AND **WO?** (WHERE?)

Wer hat noch Umschläge? Wir haben keine.	Who has got any envelopes left? We have none.
Wie viel Geld gibt es noch? Nicht viel.	How much money is left? (literally 'How much money is there still?') Not much.
Wie viele Deutsche gibt es in Chicago? Ich weiß nicht genau.	How many Germans are there in Chicago? I don't know exactly.
Was gibt es heute zum Mittagessen? Es gibt noch viel Rindfleisch von gestern.	What's for lunch today? There's a lot of beef left from yesterday.
Wo gibt es eine Tankstelle, bitte? Gleich um die Ecke.	Is there a petrol station round here, please? (literally 'Where is a petrol station, please?') Just round the corner.

Grammar summary

USE OF THE CASES

(Reference grammar 6)

You will have noticed that the form of the definite and indefinite article changes according to the context. These changes are due to the fact that a so-called 'case system' is used in the German language. Once you have mastered it, you will be able to use the German language accurately and with confidence.

In English there are few remnants of the case system still to be found in present-day usage, only the distinction between *I* and *me*, *he* and *him*, *she* and *her*, etc. and the occasional use of *whom*. There are, however, four cases in constant use in German: the nominative, the accusative, the dative and the genitive – and we have already come across the first two of these.

THE NOMINATIVE CASE (AS SEEN IN UNIT 1)

The *nominative case* (i.e. the form of the noun you find in a dictionary) is used with **sein** (*to be*), as well as for the subject of a sentence):

	Singular Masculine	Feminine	Neuter	Plural m, f, n
the:	**der**	**die**	**das**	**die**
a/an:	**ein**	**eine**	**ein**	**[–]**

THE ACCUSATIVE CASE

You have already learned that the indefinite article (**ein**) and definite article (**der**) for masculine nouns change to **einen** and **den** after the expression **es gibt** and after the verb **haben**, e.g. **Wir haben einen Tisch frei** (*We have a table free*). However, the forms of the articles in front of feminine (**eine** and **die**) and neuter nouns (**ein** and **das**) do NOT change.

▶ The accusative case is used for the direct object of the sentence. To find the direct object of a sentence, ask 'Who or what is affected by the action of the verb?'. The pronoun or noun which forms the answer to this question is the direct object. For example:

I know the man.

Ask the question 'Whom (or what) do I know?'

The answer (*the man*) is the direct object.

Hence: Ich kenne **den** Mann.

	Singular Masculine	Feminine	Neuter	Plural m, f, n
the:	**den**	**die**	**das**	**die**
a/an:	**einen**	**eine**	**ein**	**[–]**

▶ The accusative case is also used after these prepositions:

durch	*through*
für	*for*
gegen	*against, towards, to*
ohne	*without*
um	*round, around, about*
wider	*against, contrary to*
bis	*until, till*

NB If the preposition **entlang** (*along*) follows the noun, for example **Er geht die Straße entlang** (*He goes along the street*), then the noun requires the accusative case. See Unit 4 In context ('A guided tour of the town') for an example of how **entlang** can be used with the dative.

► The accusative case is also used after the following prepositions if motion is implied:

in	*into*
an	*onto, on the side of, against*
auf	*onto, on, on the top of*
über	*over, above*
unter	*under, underneath, below*
hinter	*behind, at the back/rear of*
vor	*in front of*
zwischen	*between, among*
neben	*beside, next to*

(See Unit 4 for details of when these same prepositions require the dative case.)

The negative (*no, not a*) is formed by putting **k** before **einen, eine, ein,** producing **keinen, keine, kein** for the singular accusative case. The plural form is **keine:**

	Singular			Plural
	Masculine	*Feminine*	*Neuter*	*m, f, n*
nominative:	**kein**	**keine**	**kein**	**keine**
accusative:	**keinen**	**keine**	**kein**	**keine**

Insight

The German memory game **Ich packe meinen Koffer und ich nehme ...** (*I'm packing my case and taking ...*) is a very good way to practise the accusative case because everything that comes after the verb form **ich nehme** must be in the accusative case. Ideally, you need five or six players: each person repeats what has been said before and then adds an additional item.

Imagine you are playing the game and are packing the items listed below. What would you say, using the indefinite article?

(Contd)

Ich packe meinen Koffer und ich nehme einen Mantel und ...

- **der Mantel** (*the coat*) • **das Hemd** (*the shirt*)
- **die Hose** (*trousers*) • **das Taschentuch** (*the handkerchief*)
- **das Tagebuch** (*the diary*) • **der Bleistift** (*the pencil*)
- **der Taschenrechner** (*the pocket calculator*)
- **die Taschenlampe** (*the torch/flashlight*)
- **das Fotoalbum** (*the photo album*) • **der Roman** (*the novel*)

Did you manage to remember everything? Your list should be:

Ich packe meinen Koffer und ich nehme einen Mantel, ein Hemd, eine Hose, ein Taschentuch, ein Tagebuch, einen Bleistift, einen Taschenrechner, eine Taschenlampe, ein Fotoalbum und einen Roman.

Mein Kompliment! (*Well done!*)

THE VERB **HABEN** (*TO HAVE*)

Here is the full form of the present tense:

Singular		Plural	
ich habe	*I have, I am having, I do have*	**wir haben**	*we have, etc.*
du hast	*you have, etc. (familiar)*	**ihr habt**	*you have, etc. (familiar)*
Sie haben	*you have, etc. (formal)*	**Sie haben**	*you have, etc. (formal)*
er hat	*he has, etc.*	**sie haben**	*they have, etc.*
sie hat	*she has, etc.*		
es hat	*it has, etc.*		

In context

Study this conversation between a tourist and a hotel receptionist:

Tourist	Guten Tag!
Empfangsdame	Guten Tag! Haben Sie eine Reservierung?
Tourist	Nein, leider nicht. Haben Sie ein Zimmer frei?
Empfangsdame	Für wie viele Gäste?
Tourist	Für zwei.
Empfangsdame	Wir haben leider keine Doppelzimmer mehr, aber es gibt noch zwei Einzelzimmer.
Tourist	Was kosten sie?
Empfangsdame	Fünfzig Euro pro Zimmer.
Tourist	Gibt es noch ein Hotel in der Nähe?
Empfangsdame	Jawohl! Gleich hier um die Ecke durch das Tor, dann die Straße entlang. Aber sie haben keine Zimmer frei.
Tourist	Also gut! Wir nehmen die Einzelzimmer hier. Aber nur für eine Nacht, bitte!

QUICK VOCAB

die Empfangsdame *hotel receptionist*
leider *unfortunately*
Gäste *guests, visitors*
für *for*
aber *but*
Doppelzimmer *double rooms*
mehr *more*
noch *still*
Einzelzimmer *single rooms*
Was kosten sie? *What do they cost?*
pro Zimmer *per room*
noch ein *another*
in der Nähe *in the vicinity, nearby*
gleich hier um die Ecke *just round the corner*
durch das Tor *through the gateway*
die Straße entlang *along the street*
nur für eine Nacht *only for one night*

Read this text describing the facilities available at a hotel:

Das Hotel „Vier Jahreszeiten" hat vier Sterne. Es hat zweiundzwanzig Doppelzimmer, zwölf Einzelzimmer und zehn Suiten. Jedes Zimmer hat ein Bad, eine Dusche, einen Fernseher, ein Telefon und einen Anrufbeantworter. Es gibt vier Restaurants (der Koch kommt aus Frankreich!) und zwei Bars. Außerdem haben wir einen Konferenzsaal, ein Fitnesscenter und einen Friseursalon. Weiterhin bieten wir ein Spielzimmer mit Kindermädchen für die kleinen Gäste. Es gibt auch einen Garten und eine Sonnenterrasse. Bei uns haben Sie jeden Komfort. Sie werden bei uns sicher sehr zufrieden sein!

Taking it further

GERMAN AS A 'VERB SECOND' LANGUAGE

You will notice in the passage above that the verb in a normal sentence is normally the second idea – not necessarily the second word. **Das Hotel „Vier Jahreszeiten"** is one idea, as is also **Jedes Zimmer,** and so they are followed immediately by the verb. If you start the sentence with a word or a group of words (known as a phrase) other than those which usually come before the verb, the verb is still the second idea, for example in the sentences beginning **Außerdem haben wir …** and **Bei uns haben Sie …**

QUESTIONS REGARDING QUANTITY

To ask questions relating to quantity, as in *How much information is there? How many newspapers are there?* we need to use **wie viel?** (*how much?*) or **wie viele?** (*how many?*)

Wie viele Zeitungen gibt es?	*How many newspapers are there?*
Wie viele Informationen gibt es?	*How much information is there?*

(Note that in German 'information' is often used in the plural.)

Wie viele Esszimmer hat das Hotel?	*How many dining rooms does the hotel have?*

To reply to a question like that you will need a phrase such as:

ein bisschen *a little*
viel *a lot*
genug *enough*
nichts *nothing*
keine *none*

QUICK VOCAB

Or you will need to use a number, for example **eins** (or **einen** or **eine**) (*one*), **fünf** (*five*). For further numbers, see Reference grammar 8.1.

You will also need words such as:

einige *some*
(irgend)welche *any*
jemand *somebody*
nicht genug *not enough*
niemand *nobody*
etwas *something*

Wie viel Taschengeld bekommt er? Zu viel!	*How much pocket money does he get? Too much!*
Wie viele Angestellte gibt es bei Siemens? Viele.	*How many employees does Siemens have? Lots.*

COMPOUND NOUNS

Insight

A bit of fun with compound nouns!

Children have great fun trying to invent the longest compound noun possible. Can you recognize any of the component parts of this record-breaking compound noun?

der Donaudampfschifffahrtsgesellschaftskapitänskajütenschlüssel

You can find all the following words in this one compound noun:

die Donau	*the Danube*	**die Gesellschaft**	*company, society*
der Dampf	*steam*	**der Kapitän**	*captain*
das Schiff	*ship*	**die Kajüte**	*cabin*
die Fahrt	*journey*	**der Schlüssel**	*key*
die Schifffahrt	*shipping*		

Starting almost from the end of the word, we can work out that it means: the cabin key of the captain of the Danube Steam Shipping Company.

Practice

In Exercise A, we will encounter several examples of compound nouns, for example **das Schlafzimmer, das Fahrrad, das Puppenhausmuseum, der Fahrplan, das Schwimmbad, das Kaffeehaus,** in which two or more components are joined together to form one noun.

If we examine the last example, **das Kaffeehaus,** we see that it is made up of the two nouns **der Kaffee** and **das Haus.** You will notice that the compound noun takes the same gender as the last component in the compound noun. We could, if we wished, develop this compound noun even further by adding (**die**) **Musik** onto the end, giving us **die Kaffeehausmusik** (*palm court music*).

EXERCISE A

Use the chart on the accusative case (see this unit's Grammar summary) to fill in the following gaps, using the appropriate form of *a*, *the* or *not a*. (The vocabulary below will help you to find the correct form.)

1 Haben Sie __ Bleistift da?
2 Gibt es __ Fön im Schlafzimmer?
3 Er hat __ Fahrrad parat.
4 Nürnberg hat __ Puppenhausmuseum.
5 Wir haben __ Tisch frei.
6 Jedes Zimmer hat __ Telefon.
7 Herr Meier hat __ neue Sekretärin.
8 Habt ihr __ Fahrplan zur Hand?
9 __ Schwimmbad steht Ihnen zur Verfügung.
10 Gibt es __ Kaffeehaus in der Nähe?

der Bleistift *pencil*
der Fön *hairdryer*
das Fahrrad *bicycle*
parat *ready*
das Puppenhausmuseum *doll's house museum*

der Tisch *table*
das Telefon *telephone*
die Sekretärin *secretary*
der Fahrplan *timetable*
das Schwimmbad *swimming pool*
zur Verfügung stehen *to be at your disposal*
das Kaffeehaus *café, coffee shop*

EXERCISE B

Rewrite the following sentences, starting with the given word or phrase. This has the effect of shifting the emphasis onto the first word:

1 Wir spielen Tennis am Dienstag. *We play tennis on Tuesday.*
Am Dienstag __.
2 Otto fährt immer mit dem Taxi. *Otto always travels by taxi.*
Immer __.
3 Anita besucht ihre Mutter jeden Tag. *Anita visits her mother every day.*
Jeden Tag __.
4 Mein Mann und ich denken oft an Hans. *My husband and I often think of Hans.*
Oft __.
5 Sie essen nie Rindfleisch. *They never eat beef.*
Nie __.
6 Ich muss jetzt gehen. *I must go now.*
Jetzt __.
7 Inge hat meistens keine Zeit zum Lesen. *Inge mostly has no time for reading.*
Meistens __.
8 Wir essen abends kalt. *We have a cold meal in the evening.*
Abends __.
9 Der frühere Bundeskanzler Kohl fährt im Sommer an den Wolfgangssee. *Former Chancellor Kohl goes to Lake Wolfgang in the summer.*
Im Sommer __.
10 Er macht dort eine Kur. *He 'takes a cure' there.*
Dort __.

Ten things to remember

1 Questions in German can be formed by inverting the verb (i.e. starting the sentence with the verb) or by using interrogatives such as **wer?**, **wie?**, **was?**

2 The nominative case is the form of the noun you find in a dictionary. It is used after the verb **sein** (*to be*) and for the subject of the sentence.

3 The verb **haben** (*to have*) is very important, so learn it now! It is followed by the accusative case.

4 The expression **es gibt** (*there is, there are*) is followed by the accusative case.

5 The following prepositions are always followed by the accusative case: **durch, für, gegen, ohne, um, wider, bis.**

6 The following prepositions are followed by the accusative case if they show motion: **in, an, auf, über, unter, hinter, vor, zwischen, neben.**

7 In a normal sentence, the verb should be the second 'idea'.

8 Compound nouns are formed by joining two or more words together. The compound noun takes the gender of its last component, e.g. **der Brief** (*the letter*) + **die Tasche** (*bag, pocket*) = **die Brieftasche** (*the wallet*).

9 If you want to negate the verb (i.e. say *not*), you use **nicht**, e.g. **Ich bin sportlich** → **Ich bin nicht sportlich** (*I'm sporty* → *I'm not sporty*).

10 If you want to negate the noun (i.e. say *not a* or *no*), you use the appropriate form of **kein**, *e.g.* **Ich bin Sportler** → **Ich bin kein Sportler** *(I'm a sportsman* → *I'm not a sportsman).*

4

Expressing location

In this unit you will learn how to
- *Enquire about and give information about location*
- *Enquire about and give information about distance*

Language points
- *Wo?*
- *Auf welchem?*
- *In welchem?*
- *Wie weit?*
- *The verbs* liegen, sich befinden, stehen
- *Prepositions to express location and distance*
- *Dative case*

▶ To ask the location of a place, facility or object, simply start the question with **Wo?** (*Where?*) and follow it with the verb you wish to use, and the place, facility or object, e.g. **Wo ist das Kino?** (*Where is the cinema?*)

▶ If you wish to be slightly more specific and ask 'on which?' or 'in which?', then start the sentence with **Auf welchem?/Auf welcher?** (*On which?*) or **In welchem/In welcher?** (*In which?*).

▶ To enquire about distance, start the sentence with **Wie weit ist ...?** (*How far is ...?*).

▶ To give information regarding location (e.g. *It's in the Market Square, It's at the railway station*), we often use the verb **sein** (*to be*) or **liegen** (*to be situated*), **stehen** (*to stand*), or occasionally **sich befinden** (*to be found*).

▶ We also need to use a preposition, which shows the position or location of the thing (noun). Most prepositions cause the definite article (**der, die, das** or plural **die**), the indefinite article (**ein, eine, ein**) or the possessive adjective (**mein, meine, mein** or plural **meine**) to change its form. (For fuller details on prepositions, see the Grammar summary in Units 3 and 4, and Reference grammar 6.)

ENQUIRING ABOUT LOCATION

Look at the following questions regarding location:

Wo ist die Apotheke, bitte?	*Where is the chemist's, please?*
Wo sind die Gemälde von Dürer?	*Where are the Dürer paintings?*
Wo liegt Schleswig?	*Where is Schleswig situated?*
Wo finde ich ein Telefon, bitte?	*Where can I find a telephone, please?*

Insight

Bitte is an interesting German word with several shades of meaning:

▶ In the first and last examples above, it simply means *please*.
▶ If someone offers you a coffee or a piece of cake, you say **Ja, bitte!** (*Yes, please!*) as opposed to **Nein, danke** (*No, thank you/No, thanks*).
▶ If someone thanks you for, say, holding the door open for you, it is customary to reply **Bitte schön!** (meaning *You're welcome!* or *Please don't mention it!*).
▶ If you are holding the door open for someone else, you will also say **Bitte schön!**, this time in the sense of *There you go!* or *After you!*
▶ If you feel you have not understood what the speaker has said, **Wie bitte?** (*I beg your pardon?*) suggests that you would like to hear it repeated.
▶ Sometimes you will hear **Bitte, bitte!** as a more effusive form of thanks, or with the emphasis *Please don't mention it!*

In welchem Aktenschrank befindet sich der Brief?	*In which filing cabinet is the letter to be found?*
In welcher Handtasche ist dein Pass?	*In which handbag is your passport?*
In welchem Büro arbeitest du?	*In which office do you work?*

GIVING INFORMATION ABOUT LOCATION

Now have a look at these examples of location and their English translations before going on to the Grammar summary.

> ### Insight
> The forms **an dem**, **in dem** and **zu dem** can be, and regularly are, contracted to **am**, **im** and **zum** respectively. In fact, they *must be* contracted if the article is not stressed. (This obviously refers only to the masculine and neuter forms.) This is standard German and is in no way informal or colloquial.

Die Apotheke ist an dem (am) Marktplatz.	*The chemist's is on the Market Square.*
Das nächste Telefon ist in der Post.	*The nearest phone is in the post office.*
Sie arbeitet in einer Bank.	*She's working in a bank.*
Er schläft fest in seinem Bett.	*He is fast asleep in his bed.*
Es gibt zu viele Autos in unseren Städten.	*There are too many cars in our towns.*

THE LOCATION OF TOWNS AND AREAS

To give information about the location of towns, the verb **liegen** is often used. This information can involve the points of the compass or more specific geographic locations:

Schleswig liegt in Norddeutschland.	*Schleswig is in North Germany.*
München liegt in Süddeutschland.	*Munich is in South Germany.*
Die Insel Rügen liegt im Nordosten.	*The island of Rügen is in the North East.*

Karlsruhe liegt im (in dem) Südwesten.	*Karlsruhe is in the South West.*
Oberammergau liegt in den Alpen.	*Oberammergau is in the Alps.*
Berlin liegt an der Spree.	*Berlin is on the (River) Spree.*
Königswinter liegt an dem (am) Rhein.	*Königswinter is on the Rhine.*

QUESTIONS ABOUT DISTANCE

To enquire how far it is to a particular amenity within a neighbourhood, for example the post office, the university or the football stadium, you can ask:

Wie weit ist der Flughafen von hier?	*How far is the airport from here?*
Wie weit ist es zum Flughafen?	*How far is it to the airport?*

If you wish to ask how far it is to a town or country, you ask:

Wie weit ist Kiel von hier?	*How far is Kiel from here?*
Wie weit ist es nach Kiel?	*How far is it to Kiel?*

Various expressions of distance:

Der Flughafen ist weit entfernt.	*The airport is far away.*
Bonn ist nicht weit entfernt.	*Bonn is not far away.*
Potsdam ist ungefähr 30 Kilometer von Berlin entfernt.	*Potsdam is approximately 30 kilometres from Berlin.*

Grammar summary

THE DATIVE CASE

(Reference grammar 6.3)

In some of the examples above, der, die, das and the plural die as we met them in Unit 1 (the nominative case) underwent a change – under the influence of the preposition an or in – to dem, der, dem or den. These are examples of the dative case.

The dative case is used:

- ▶ after certain prepositions (listed below)
- ▶ to indicate the indirect object of the sentence. The indirect object is the recipient or beneficiary of the action of the verb, e.g. in the sentence *I told the child a story*, the recipient of the verb's action (i.e. *the telling*) is *the child*, so the child is the indirect object and must therefore be in the dative case. Often, you can identify the indirect object by putting 'to' or 'for' in front of it, e.g. *I told a story **to the child**.*
- ▶ after some verbs, e.g. **helfen** (*to help*), **glauben** (*to believe*), **folgen** (*to follow*), **schaden** (*to damage, to harm*), **begegnen** (*to meet*), e.g. **der Lehrer hilft dem Kind** (*the teacher is helping the child*), **der Hund folgt dem Mann** (*the dog is following the man*).

Insight

Once again, we realize how important it is to learn the gender with each new noun (i.e. whether it is labelled in the dictionary as **der**, **die** or **das**). Look at the following examples and see how the definite article changes in the dative case:

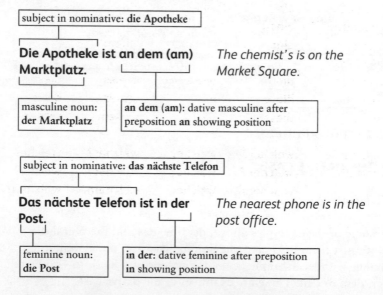

subject in nominative: **die Apotheke**

Die Apotheke ist an dem (am) Marktplatz.

The chemist's is on the Market Square.

masculine noun: **der Marktplatz**

an dem (am): dative masculine after preposition **an** showing position

subject in nominative: **das nächste Telefon**

Das nächste Telefon ist in der Post.

The nearest phone is in the post office.

feminine noun: **die Post**

in der: dative feminine after preposition **in** showing position

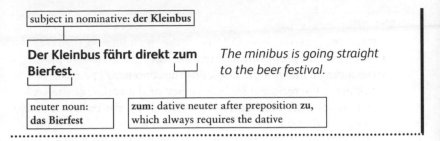

subject in nominative: der Kleinbus

Der Kleinbus fährt direkt zum Bierfest.

The minibus is going straight to the beer festival.

neuter noun: das Bierfest

zum: dative neuter after preposition **zu**, which always requires the dative

THE CASES

The following chart summarizes the cases we have learned so far:

	Singular			Plural
	Masculine	*Feminine*	*Neuter*	*m, f, n*
the:				
nominative	**der**	**die**	**das**	**die**
accusative	**den**	**die**	**das**	**die**
dative	**dem**	**der**	**dem**	**den**
a/an:				
nominative	**ein**	**eine**	**ein**	–
accusative	**einen**	**eine**	**ein**	–
dative	**einem**	**einer**	**einem**	–
this/these:				
nominative	**dieser**	**diese**	**dieses**	**diese**
accusative	**diesen**	**diese**	**dieses**	**diese**
dative	**diesem**	**dieser**	**diesem**	**diesen**
which?:				
nominative	**welcher?**	**welche?**	**welches?**	**welche?**
accusative	**welchen?**	**welche?**	**welches?**	**welche?**
dative	**welchem?**	**welcher?**	**welchem?**	**welchen?**

In the chart above, you will notice the **-n** ending on the three dative plural forms. Please learn the rule that all dative plural forms must end with **-n**. Look at these two examples:

▶ The plural of **das Kind** *(the child)* is **-er** *(**Kinder**) (children)*.

The preposition **mit** (with) is always followed by the dative case. So if you want to *say I'm going to Stuttgart with the children*, you have to say **Ich fahre mit den Kindern nach Stuttgart.**

▶ The plural of **der Berg** *(the mountain)* is **-e** *(**Berge**) (mountains)*.

When the preposition **in** *(in)* is used to show location or position, it is followed by the dative case. So if you want to say *He is camping in the mountains*, you have to say **Er zeltet in den Bergen.**

For more details, see Taking it further.

PREPOSITIONS WHICH ALWAYS REQUIRE THE DATIVE CASE

The dative case is used after the following prepositions:

aus	*out of, from*
außer	*except for, apart from*
bei	*at, at the house of, with*
mit	*with*
nach	*after, to* (a town or country)
seit	*since, for* (a length of time)
von	*from*
zu	*to* (a local amenity)
gegenüber	*opposite*
entlang	*along* (when used before the noun)

bei (*with, at the house of, at*):

Er wohnt bei seiner Freundin.   *He lives with his girlfriend.*

gegenüber (*opposite*):

Er wohnt dem Gefängnis gegenüber.   *He lives opposite the prison.*

NB Gegenüber can appear either before or after the noun.

Insight

Seit is often used with the present tense in German sentences, whereas we use the perfect tense in English:

Ich studiere Deutsch seit zwei Jahren.	*I have been studying German for two years.*
Er wohnt seit dem Krieg zufrieden in Berlin.	*He has been happily living in Berlin since the war.*

Did you notice that, in the second example, the word order is different in German and English? Word order is very important in German.

PREPOSITIONS WHICH REQUIRE THE DATIVE CASE WHEN THEY SHOW LOCATION OR POSITION

The nine prepositions which we came across in Unit 3 take the dative case if they show location, position or a static condition:

in	*in*	**hinter**	*behind*
an	*on, on the side of*	**vor**	*in front of*
auf	*on, on top of*	**zwischen**	*between*
über	*over, above*	**neben**	*next to, beside*
unter	*under*		

an (*on, on the side of*):

Ihr zweites Zuhause ist an der Küste.   *Her second home is on the coast.*

auf (*on*):

Die Buchhandlung ist auf der rechten Seite.   *The bookshop is on the right-hand side.*

unter (*under*):

Der Koffer ist unter dem Bett. *The case is under the bed.*

hinter (*behind/at the back of*):

Die Taxis stehen hinter den Telefonzellen. *The taxis are (standing) behind the telephone boxes.*

vor (*in front of*):

Die Toiletten sind vor dem Café. *The toilets are in front of the café.*

zwischen (*between*):

Die Bank ist zwischen der Kirche und der Post. *The bank is between the church and the post office.*

neben (*next to*):

Das Reisebüro ist neben dem Dom. *The travel agency is next to the cathedral.*

Insight

Remember that these prepositions require the accusative case when they show motion or movement from one place to another (see Unit 3).

A rather silly but effective way to remember when these prepositions take the accusative case and when they take the dative case is to think of the two university higher degrees, the MA and the P(h)D:

▶ **MA:** if these prepositions show **M**otion, they take the **A**ccusative case.
▶ **PhD:** if the same prepositions show **P**osition, they take the **D**ative case.

For examples of this usage, see Reference grammar 6.

In context

Looking for a bank

Tourist	Entschuldigung! Gibt es eine Bank hier in der Nähe?
Polizist	Ja, klar. Es gibt eine am Marktplatz.
Tourist	Wo ist der Marktplatz, bitte?
Polizist	Gar nicht weit von hier, nur zwei Minuten zu Fuß. Er ist direkt hinter dem Bahnhof dort drüben.
Tourist	Vielen Dank!
Polizist	Nichts zu danken!

klar (colloquial) *of course*
direct *directly*
der Bahnhof *the railway station*
Vielen Dank *Many thanks*
Nichts zu danken *It's a pleasure*

A guided tour of the town

Meine Damen und Herren. Unsere Stadttour von Leipzig beginnt hier am Augustusplatz vor dem restaurierten Mendebrunnen. Links sehen Sie das Gewandhaus und rechts das Opernhaus. Da vorne ist das Hochhaus der Universität. (Man nennt es hier den Weisheitszahn!) Wir fahren jetzt entlang der Schillerstraße am Ägyptischen Museum vorbei. In wenigen Minuten erreichen wir die Thomaskirche, in der Johann Sebastian Bach Thomaskantor war. Seine Grabstätte befindet sich seit 1950 in der Kirche. Vor der südlichen Seite der Kirche sehen wir das Bachdenkmal. Nach dieser Tour können Sie ein Bier in Auerbachs Keller trinken. Er ist gar nicht weit vom Markt entfernt. Das berühmte Messegelände liegt außerhalb der Stadtmitte. Am besten fahren Sie mit einem Linienbus dorthin.

restauriert *restored*
der Brunnen *fountain, well*
das Gewandhaus *famous concert hall in Leipzig, housing a magnificent organ*

das Opernhaus *the opera house*
da vorne *in front, there*
das Hochhaus der Universität *university skyscraper*
der Weisheitszahn *wisdom tooth* (used figuratively here)
das Ägyptische Museum *the Egyptian Museum*
vorbel/fahren an + (*dative*) *to drive past*
in wenigen Minuten *in a few minutes*
erreichen *to reach*
in der ... *in which ...* (note that the verb is sent to the end of this
  relative clause. For more details, see Unit 5.)
der Kantor *choirmaster, cantor*
die Grabstätte *grave, tomb*
südlich *southern*
das Denkmal *statue, monument*
Auerbachs Keller *Auerbach's Cellar* (famous restaurant mentioned in
  Goethe's play "Faust")
berühmt *famous*
das Messegelände *exhibition centre*
außerhalb + genitive *outside of* (See Reference grammar 6.4)
der Linienbus *public service bus*
dorthin/fahren *to go (to) there*

Taking it further

DATIVE PLURAL

In the dative plural, the noun itself must end in -**n**. If the plural
naturally ends in -**n**, there is no need to add another one. Look at
the following examples:

Wir fahren mit den Kindern nach   *We are travelling to France with*
Frankreich.   *the children.*

The plural of **das Kind** is **die Kinder**. Because the plural form
Kinder is in the dative case (it comes after the preposition **mit**),
an additional -**n** must be added.

Ich wandere gern in den Bergen. *I like hiking in the mountains.*

The plural of **der Berg** is **die Berge.** This plural noun is in the dative case here, because when the preposition **in** shows position or location, it must be followed by the dative.

Das ist ein Bild von meinen Brüdern. *That is a picture of my brothers.*

The plural of **der Bruder** is **die Brüder.** Here, it is in the dative case because it follows the preposition **von.**

Viele Plastiken von Barlach befinden sich in den Kirchen von Norddeutschland.	*Many of Barlach's sculptures are to be found in North Germany's churches.*

The plural of **die Kirche** is **die Kirchen,** so no additional **-n** needs to be added to show that it is in the dative plural.

PERSONAL PRONOUNS

In later units we will come across examples of the personal pronouns in these three cases. You may well be interested to see them in chart form here, and compare them with their English equivalents.

Singular					
Person 1st	2nd		3rd		
Nom. **ich** (*I*)	**du** (*you*)	**Sie** (*you*)	**er** (*he*)	**sie** (*she*) **es** (*it*)
Acc. **mich** (*me*)	**dich** (*you*)	**Sie** (*you*)	**ihn** (*him*)	**sie** (*her*) **es** (*it*)
Dat. **mir** (*(to) me*)	**dir** (*(to) you*)	**Ihnen** (*(to) you*)	**ihm** (*(to) him*)	**ihr** (*(to) her*) **ihm** (*(to)it*)

Plural			
Person 1st	2nd		3rd
Nom. **wir** (*we*)	**ihr** (*you*)	**Sie** (*you*)	**sie** (*they*)
Acc. **uns** (*us*)	**euch** (*you*)	**Sie** (*you*)	**sie** (*they*)
Dat. **uns** (*(to) us*)	**euch** (*(to) you*)	**Ihnen** (*(to) you*)	**ihnen** (*(to) them*)

Practice

EXERCISE A

Join the following sentence halves together:

1	Hamburg liegt	A	zum Flughafen?
2	Ich arbeite in	B	am Rhein.
3	Der ICE kommt	C	von Griechenland.
4	Bonn liegt	D	in Norddeutschland.
5	Athen ist die Hauptstadt	E	am Marktplatz.
6	Wie weit ist es	F	die Hauptstadt von Island.
7	Die Bushaltestelle ist	G	auf Gleis 4 an.
8	Reykjavik ist	H	einer Bank.
9	Er wandert gern	I	arbeiten Sie?
10	In welchem Büro	J	in den Bergen.

EXERCISE B

Rewrite the following sentences replacing the underlined nouns with the appropriate pronoun.

For example: <u>Die Frau</u> hat nur einen Sohn. → **Sie** hat nur einen Sohn.

For help, refer to the charts in Taking it further.

1 <u>Frau Müller</u> ist sehr krank. → __ ist sehr krank.
2 <u>Die Schulkinder</u> sind sehr faul. → __ sind sehr faul.
3 <u>Hans Schmidt</u> arbeitet in einem Hotel. → __ arbeitet in einem Hotel.
4 Wir fahren mit <u>Hans und Lotte</u> nach Hamburg. → Wir fahren mit __ nach Hamburg.
5 Frau Braun besucht <u>den Arzt</u>. → Frau Braun besucht __.
6 Heinrich wohnt bei <u>Oma</u>. → Heinrich wohnt bei __.
7 <u>Meine Mutter</u> hat am neunten Oktober Geburtstag. → __ hat am neunten Oktober Geburtstag.

8 <u>Seine Eltern</u> sind sehr nett. → __ sind sehr nett.

9 Inge spielt Tennis mit <u>Fritz</u>. → __ spielt Tennis mit __.

10 Der Brief ist für <u>den Chef</u>. → Der Brief ist für __.

QUICK VOCAB

krank *ill*
faul *lazy*
arbeiten *to work*
Oma *grandmother*
Geburtstag haben *to have one's birthday*
Eltern, die *parents*
Brief, der *letter*
Chef, der *boss*

Ten things to remember

1 The word **bitte** has several shades of meaning. It normally means *please* but can also mean *You're welcome*.

2 The dative forms of the singular and plural definite articles are **dem, der, dem, den**.

3 You can shorten **an dem** → **am, in dem** → **im** and **zu dem** → **zum**.

4 The verb **liegen** (*to lie*) is often used to express location.

5 Do learn the gender and plural of each new noun you come across.

6 The dative case is used to express the indirect object of the sentence.

7 The following prepositions always require the dative case: **aus, außer, bei, mit, nach, seit, von, zu, gegenüber**.

8 The following prepositions take the dative case if they show location, position or a static condition: **in, an, auf, über, unter, hinter, vor, zwischen, neben.**

9 Some verbs are followed by the dative case, e.g. **helfen, glauben, folgen, schaden, begegnen.**

10 All dative plural nouns must end with -n.

5

Talking about the present

In this unit you will learn how to
- *Talk about something which is happening now*
- *Talk about something which is true as of now, but not necessarily at this specific time*
- *Describe a regular or habitual activity*
- *Express universal truths and well-known facts*
- *Present information about the past in a dramatic present form*

Language points
- *The present tense of regular verbs*
- *The present tense of irregular verbs*
- *Relative clauses*
- *Separable verbs*

▶ You would naturally choose the present tense to talk about an activity, action, state of affairs or event which is happening just now, for example: *It's snowing, He's arriving, The train is just leaving.*

▶ You would also use the present tense to describe an activity, action, state of affairs or event which is true as of now, but is not necessarily happening at this specific moment, for example: *I'm reading a novel by Böll, My son's studying medicine, They understand the problem.*

▶ The present tense would also be your natural choice to describe a regular or habitual action or activity that you do or are doing, for example: *I read the newspaper every morning,*

He works every Saturday, You always look half-starved,
They go to the mosque on Fridays.

▶ The present is also used for expressing universal truths and proven facts, for example: *Children love chips and ice cream, Blood is thicker than water, Time heals, Practice makes perfect, The earth is round.*

▶ The so-called dramatic present is sometimes used either to bring historical narrative to life or to present an incident from the past more vividly, for example: *And then the Vikings simply come up the river and set fire to the whole settlement, I get out of the car and see water streaming out of the front door.*

TALKING ABOUT SOMETHING WHICH IS TRUE OR IS HAPPENING JUST NOW

Es ist heute kalt.	*It's cold today.*
Sie ist wirklich krank.	*She's really ill.*
Schh! Das Baby schläft.	*Shh! The baby's asleep.*

TALKING ABOUT SOMETHING WHICH IS HAPPENING OR TRUE, BUT NOT NECESSARILY AT THIS PRECISE MOMENT

Ich komme gleich.	*I'm on my way/I'm coming immediately.*
Mein Sohn studiert Medizin.	*My son's studying medicine.*
Sie sucht ihren idealen Mann.	*She's looking for her ideal man.*
Wir lernen kochen.	*We're learning to cook.*

DESCRIBING A REGULAR ACTIVITY OR HABITUAL ACTION

Ich arbeite samstags.	*I work on Saturdays.*
Er liest die Zeitung jeden Morgen.	*He reads the newspaper every morning.*
Er trinkt.	*He drinks/he's a regular drinker.*
Renate isst jeden Tag Nudeln.	*Renate eats pasta every day.*
Freitags gehen sie in die Moschee.	*They go to the mosque on Fridays.*

EXPRESSING UNIVERSAL TRUTHS AND PROVEN FACTS

Kinder essen gern Pommes frites. *Children like eating chips.*
Blut ist dicker als Wasser. *Blood is thicker than water.*

Insight

You will be pleased to hear that the formation of the present tense is easier in German than in English! For example, the single German sentence **Ich lese die Zeitung** can be translated into English in three ways:

▶ *I read the newspaper* (i.e. regularly, but not necessarily just now)
▶ *I am reading the newspaper* (i.e. at the moment, so please don't keep interrupting me)
▶ *I **do** read the newspaper* (emphasizing the fact that you really do read it).

PRESENTING INFORMATION ABOUT THE PAST IN A DRAMATIC PRESENT FORM

Und dann kommen die Wikinger *Then the Vikings come and burn*
und brennen die Siedlung nieder. *the settlement down.*
Ich steige aus dem Auto und sehe *I get out of my car and see water*
Wasser aus der Haustür strömen. *streaming out of the front door.*

Grammar summary

THE PRESENT TENSE OF REGULAR VERBS

English has various ways of expressing the present tense, such as: *I cook, I am cooking* or *I do cook*. German has only one form to translate these three: **Ich koche.**

This verb **kochen** (*to cook*) consists of the stem **koch-** plus various endings, which are shown below in bold. This provides the pattern for several other verbs in the present tense, in that the various forms of the verb all have the same endings as below and can therefore be worked out.

Several other verbs which also follow this pattern in the present tense are, for example:

kaufen *to buy*   **sparen** *to save*
lernen *to learn*   **spielen** *to play*
klopfen *to knock*   **studieren** *to study*
machen *to make* or *to do*   **suchen** *to look for*
malen *to paint*   **verkaufen** *to sell*
sagen *to say*   **wohnen** *to live*

Singular	
ich koche	*I cook, I am cooking, I do cook*
du kochst	*you cook, you are cooking, etc.*
Sie kochen	*you cook, you are cooking, etc.*
er kocht	*he cooks, he is cooking, etc.*
sie kocht	*she cooks, she is cooking, etc.*
es kocht	*it cooks, it is cooking, etc.*

Plural	
wir kochen	*we cook, we are cooking, etc.*
ihr kocht	*you cook, you are cooking, etc.*
Sie kochen	*you cook, you are cooking, etc.*
sie kochen	*they cook, they are cooking, etc.*

Have another look at the examples on the preceding pages and check that the endings are the same as those in the box above.

HOW TO FIND THE STEM OF THE VERB

If we subtract the endings from the infinitive (the verb form which we find in the dictionary with the meaning *to cook* (**kochen**), *to* *play* (**spielen**), *to pay* (**bezahlen**), etc.), we are left with the so-called stem of the verb: **koch-, spiel-, bezahl-,** etc.

If the stem of a regular verb ends in **d** or **t**, e.g. **reden** (*to speak*), **arbeiten** (*to work*), or a combination of **m** or **n** preceded by another consonant, e.g. **atmen** (*to breathe*), **regnen** (*to rain*), an **e** is added before the endings of the **du, er, sie, es** and **ihr** forms in the present tense, for ease of pronunciation. For example:

arbeiten (*to work*)

Mein Vater arbeitet bei Bosch.   *My father works for Bosch.*

atmen (*to breathe*)

Oma atmet sehr langsam.   *Grandma is breathing very slowly.*

finden (*to find*)

Er findet seine Fahrkarte nicht.   *He can't find his ticket.*

öffnen (*to open*)

Die alte Frau öffnet ihre Haustür nicht.   *The old lady isn't opening her front door.*

senden (*to send, transmit*)

CNN sendet rund um die Uhr.   *CNN broadcasts round the clock.*

---

arbeiten *(to work)*

Singular		Plural	
ich arbeite	*I work, am working*	**wir arbeiten**	*we work, are working*
du arbeitest	*you work, are working*	**ihr arbeitet**	*you work, are working*
Sie arbeiten	*you work, are working*	**Sie arbeiten**	*you work, are working*
er arbeitet	*he works, is working*	**sie arbeiten**	*they work, are working*
sie arbeitet	*she works, is working*		
es arbeitet	*it works, is working*		

THE PRESENT TENSE OF IRREGULAR VERBS

(Reference grammar 9.1 and 10.7)

Insight

Although we noticed some slight variations in the endings of
the regular verbs above to ease pronunciation, the stem was
always based on the infinitive form.

Other verbs, however, change their stem vowel in the second
(**du**) and third (**er, sie, es**) person singular, so that these forms
are different from the stem and thus also from the infinitive.
We cannot work these out, but have to refer to a verb list,
such as that in Reference grammar 10.7, to be sure of the
correct form.

Look at the vowel changes in the following verbs.

fahren (*to go, travel*)

ab/fahren (*to depart, set off*)

Fährst du gleich ab?	*Are you setting off straight away?*
Nein, ich fahre erst morgen.	*No, I'm not going until tomorrow.*
Der Zug fährt um 12 Uhr von	*The train departs from platform 5*
Gleis 5 ab.	*at twelve o'clock.*

Insight

You will have noticed that there is a prefix **ab** at the
beginning of the infinitive in the example above. If you add a
prefix to a verb, it changes the verb's meaning, e.g.

kommen (*to come*) → **an/kommen** (*to arrive*),
bekommen (*to get, receive*), **entkommen** (*to escape*).

In grammar books, verbs which start with a prefix are
sometimes written as one word in the infinitive and are known
as inseparable verbs, e.g. **bekommen, verkaufen** (*to sell*).

Sometimes they are written with a slash between the prefix and the verb: these verbs are known as separable verbs, e.g. **an/kommen, ein/laden** (*to invite*).

A few German verbs which begin with a prefix can be either separable or inseparable, depending on their meaning, e.g. **übersetzen** (*to translate*) and **über/setzen** (*to ferry over*).

fangen (*to catch*)

Unsere Katze fängt zu gerne Mäuse.	*Our cat likes catching mice too much.*

schlafen (*to sleep*)

Das Mädchen schläft nicht gut.	*The girl doesn't sleep well.*

geben (*to give*)

aus/geben (*to spend*)

Meine Tochter gibt sehr viel Geld für Kosmetika aus.	*My daughter spends a lot of money on cosmetics.*
Der Chef gibt mir keinen Tag frei.	*The boss doesn't give me a day off.*

(Do you remember the expression **es gibt** from Unit 3? It is the third person singular of this verb, **geben**.)

essen (*to eat*)

Du isst viel zu wenig.	*You're eating far too little.*
Er isst Lachs so gern.	*He likes eating salmon so much.*

lesen (*to read*)

Liest du *Focus*?	*Do you read Focus?*
Meine Frau liest den *Spiegel* jede Woche.	*My wife reads the Spiegel every week.*

sehen (*to see*)

aus/sehen (*to look*)

Siehst du den Baum da?	*Can you see the tree there?*
Er sieht sehr müde aus.	*He looks very tired.*

laufen (*to run*) (**laufen** is also used for *to go, to walk*)

Der Vertreter läuft aus dem Büro.	*The company representative runs out of the office.*
Läufst du oft in die Stadt?	*Do you often walk into town?*

Remember that only the **du-**, and **er-, sie-, es-**forms change. All the other forms are predictable and have the same vowel as the stem. For example:

Ich fahre nicht gern Rad.	*I don't like cycling.*
Wir fahren heute nach Schwerin.	*We're going to Schwerin today.*
Lesen Sie nichts?	*Don't you read anything? (literally 'Do you read nothing?')*

In context

Read the following article in which Ilse explains why she always returns to the same Greek island for her holidays. The vocabulary following the article will help you.

Meine Freunde und Kollegen wechseln ihr Urlaubsziel von Jahr zu Jahr. Ich selbst fahre seit zwölf Jahren auf die gleiche Insel, die kaum jemand kennt, in Griechenland. Wollt ihr wissen, warum ich immer wieder hinfahre?

Ich kenne die Kinder des Dorfes, ich kenne die schwarzgekleideten Großmütter, ich kenne die Wirte. Wenn ich ankomme, freuen sich alle, und ich habe das Gefühl im Urlaub nach Hause zu kommen. „Fährst du schon wieder nach Griechenland?" spotten meine Freunde. „Willst du nichts anderes kennen lernen? Die Welt ist groß ..."

Ich weiß es besser. Diese Insel, die ich jedes Jahr besuche, ist mein Platz an der Sonne. Aber ich sage dir nicht, wo sie liegt!

die Freunde *friends*
die Kollegen *colleagues*
wechseln *change*
das Urlaubsziel *holiday destination*
von Jahr zu Jahr *from year to year*
ich selbst *I myself*
Ich fahre seit zwölf Jahren zu ... *For twelve years I have been going/travelling to ...*
die gleiche Insel *the same island*
kaum jemand *scarcely anybody*
immer wieder *again and again, time after time*
hin/fahren *to go/travel there*
die Kinder des Dorfes *the children of the village* (see the genitive case in Unit 12)
die schwarzgekleideten Großmütter *the grandmothers dressed in black*
der Wirt *the landlord*
Wenn ich ankomme, freuen sich alle. *Whenever I arrive, everyone is pleased.*
das Gefühl *the feeling*
nach Hause kommen *to come home*
schon wieder *yet again*
spotten *to mock*
nichts anderes *nothing else*
die Welt *the world*
besser *better*
mein Platz an der Sonne *my place in the sun*
ich sage dir nicht *I'm not telling you*
sie liegt *it's situated*

QUICK VOCAB

Taking it further

RELATIVE CLAUSES

(Reference grammar 15.2)

> **Insight**
>
> A relative clause is a subordinate clause which refers back to or depends on a preceding noun or noun phrase. For example, in the sentence *The island (that) I visit every year is very remote*, 'the island' is the noun being referred back to; and in the sentence *The paradise island in the sun, which I mentioned last week, is very remote*, 'the paradise island in the sun' is the noun phrase being referred back to.
>
> You will realize that we sometimes omit the relative pronoun in English (as in the first example above) but this never happens in German.
>
> English also distinguishes between a human relative pronoun (*who, whom, whose*) and an inanimate relative pronoun (*which, that*), whereas German does not.

Have another look at the sentences:

Ich fahre seit zwölf Jahren auf die gleiche Insel, die kaum jemand kennt.   *For 12 years I have been going to the same island, which scarcely anyone knows.*

and:

Diese Insel, die ich jedes Jahr besuche, ist mein Platz an der Sonne.   *This island, which I visit every year, is my place in the sun.*

In these sentences, **die** (*which*) is a relative pronoun and it introduces the relative clause **die kaum jemand kennt** or **die ich jedes Jahr besuche.** You will notice that the relative pronoun **die** is preceded by a comma, and that it sends the verb to the end of the clause, which also ends with a comma if the sentence continues.

First of all, have a look at the chart of relative pronouns, and then study the following examples of relative clauses. See if you can work out how they relate back to the main clause.

Relative pronouns				
Singular	masculine	feminine	neuter	Plural m, f, n
nominative	der	die	das	die
accusative	den	die	das	die
dative	dem	der	dem	denen
genitive*	dessen	deren	dessen	deren

* For more on the genitive, see Unit 12.

Der Wein, der aus diesem Gebiet kommt, ist lieblich.   *The wine which comes from this region is sweet.*

The relative pronoun here is in the nominative case, because it is the subject of the relative clause in which it stands. To check this, replace the pronoun with the noun to which it refers, viz. 'The wine comes from this region'. The wine is clearly the subject of this sentence. The relative pronoun is masculine singular, because it is referring or relating back to **der Wein** in the main clause.

Der Wein, den wir trinken, ist herb.   *The wine which we are drinking is dry.*

The relative pronoun, **den**, is in the accusative case, because it is the direct object of the verb in the relative clause. The pronoun is masculine singular, because it is referring back to **der Wein**.

Der Wein, mit dem wir diese Weinprobe beenden, ist eine Spätlese.   *The wine with which we are concluding this wine tasting is a late vintage.*

The relative pronoun is in the dative case, because it is straight after the preposition **mit**. It is masculine singular, because it is referring back to **der Wein**.

Viele Weinsorten, die wir exportieren, sind für die Deutschen zu süß.	*Many of the wines which we export are too sweet for the Germans.*
Die Weinreben, aus denen wir diesen Wein machen, wachsen in den Weingärten um Rüdesheim.	*The vines from which we make this wine grow in the vineyards around Rüdesheim.*

The same relative pronoun can also be translated as *who* or *whom* if referring to a person:

Die Dame, *die* **jetzt redet, ist Professorin für Tiefbau.**	*The lady who is speaking at the moment is the civil engineering professor.*
Die Dame, *die* **ich meine, ist Professorin für Hochbau.**	*The lady (whom) I mean is the structural engineering professor.*
Die Dame, mit *der* **ich verabredet bin, ist die neue Professorin für Jura.**	*The lady (with whom) I have arranged to meet, is the new law professor.*
Die Damen, *die* **morgen ankommen, sind alle aus China.**	*The ladies who are arriving tomorrow are all from China.*

SEPARABLE VERBS

In this unit, we have come across several so-called separable verbs, for example **ab/fahren, ab/trocknen, fern/sehen, aus/sehen, nieder/brennen**. A prefix, such as **ab-, an-, aus-, ein-, fern-, nieder**, is to be found at the beginning of the infinitive form of a separable verb. It will be followed by a slash (/) to show that it is separable. This prefix changes the meaning of the basic verb. For example:

fahren = *to travel, to go*	**ab/fahren** = *to depart, to set off*
kommen = *to come*	**an/kommen** = *to arrive*
geben = *to give*	**aus/geben** = *to spend (money)*
sehen = *to see*	**aus/sehen** = *to look (like)*
	fern/sehen = *to watch TV*

When a separable verb is used as a finite verb (i.e. as a working verb in a main clause), the prefix splits from the rest of the verb and goes to the end of the clause:

ab/fahren:

Der Zug fährt um 12 Uhr ab. *The train leaves at 12 o'clock.*

aus/geben:

Er gibt sehr viel Geld aus. *He spends a lot of money.*

Practice

EXERCISE A

Choose one of the verb forms from the box below to complete these sentences:

1 Inge __ gerade nach Hannover.
2 Seit dem Unfall (*accident*) __ ich keinen Alkohol mehr.
3 Heute __ es schön. Die Sonne __.
4 Der Zug aus Köln __ um 12 Uhr auf Gleis 2 an.
5 Das Baby __ in dem Kinderwagen.
6 Was __ Sie da? Einen Roman (*novel*)?
7 Am Samstagabend __ wir immer in einem Restaurant.
8 __ ihr für die Englandreise, oder __ ihr schon genug Geld?
9 Fritz und Hanno __ Jura (*law*) an der Universität Marburg.
10 Was __ du jetzt?
11 Der Schüler __ schon zwanzig Minuten an der Bushaltestelle.
12 Wie lange __ Otto schon Klavier?

> • machst • scheint • essen • spielt • studieren • wartet • fährt
> • spart • trinke • ist • kommt • lesen • schläft • habt

Complete the following sentences by changing the infinitive in brackets into a finite verb:

For example: Ich (gehen) __ in die Stadt. *I'm going into town.*
Ich gehe in die Stadt.

1 (Kommen) __ du mit? *Are you coming with us?*
2 Mein Mann (nehmen) __ Zucker in den Tee. *My husband takes sugar in his tea.*
3 (Sehen) __ du den Mann da? *Do you see the man there?*
4 Der Chef (fahren) __ oft nach Berlin. *The boss often travels to Berlin.*
5 Wir (fern/sehen) __ abends __. *We watch TV in the evening.*
6 Der Zug (ab/fahren) __ um 12 Uhr __. *The train departs at 12 o'clock.*
7 Wir (ein/kaufen) __ am liebsten bei Aldi __. *We like shopping most at Aldi.*
8 Jakob (an/kommen) __ heute Nachmittag __. *Jakob arrives this afternoon.*
9 Man (aus/geben) __ zu Weihnachten zu viel Geld __. *One spends too much money at Christmas.*
10 Ich (ein/schlafen) __ sofort __. *I go to sleep immediately.*

Ten things to remember

1 There is only one form of the present tense in German: **Hans arbeitet fleißig.** This can be translated into English in any of the following three ways: *Hans works hard, Hans is working hard* or *Hans **does** work hard.*

2 Some German verbs are regular, e.g. **kochen** (*to cook*), **spielen** (*to play*). This means that the stem of the verb comes from the infinitive (e.g. **koch-, spiel-**), and various forms and tenses can be worked out according to rules.

3 The stem of some regular verbs ends in **d** or **t**, e.g. **reden** (*to speak*), **arbeiten** (*to work*), or a combination of **m** or **n** preceded by another consonant, e.g. **atmen** (*to breathe*), **regnen** (*to rain*). In this case, an **e** is added before the endings of the **du, er, sie, es** and **ihr** forms in the present tense, for ease of pronunciation, e.g. **er arbeitet, es regnet.**

4 Some German verbs are irregular and so their various forms are unpredictable. You should always refer to the verb list to check the forms of irregular verbs such as **sein** (*to be*), **haben** (*to have*), **bleiben** (*to stay*), **geben** (*to give*) and **gehen** (*to go*).

5 Some German verbs which begin with a prefix are separable, e.g. **an/kommen** (*to arrive*), **ab/fahren** (*to depart, set off*), **an/bieten** (*to offer*), **ein/laden** (*to invite*).

6 Some German verbs which begin with a prefix are inseparable, e.g. **beschreiben** (*to describe*), **empfehlen** (*to recommend*), **verdienen** (*to earn*).

7 A few German verbs which begin with a prefix can be either separable or inseparable, depending on their meaning, e.g. **übersetzen** (*to translate*) and **über/setzen** (*to ferry over*).

8 Relative clauses in German always start with a relative pronoun, which is preceded by a comma.

9 The relative pronoun sends the verb to the end of the clause, which also finishes with a comma if the sentence continues, e.g. **Der Mann, den der Arzt besucht, ist sehr krank.** (*The man whom the doctor is visiting is very ill.*)

10 Never confuse the chart of relative pronouns with the chart for the definite article. There are important differences!

6

Expressing likes and dislikes

In this unit you will learn how to
- **Express likes and dislikes**
- **Ask questions about likes and dislikes**

Language points
- **Various verbs followed by gern**
- **The verbs mögen, gefallen, lieben and schätzen**
- **Pronouns in the accusative and dative**

EXPRESSING LIKES USING THE WORD **GERN**

Insight
You have already come across several examples of the adverb
gern(e), for example **Ich spiele gern Schach** (*I like playing
chess*).

▶ Used on its own, often in the form **gerne**, in response to a
question asking if you would like to do something, it means
with pleasure, willingly, readily.
▶ When used after a verb, **gern** expresses the idea of enjoying the
action portrayed. Look at the following examples, using the
different forms of the verb **spielen** (*to play*):

Ich spiele gern Fußball.	*I enjoy/like playing football.*
Er spielt gern Gitarre.	*He likes/enjoys playing the guitar.*
Wir spielen gern zusammen.	*We like playing together.*

Insight

Gern(e) is a particularly useful word to express personal likes and can be intensified in meaning by the addition of other adverbs, e.g. **Ich koche sehr gern** (*I like/enjoy cooking a lot*), **Ich koche besonders gern** (*I particularly like/enjoy cooking*) and more colloquially **Ich koche furchtbar gern** (*I like/enjoy cooking an awful lot*).

ENQUIRING ABOUT LIKES USING **GERN**

Spielt sie gern Klavier?	*Does she like playing the piano?*
Sie spielen gern Golf, ja?	*You like playing golf, don't you?*

EXPRESSING DISLIKES

The word **ungern** can be used in the above examples to change the meaning to: *I cook with reluctance, He swims very reluctantly, They don't like playing chess.*

Ich koche ungern.	*I don't like cooking.*
Er schwimmt sehr ungern.	*He swims very reluctantly.*

It is also possible to use **nicht gern** to express dislike, as in these sentences:

Er geht nicht gern in die Schule.	*He doesn't like going to school.*
Wir spielen nicht gern Tischtennis.	*We don't like playing table tennis.*

EXPRESSING AND ENQUIRING ABOUT LIKES

The verb **mögen** is also used to express liking and is followed sometimes by an infinitive at the end of the clause, sometimes by a noun or pronoun (See this unit's Grammar summary for the full verb):

Ich mag gern Turnen.	*I enjoy doing gym.*
Du magst Blumenkohl, nicht?	*You like cauliflower, don't you?*

Insight

The use of this verb **gefallen** is a little more complicated than some, so it is worth learning some examples until you get a feel for how it works:

Das Essen im Krankenhaus gefällt mir nicht.	*I don't like the food in hospital.*
Das Klima im Norden gefällt ihm nicht.	*He doesn't like the climate in the north.*

Have you noticed that these examples literally translate as 'The food in hospital does not please me/is not pleasing to me' and 'The climate in the north does not please him/is not pleasing to him'? This is because the verb **gefallen** requires the dative case.

The irregular verb **gefallen** is also often used with the impersonal pronoun **es** (*it*) plus a personal pronoun in the dative case: **mir** (*me, to me*), **dir** (*you, to you*), **ihm** (*him, to him*), **ihr** (*her, to her*), **ihm** (*it, to it*), **uns** (*us, to us*), **euch** (*you, to you*), **Ihnen** (*you, to you*), **ihnen** (*them, to them*). (See Unit 4 Taking it further, and Reference grammar 4.) For example:

Es gefällt ihm hier nicht.	*He doesn't like it here.*
Es gefällt ihr, wie er spricht.	*She likes the way he speaks.*

The impersonal pronoun **es** can, of course, be replaced by a noun of your choice, for example:

Wien gefällt ihm besonders gut.	*He particularly likes Vienna.*
Die deutsche Sprache gefällt mir gut.	*I like the German language.*

ENQUIRING ABOUT LIKES USING THE VERB **GEFALLEN**

You can also use this verb to ask how somebody likes something:

Gefällt Ihnen das Hotelzimmer?	*Do you like the hotel room?*
Wie gefällt dir der Film?	*How do you like the film?*

LUST HABEN *(TO FEEL LIKE DOING, TO BE IN THE MOOD TO)*

Hast du Lust, Eis zu essen?	*Do you feel like (eating) an ice cream?*
Wir haben heute keine Lust zu arbeiten.	*We don't feel like working today.*

Insight

Do note that the German word **die Lust** does not have the same meaning as the English word *lust*! In German, it is used to express your present inclination to do something:

Ich habe jetzt Lust auf eine Tasse Tee.	*I feel like a cup of tea now.*
Hast du Lust zum Schwimmen?	*Do you feel like going for a swim?*

LIEBEN *(TO LOVE)*

This regular German verb is not so widely used as its English or French counterparts. It is mostly used with reference to people or pets:

Sie liebt ihr Patenkind sehr.	*She loves her godchild very much.*
Er liebt seine Katze so.	*He loves his cat dearly.*

Insight

Lieben is the verb used to express being in love with someone, e.g. **Ich liebe dich** (*I love you*), or to ask if someone loves you: **Liebst du mich?** (*Do you love me?*)

(Contd)

At German funfairs you will see big decorated gingerbread hearts on sale with a ribbon to be worn round the neck. The words **Ich liebe dich** are picked out in bold white icing in the middle.

Compound nouns using **Lieblings-** (*favourite*) are much more widely used than the verb **lieben**. For example:

Seine Lieblingsfarbe ist Purpur.	*His favourite colour is purple.*
Ihre Lieblingsgruppe ist „Um Mitternacht".	*Her favourite (pop) group is Round Midnight.*
Mein Lieblingsfach war immer Chemie.	*My favourite subject was always chemistry.*

EXPRESSING A HIGH REGARD USING **SCHÄTZEN**

You can express a high regard for someone by using the regular verb **schätzen** (*to value, to think highly of*) as in the following examples:

Sie schätzt ihren Pfarrer sehr.	*She holds her vicar/minister in high regard.*
Thomas schätzt seinen Physiklehrer sehr.	*Thomas thinks very highly of his physics teacher.*

Insight

The noun from the verb **schätzen** is **der Schatz** (*the treasure*). This and the diminutive form **(das) Schätzchen** (literally *'little treasure'*) are used as the term of endearment *darling*.

The same verb **schätzen** has a second meaning: *to estimate* or *to reckon*:

Wie alt schätzt du sie?	*How old do you reckon she is?*
Ich schätze sie auf 30.	*I reckon she's 30.*

Grammar summary

Look at the following examples, which show how many other verbs can be used with **gern** to express the idea of enjoying or liking doing something.

VERBS WITH **GERN**

haben (*to have*)

gern haben (*to like*) (for the full form of **haben,** see Unit 3 Grammar summary)

Ich habe ihn sehr gern.	*I like him a lot.*
Sie hat Rockmusik sehr gern.	*She likes rock music very much.*

sein (*to be*) (for the full form of **sein,** see Unit 1 Grammar summary)

Das Kind ist gern bei seiner Oma.   *The child likes it at his grandma's.*

Regular verbs

hören (*to hear*)
Was für Musik hören Sie gern?   *What sort of music do you enjoy listening to?*

malen (*to paint*)
Er malt sehr gern.   *He enjoys painting very much.*

reisen (*to travel*)
Reist du auch gern?   *Do you also like travelling?*

For further details about the formation of regular verbs, see Unit 5 Grammar summary.

Irregular verbs

lesen (*to read*)
Liest du gern?   *Do you enjoy/like reading?*

fahren (*to drive, to travel*)
Er fährt sehr gern schnell.   *He likes driving fast.*

For further details about the formation of irregular verbs, see Unit 5 Grammar summary.

THE VERB **MÖGEN**

Here is the full form of the verb **mögen** (*to like*):

Singular		Plural	
ich mag	*I like*	**wir mögen**	*we like*
du magst	*you like*	**ihr mögt**	*you like*
er mag	*he likes*	**Sie mögen**	*you like*
sie mag	*she likes*	**sie mögen**	*they like*
es mag	*it likes*		

Insight

The verb **mögen** is one of the six so-called modal verbs, which all have irregular forms. You will notice above that the first and third person forms (i.e. **ich** and **er, sie, es**) are identical, and that the vowel in the singular is different from the plural (i.e. **mag, mögen**).

Modal verbs are sometimes followed by an infinitive at the end of the clause:

Ich mag nicht daran denken.   *I don't like to think about it.*

Sometimes this second verb does not appear in actual speech or writing, but it is still implied in the thought. (For details of other modal verbs, see Units 8 and 9.)

In speech, you will regularly come across the subjunctive form of this verb: **ich möchte** (*I should like*) used as an idiom. (See also Unit 7.)

In context

Read this letter from a German girl to a new penfriend abroad.

Liebe Anna,

Ich bin deine neue Brieffreundin. Ich bin vierzehn Jahre alt und ich wohne in Pockau. Ich habe einen Bruder und eine Schwester. Wir haben einen Hund. Er heißt Raudi. Ich liebe ihn sehr.

Ich schwimme gern. Ich spiele sehr gern Tennis und es gibt einen Tennisplatz hier in der Nähe. Ich höre gern Musik, besonders Popmusik. Pur ist meine Lieblingsgruppe. Was machst du gern? Was für Musik hörst du gern?

Ich mag die Schule nicht sehr und ich lerne nicht gern Mathe. Geschichte finde ich gar nicht interessant und Erdkunde ist einfach langweilig! Aber ich finde Kunst echt toll und Turnen gefällt mir gut. Hast du Lust, nach Deutschland zu kommen? Schreib mir bitte bald.

Deine Waltraud

deine neue Brieffreundin *your new penfriend*
der Hund *dog*
besonders *especially*
die Lieblingsgruppe *favourite pop group*
die Schule *school*
Mathe *maths*
gar nicht *not at all*
interessant *interesting*
Geschichte *history*

QUICK VOCAB

Now read this magazine interview with a famous Swiss personality:

Interviewerin	Grüezi, Norbert Eichler! Wie wunderbar, dass Sie mit uns sprechen! Sie haben sicher nicht sehr viel Freizeit. Aber was haben Sie als Hobby?
N.E.	Na ja, im Winter fahre ich leidenschaftlich gern Ski und im Sommer wandere ich sehr gern im Berner Oberland. Curling gefällt mir auch sehr. Ich liebe die Natur.
Interviewerin	Sie sind also sehr sportlich. Was machen Sie noch?
N.E.	Ich schätze meine Familie sehr. Abends spielen wir sehr gern zusammen, „Elfer raus", „Mensch ärgere dich nicht", „Uno" usw. Manchmal auch Skat oder Schach. Ich koche auch gern, wenn möglich Schweizer Spezialitäten wie Geschnetzeltes, Raclette oder Fondue.
Interviewerin	Vielen Dank für das Gespräch, Norbert! Viel Spaß beim Skifahren!

manchmal *sometimes*
Skat *a card game*
Schach *chess*
Schweizer *Swiss*
die Spezialität *speciality*
Geschnetzeltes *slivers of meat served in a cream sauce*
Raclette *a Swiss cheese dish*
Vielen Dank *many thanks*
das Gespräch *the conversation*
Viel Spaß beim Skifahren! *Have fun skiing!*

Taking it further

THE USE OF ACCUSATIVE PERSONAL PRONOUNS

Each time we have used a verb, we have come across a personal pronoun (**ich, du, er, sie, es, wir, ihr, Sie, sie**) which is used as a subject in the nominative case.

The accusative personal pronouns are **mich, dich, ihn, sie, es, uns, euch, Sie, sie** (*me, you, him, her, it, us, you, them*). We can use them in a sentence such as *I like him very much* or *He doesn't like it at all*, where they function as direct objects.

Look at the following questions and answers to illustrate the use of these. (In speech these questions could obviously be answered with a *yes* (**ja**) or *no* (**nein**), but the full answers illustrate the use of the pronouns very clearly.)

Mag er den Lehrer? Ja, er mag ihn sehr.   *Does he like the teacher? Yes, he likes him a lot.*

Du magst den Film nicht, oder? Doch, ich mag ihn sehr.   *You don't like the film, do you? Oh yes, I like it a lot.*

(You use **doch** instead of **ja**, when a negative answer is expected, but it turns out to be positive.)

Magst du die Königin? Oh ja.	Do you like the Queen? Yes, indeed.
Ich mag sie sehr.	I like her very much.
Isst du gern Eis? Nein, ich finde	Do you like eating ice cream? No,
es zu kalt.	I find it too cold.
Wie finden Sie Annas Eltern?	What do you think of Anna's
Ich finde sie zu streng.	parents? I find them too strict.

In this unit, we have also encountered personal pronouns in the dative case when using the verb **gefallen**. The dative personal pronouns are **mir, dir, ihm, ihr, ihm, uns, euch, Ihnen, ihnen.** We have used them in sentences such as:

| **Das Essen gefällt mir nicht.** | I do not like the food/The food does not please me. (literally 'The food is not pleasing to me.') |
| **Das Klima im Norden gefällt ihm nicht.** | He doesn't like the climate in the north. (literally 'The climate in the north is not pleasing to him.') |

The German title of Shakespeare's play *As You Like It* is translated into German as **Wie es Euch gefällt** (literally *'As it pleases (to) you'*).

Practice

EXERCISE A

Imagine that you are visiting a family in Vienna, who want to know your likes and dislikes so that they can plan the programme for your stay.

Using the icons and the vocabulary list to help you, form a sentence in response to questions 1–10. (The first is done for you.)

☺ besonders gut + gefallen   ✿ gern + a verb
❀ nicht gern + a verb   ☹ gar nicht + gefallen
😊 nicht sehr interessant + finden

1 Mögen Sie Gulasch? ✿ **Ja, ich mag or (ich esse) gern Gulasch.**
2 Schwimmen Sie gern? ❀
3 Wie finden Sie Jazz? 😊
4 Hören Sie gern die Musik von Strauwß? ✿
5 Gefällt Ihnen die moderne Kunst? ☹
6 Wie gefallen Ihnen die Kaffeehäuser von Wien? ☺
7 Besuchen Sie gern Museen? ❀
8 Wie gefällt Ihnen der Prater? ☹
9 Wie finden Sie die Oper? 😊
10 Gefällt Ihnen die blaue Donau? ☺

QUICK VOCAB

der or **das Gulasch** *goulash*
die moderne Kunst *modern art*
das Kaffeehaus *coffee shop*
das Museum (plural: **die Museen**) *the museum*
der Prater *permanent funfair by the River Danube in Vienna*
die Oper *the opera*
die blaue Donau *The Blue Danube*

EXERCISE B

Reread the magazine interview in 'In context' and decide whether the following statements are **richtig** (true) or **falsch** (false). If they are false, write out the correct answer.

1 Sein Vorname ist Herbert.
R F _____
2 Norbert Eichler kommt aus der Schweiz.
R F _____
3 Er fährt nicht gern Ski.
R F _____
4 Im Sommer wandert er gern in den Alpen.
R F _____

5 Er liebt die Natur.

R F _____

6 Er ist nicht sportlich.

R F _____

7 Norbert schätzt seine Familie sehr.

R F _____

8 Abends spielen sie Curling.

R F _____

9 Er kocht gern.

R F _____

10 Geschnetzeltes, Raclette und Fondue sind deutsche Spezialitäten.

R F _____

Ten things to remember

1 The adverb **gern** is often used with a verb to express liking doing something, e.g. **Ich schwimme gern.** (*I like swimming.*)

2 You can intensify the meaning of **gern** by adding another adverb such as **sehr** (*very*), **besonders** (*particularly, especially*) or even **furchtbar** (literally 'frightfully', but in this context it means *a lot*), e.g. **Ich schwimme sehr gern, Ich schwimme besonders gern, Ich schwimme furchtbar gern.**

3 The verb **gefallen** means *to please* but is often used in the sense of *to like*. It requires the dative case.

4 The verb **gefallen** is also often used with the impersonal pronoun **es**, e.g. **Wie gefällt es dir hier? Es gefällt mir gut hier, danke!** (*How do you like it here? I like it a lot here, thanks!*)

5 **Lust haben** expresses your present inclination to do something (i.e. whether you feel like doing it now), e.g. **Hast du Lust zum Schwimmen? Nein, ich habe keine Lust dazu.** (*Do you feel like going swimming? No, I don't feel like it.*)

6 The verb **lieben** is used to express your love for a person or animal.

7 The verb **schätzen** has two different meanings: 1) *to treasure, to value* 2) *to estimate, to reckon*.

8 The verb **mögen** (*to like to*) is one of a group of six modal verbs which have peculiar forms.

9 The accusative personal pronouns are **mich, dich, ihn, sie, es, ihn, uns, euch, Sie, sie,** e.g. **Liebst du mich? Ja, ich liebe dich.** (*Do you love me? Yes, I love you.*)

10 The dative personal pronouns are **mir, dir, ihm, ihr, ihm, uns, euch, Ihnen, ihnen,** e.g. **Wie gefällt es dir in Hamburg? Es gefällt mir gut in Hamburg.** (*How do you like it in Hamburg? I like it in Hamburg.*)

7

Expressing wants and preferences

In this unit you will learn how to
- *Express wants and preferences*
- *Ask questions about wants and preferences*

Language points
- *The verb* wollen
- *The idiomatic use of* möchten
- *The use of* lieber *to express preferences*
- *The verb* vor/ziehen
- *Other ways of expressing preferences*

EXPRESSING WANTS USING **WOLLEN**

Ich will unbedingt Kaffee trinken.   *I really want to drink some coffee.*
Sie will ja ein Auto kaufen.   *She wants to buy a car.*

Insight

The two examples above show the use of **unbedingt** (*absolutely*, *definitely*, *really*) and **ja** (*yes*). These are known as modal particles and are common in speech. They are not translated directly and do not change the overall meaning of a sentence, but they do show the mood or attitude of the speaker.

Other examples of modal particles are: **aber** (*but*, *however* – literally 'but'), **denn** (*because*, *as*), **doch** (*but*), **mal** (*just*, e.g. **Komm mal her!** *Just come here!*), **schon** (*already*, *yet*).

ENQUIRING ABOUT WANTS USING THE VERB **WOLLEN**

Willst du auch nach Spanien fahren?	*Do you also want to go to Spain?*
Will er nicht bei Hans übernachten?	*Doesn't he want to stay at Hans' house?*

Insight

The verb **wollen** is used when you wish to express what you want to do in fairly strong terms:

Ich will hier bleiben.   *I want to stay here.*

This is a direct way of speaking but is not necessarily impolite.

THE USE OF THE CONJUNCTION **DASS** *WITH* **WOLLEN**

Notice the way that German uses the conjunction **dass** to express the following:

Ihr Mann will, dass sie zu Hause bleibt.	*Her husband wants her to stay at home. (literally 'Her husband wants that she stay at home.')*
Mein Sohn will nicht, dass ich zu laut spreche.	*My son doesn't want me to talk too loudly.*

Insight

You will notice that **dass** is a conjunction which sends the verb to the end of the clause. Further examples of such conjunctions are: **weil** (*because*), **wenn** (*if, whenever*), **ob** (*whether*), **obwohl** (*although*) and **als** (*when* – when referring to the past). If they appear mid-sentence, they are preceded by a comma.

EXPRESSING POLITE REQUESTS USING **ICH MÖCHTE**, ETC.

ich möchte (*I should like*)

> ## Insight
>
> It is possible to express likes and preferences in a more subtle and certainly more polite way using the verb forms **ich/er/sie/es möchte, du möchtest, ihr möchtet, wir/Sie/sie möchten.** This is in fact the simple past subjunctive form of the verb **mögen** (see Unit 6). In this context, it is simply used as an idiom, and you do not need to understand how it is formed.

You are very likely to be asked in a café or a restaurant: **Was möchten Sie?** (*What would you like?*). Another verb is implied in this question (most probably to order), but it is not always said.

Look at the following examples of this verb:

Ich möchte bitte Käsekuchen.   *I should like cheesecake, please.*
Wir möchten bezahlen, bitte!   *We'd like to pay, please.*

ENQUIRING POLITELY ABOUT WANTS USING **MÖCHTEN**

Möchtest du Tee, Hans?   *Would you like tea, Hans?*
Möchtet ihr Apfelsaft?   *Would you like apple juice?*

EXPRESSING PREFERENCES USING **LIEBER** OR **AM LIEBSTEN**

You can express what you prefer doing by using the same structures as above, replacing **gern** with **lieber,** for example:

Sie möchte lieber keinen   *She would prefer to drink no alcohol.*
   Alkohol trinken.
Er spielt lieber Handball.   *He prefers playing handball.*
Wir trinken lieber Bier.   *We prefer (we'd prefer) to drink beer.*
Ich würde lieber in die Schweiz   *I'd prefer to go to Switzerland rather*
   fahren als nach Schweden.   *than Sweden.*
Er bleibt am liebsten zu Hause.   *He likes staying at home best of all.*

Du hörst lieber CDs, oder?	*You prefer listening to CDs, don't you?*
Essen Sie lieber rote Grütze als Eis?	*Would you prefer (to eat) fresh red fruit pudding rather than ice cream?*

Insight

In the above examples, the word **lieber** is used as the comparative form of the adverb **gern**, which we have already learned:

Ich trinke doch gern Tee, aber ich trinke lieber Bier.	*I do like drinking tea but I prefer (drinking) beer.*

Please do not confuse this with the nominative masculine adjective **Lieber** (*Dear*), which is used at the start of an informal letter:

Lieber Hans	*Dear Hans*
Lieber Herr Braun	*Dear Mr Brown*

The superlative form is **am liebsten:**

Ich trinke Wein am liebsten.	*I like wine best of all.*

Grammar summary

The verb **wollen** is another one of the six modal verbs. The formation of **wollen** is similar to that of **mögen** (see Unit 6), in that there is no ending in the first and third person singular, and there is a vowel change from the singular to the plural.

The full form of **wollen** is as follows:

wollen (to want to) Singular		Plural	
ich will	I want to	wir wollen	we want to
du willst	you want to	ihr wollt	you want to
er will	he wants to	Sie wollen	you want to
sie will	she wants to	sie wollen	they want to
es will	it wants to		

Insight

You will have noticed that the I, he, she and it forms of **wollen** look like the English future tense. You must resist the temptation to translate it in this way. **Ich will** means I want to, in the same way as the response in the 1662 Prayer Book version of the Church of England marriage ceremony presumably means I will in the sense of 'I want to' rather than 'I have the intention of doing so in future'!

In context

IN A RESTAURANT

Herr Schneider	Die Speisekarte, bitte.
Kellner	Jawohl. Ich bringe sie gleich.
Herr Schneider	Danke.
Herr Schneider and his wife call the waiter and order their meal.	
Herr Schneider	Ich möchte gern eine Gulaschsuppe und nachher den Fisch, bitte.
Kellner	Wie mögen Sie ihn? Gebraten oder gegrillt?
Herr Schneider	Lieber gegrillt. Das ist gesund und schmeckt besser.
Kellner	Gut. Und was möchten Sie, gnädige Frau?
Frau Schneider	Zuerst möchte ich am liebsten den Thunfischsalat und dann das Hähnchen, bitte. Aber gibt es nur Pommes frites als Beilage? Ich esse sie nicht gern.

Kellner	Es gibt auch Salzkartoffeln heute Abend und Blumenkohl, Bohnen und Salat.
Frau Schneider	Ich möchte gern den Salat aber sind Eier in der Mayonnaise? Ich bin allergisch gegen Eier. Vielleicht nehme ich die Bohnen.
Herr Schneider	Gut, mein Schatz, was möchtest du am liebsten trinken?
Frau Schneider	Lieber keinen Alkohol; vielleicht nur eine Flasche Mineralwasser.
Herr Schneider	Und ich trinke ein Glas Weißwein.
Kellner	Ist in Ordnung. Einen Moment, bitte. Es kommt gleich.

Insight

You will see from the conversation above that Frau Schneider is allergic to eggs. In German, this is expressed by using a different preposition from the one we use in English: **allergisch gegen etwas sein** literally means 'to be allergic *against* or *towards* something'.

Other examples to remember are: **anders als** (*different from*), **fähig zu** (*capable of*), **stolz auf** (*proud of*), **typisch für** (*typical of*) and **verlobt sein mit** (*to be engaged to*).

And if you want tablets for your headache, you would ask: **Haben Sie bitte Tabletten gegen Kopfschmerzen?** (literally *'Have you (any) tablets against (a) headache, please?'*).

die Gulaschsuppe *goulash soup*
nachher *afterwards*
der Fisch *fish*
gebraten *baked/fried*
gegrillt *grilled*
gesund *healthy*
es schmeckt besser *it tastes better*
zuerst *first of all*

der Thunfischsalat *tuna salad*
das Hähnchen *chicken*
nur *only*
Pommes frites *chips*
als Beilage *as an accompaniment*
Salzkartoffeln *boiled potatoes (literally 'salt potatoes')*
heute Abend *this evening*
der Blumenkohl *cauliflower*
die Bohnen *(pl.) beans*
der Salat *salad*
das Ei *(pl.* Eier*) egg(s)*
allergisch gegen *allergic to*
der Schatz *darling (literally 'treasure')*
eine Flasche Mineralwasser *a bottle of mineral water*

Taking it further

MAKING POLITE REQUESTS USING **HÄTTE**

A level of politeness can be achieved by using the past subjunctive of the verb **haben** in the following way:

Meine Frau hätte gern eine Kaltschale.	*My wife would like a cold sweet soup (often cherry).*
Wir hätten gern ein Zimmer mit Badewanne.	*We'd like a room with a bath.*

Expressing preferences using **vor/ziehen**:

Ich ziehe Beethoven den Beatles vor.	*I prefer Beethoven to the Beatles.*
Sie zieht Wein dem Bier vor.	*She prefers wine to beer.*

Vorsicht! *Be careful!* In the previous two sentences, the direct object in the accusative case (**Beethoven, Wein**) precedes the indirect object in the dative case (**den Beatles, dem Bier**). But this word order is an exception and is not true of other structures which have two nouns after the verb, such as:

Der Lehrer schenkt dem Schüler das Buch.
The teacher gives the book to the boy.

Here, the indirect object in the dative case precedes the direct object in the accusative case.

Der Chef gibt seiner Sekretärin einen Kuss.
The boss gives his secretary a kiss.

Der Mann kauft seinem Sohn ein Fahrrad.
The man buys his son a bicycle.

....

Insight

If you wish to check whether something is an indirect object or not, try rephrasing the English version, prefacing what you think is the indirect object with either 'to the' or 'for the'. If the result sounds natural, even if a little stilted (for example *The boss gives a kiss to his secretary, The mother sings a lullaby to the baby, The man buys a bicycle for the boy*), this noun phrase is the indirect object of the sentence and will require the dative case. For full details about word order, see Reference grammar 14.

....

EXPRESSING WISHES USING **SICH ETWAS WÜNSCHEN**

Ich wünsche mir einen gut bezahlten Beruf.
I wish for a well-paid job.

Was wünschst du dir zum Geburtstag?
What would you like for your birthday?

Sie wünscht sich einen reichen Mann.
She'd like a rich husband.

(See Unit 11 for more reflexive verbs.)

ENQUIRING ABOUT WISHES USING **WÜNSCHEN**

Ich wünsche dir vor allem Gesundheit und ein langes Leben.	*I wish you above all health and a long life.*
Wir wünschen Ihnen alles Gute zum Neuen Jahr.	*We wish you all the best for the New Year.*

Practice

EXERCISE A

The woman of my dreams

You are looking for a partner at an introduction agency and are being asked about your interests and preferences. Answer each of the questions you are asked, using the personal details in the box:

> You are called *Willi Winkelmann*, are 30 years old and live in Zurich, Switzerland. You are divorced and have a dog. You enjoy playing the guitar and prefer classical music to pop music. Of course you enjoy drinking beer, but do not like wine. Your favourite food is boiled knuckle of pork with pickled cabbage, but unfortunately you are allergic to fish. You don't like hotels but prefer camping, particularly in Greece and Spain. The woman of your dreams is a kind blonde who loves dogs, likes drinking beer and enjoys fresh air.

QUICK VOCAB

geschieden *divorced*
Gitarre spielen *to play the guitar*
die Popmusik *pop music*
klassische Musik *classical music*
das Bier *beer*
der Wein *wine*
das Eisbein mit Sauerkraut *boiled knuckle of pork with pickled cabbage*

allergisch gegen *allergic to*
zelten *to camp*
Griechenland *Greece*
Spanien *Spain*

Interviewer	Guten Tag! Wie heißen Sie, bitte?
Willi Winkelmann	Ich heiße Willi Winkelmann.
Interviewer	Gut, und wie alt sind Sie, Herr Winkelmann?
Willi Winkelmann	Ich ___.
Interviewer	Wo wohnen Sie?
Willi Winkelmann	Ich ___.
Interviewer	Sind Sie verheiratet?
Willi Winkelmann	Nein, ___.
Interviewer	Haben Sie Haustiere (*pets*)?
Willi Winkelmann	Ja, ___.
Interviewer	Was machen Sie gern in Ihrer Freizeit? (*free time*)
Willi Winkelmann	Ich ___.
Interviewer	Hören Sie gern Popmusik?
Willi Winkelmann	Ich ___.
Interviewer	Trinken Sie viel (*much*)?
Willi Winkelmann	Ich ___.
Interviewer	Was ist Ihr Lieblingsessen?
Willi Winkelmann	Mein ___.
Interviewer	Haben Sie irgendwelche Allergien (*any allergies*)?
Willi Winkelmann	Ich bin ___.
Interviewer	Übernachten Sie gern in Hotels?
Willi Winkelmann	Nein, ich ___.
Interviewer	Wo zelten Sie am liebsten (*where do you most like camping*)?
Willi Winkelmann	In ___ und in ___.
Interviewer	Wie ist Ihre Traumfrau?
Willi Winkelmann	Sie ist ___, liebt ___ und frische Luft, ___ gern Bier, kurz gesagt (*in short*) eine nette Blondine.

EXERCISE B

German friends have sent you details about a young girl who would like an au pair job in England. Can you translate the information into English for a family who are looking for an au pair?

Anneliese will ein Jahr lang in England bleiben. Die Schule gefällt ihr gar nicht, und sie studiert sehr ungern. Aber ihre Mutter will, dass sie Englisch lernt. Sie würde am liebsten in einer Großstadt wie London oder Manchester wohnen, und sie möchte gern bei einer Familie mit Kleinkindern wohnen. Sie hört gern Musik und zieht englische Popmusik der deutschen Popmusik vor. Sie ist keine Vegetarierin, aber sie isst lieber kein Fleisch. Sie hätte gern ein Einzelzimmer, und sie will auf gar keinen Fall Hausarbeit machen.

Ten things to remember

1 The verb **wollen** (*to want to*) is one of the six modal verbs. It is conjugated in an unusual way and is sometimes followed by an infinitive at the end of the clause.

2 Never be tempted to confuse the singular form of **wollen** (i.e. **ich will, er will**) with the English future tense!

3 Several conjunctions send the verb to the end of the clause, e.g. **als, dass, ob, obwohl, weil, wenn**. Whenever they appear mid-sentence, they are preceded by a comma.

4 The phrase **ich möchte** is an idiomatic use of the verb **mögen**. It is a polite expression meaning *I should like to*.

5 The adverb **lieber** is the comparative form of **gern**. It is used with a verb to express a preference.

6 Do not confuse the adverb **lieber** with the nominative masculine adjective **Lieber** (*Dear*) at the beginning of an informal letter, e.g. **Lieber Hans** (*Dear Hans*), **Lieber Herr Braun** (*Dear Mr Brown*).

7 The phrase **am liebsten** is used with a verb to express the strongest preference.

8 Some adjectives are followed by different prepositions in German and English, e.g. **anders als** (*different from*), **fähig zu** (*capable of*), **stolz auf** (*proud of*), **typisch für** (*typical of*), **verlobt mit** (*engaged to*).

9 If you wish to check an indirect object, try rephrasing the English version, prefacing what you think is the indirect object with either 'to the' or 'for the'. If the result sounds natural, even if a little stilted (for example *The boss gives a kiss to his secretary*), the noun phrase is the indirect object of the sentence and will require the dative case.

10 Some common words are used in speech to add emphasis but are not necessarily translated, e.g. **denn, doch, ja, mal, unbedingt**.

8

Expressing permission and ability

In this unit you will learn how to
- **Make statements about permission and ability**
- **Ask questions about permission and ability**

Language points
- **The verbs dürfen and können**
- **The indefinite pronoun man**

In this unit we will learn two more verbs which are similar to **mögen** (see Unit 6) and **wollen** (see Unit 7). In fact, there are numerous ways of translating these verbs, but we are mainly going to restrict ourselves to the areas of permission, ability and obligation.

MAKING STATEMENTS ABOUT PERMISSION

In order to express permission, the verb **dürfen** is often used. This infinitive form is normally translated as *to be allowed to, to be permitted to*, but depending on the context the individual parts of the verb are also rendered in the following ways: *I may, I can, I am allowed to, I am permitted to.*

Ich darf keine Butter essen.   *I am not allowed to eat butter.*

ASKING QUESTIONS ABOUT PERMISSION

You will have noticed in the above examples that **dürfen** is normally followed by another infinitive at the end of the clause, for example **Ihr dürft schon gehen**. But, as we noted with **wollen** and **mögen**, the infinitive is not always stated, even though it is implied.

Darf ich Sie nach Hause bringen? *May I/Can I take you home?*

Insight

This example also shows that German uses the verb **bringen** (*to bring*) whereas English uses *to take*:

Renate bringt ihren Sohn zum Bahnhof.	*Renate is taking her son to the railway station.*
Darf er im Krankenhaus rauchen?	*Can/is he allowed to smoke in hospital?*
Dürfen wir Sie um das Geld bitten?	*Can/may we ask you for the money?*

Insight

The polite question **Darf ich?** (*May I?* – i.e. *May I join in? May I have one?*) opens many social doors in German. There are also many extended forms in frequent use:

Darf ich bitten?	*May I have the pleasure (of this dance)?*
Darf ich zu Tisch bitten?	*Lunch/dinner is served.*
Darf ich reden?	*Am I allowed to speak?*
Darf ich mal gucken?	*May I have a little look?*
Darf ich durch?	*May I get through?*

Grammar summary

Here is the full form of the verb **dürfen**:

Singular		Plural	
ich darf	I may/can, I am permitted to	**wir dürfen**	we may, etc.
du darfst	you may, etc.	**ihr dürft**	you may, etc.
er darf	he may, etc.	**Sie dürfen**	you may, etc.
sie darf	she may, etc.	**sie dürfen**	they may, etc.
es darf	it may, etc.		

Insight

In shops, you will often hear the question **Was darf es sein?** (*What is it to be? What can I do for you? How can I help you?*). You would not use the verb **dürfen** in your reply, but rather a phrase such as **Ich möchte ...** (*I should like ...*) or **Haben Sie ...?** (*Have you ...?*).

NB **Dürfen** changes its meaning when used in the negative form. (See Unit 9 Taking it further.)

GRANTING PERMISSION USING **KÖNNEN**

Können is used to express permission in the same way as *can* in English.

Du kannst bei uns übernachten.	*You can spend the night with us.*
Ihr könnt gerne heute Abend ins Kino gehen.	*You can go to the cinema this evening with pleasure.*
Selbstverständlich können Sie hier rauchen.	*Of course you can smoke here.*

IS IT EXPRESSING PERMISSION OR ABILITY?

Before looking in detail at the verb **können** (*to be able to*), we must explain some of the overlap that exists between this verb and **dürfen**, and indeed between their English counterparts. Literally, **können** is used to show ability, for example 'My three-year old daughter *can* already swim', 'I *can* easily sing the alto part', 'They *can* fix it tomorrow'. These sentences clearly show the ability to perform an action.

But in spoken language, **können**, as well as its English counterpart, is also used to express or enquire about permission.

As we saw above in the examples, **dürfen** is sometimes translated as *Can I take you home? You can get up tomorrow*, in the sense of *Am I allowed to take you home? You have permission to get up tomorrow*. **Dürfen** gives a polite tone to the language, but **können** is very often used in its place. Thus you will hear the following examples in speech:

Kann ich Sie nach Hause bringen? *Can I take you home?*
Kann ich rauchen? *Can I smoke?*

In these examples, **dürfen** and **können** have a very similar meaning and can be interchanged, affecting only the level of politeness of the language.

EXPRESSING ABILITY WITH **KÖNNEN**

Insight

Können expresses ability in various ways. It can simply mean that someone is either old enough, big enough, clever enough or strong enough to do something. It can also suggest that they know or understand how to do something, or have the right or power to do it.

Ich kann schlecht hören.	*I hear with difficulty. (literally 'I can hear badly.')*
Du kannst gut Rad fahren.	*You can ride (a bicycle) well.*
Alina kann fließend Russisch (sprechen).	*Alina can speak fluent Russian.*
Wir können morgen kommen.	*We can come tomorrow.*
Sie können schon Auto fahren, oder?	*You can already drive a car, can't you?*

Können can also be used without being followed by an infinitive, although a second verb is implied, as in:

Ich kann nicht weiter.	*I can't (go) any further/I can't go on.*
Er kann kein Deutsch.	*He can't (speak) German.*
Sie kann das schon.	*She can already (do it).*

ASKING QUESTIONS ABOUT ABILITY

Questions about ability can be asked either by inverting the verb or by using one of the words we learned in Unit 1.

Kannst du Schach spielen?	*Can you play chess?*
Können sie nicht länger warten?	*Can't they wait any longer?*
Wie kann ich Ihnen helfen?	*How can I help you?*
Wer kann kochen?	*Who can cook?*

Here is the full form of the verb **können**:

Singular		Plural	
ich kann	*I can/am able to*	**wir können**	*we can/are able to*
du kannst	*you can/are able to*	**ihr könnt**	*you can/are able to*
er kann	*he can/is able to*	**Sie können**	*you can/are able to*
sie kann	*she can/is able to*	**sie können**	*they can/are able to*
es kann	*it can/is able to*		

In context

AN INTERVIEW FOR A JOB

Der Chef Guten Morgen, Frau Braun! Sie dürfen gerne Platz nehmen. Darf ich fragen: Warum wollen Sie bei uns arbeiten?

Frau Braun Also, ich kann fließend Französisch sprechen, und ich kann sowohl auf Französisch als auch auf Deutsch Geschäftsbriefe schreiben.

Der Chef Sie können auch Englisch, oder?

Frau Braun Nein, leider nicht. Aber mein Mann und ich wollen es lernen.

Der Chef Möchten Sie etwas fragen?

Frau Braun Darf man im Büro rauchen?

Der Chef Nein, unbedingt nicht. In unserem Büro gibt es ein Rauchverbot. ... Können Sie gleich bei uns anfangen?

fließend Französisch *fluent French*
sowohl ... als auch *both ... and*
auf Französisch *in French*
auf Deutsch *in German*
der Geschäftsbrief *business letter*
leider nicht *unfortunately not*
etwas fragen *to ask something/anything*
das Büro *the office*
rauchen *to smoke*
unbedingt nicht *absolutely not*
das Rauchverbot *smoking ban*
gleich *immediately*
an/fangen *to begin, start*

QUICK VOCAB

Taking it further

OTHER EXPRESSIONS WHICH SUGGEST PERMISSION GIVEN

ruhig (*feel free to, you're welcome to*) (*normally means 'calm, quiet'*)

Du kannst den Rest des Essens ruhig **mitnehmen.**	*Feel free to take the rest of the food with you.*

ohne weiteres (*it's quite all right, it's no problem*)

Er kann ohne weiteres **hereinkommen.**	*It's quite all right for him to come in.*

von mir (uns) aus (*as far as I am/we are concerned*)

Von uns aus **kannst du nach dem Faschingsball bei Trudi schlafen.**	*As far as we are concerned, you can sleep at Trudi's after the Carnival Ball.*

schon (*of course, it's all right*) (*no exact English equivalent*)

Du kannst schon **gehen.**	*You can go.*

THE INDEFINITE PRONOUN **MAN**

Insight

The indefinite pronoun **man** translates into English as *one* or *you*. (Compare the French word '*on*'.) Do be careful in speech to distinguish between this indefinite pronoun **man** and the masculine noun **Mann**, as they both sound the same. **Man** is often used with modal verbs and also as an alternative to the passive voice (see Unit 19).

Look at the following:

Man darf hier rauchen.	*You can smoke here.*
Man kann nur hoffen.	*One can only hope.*
Man muss in der Schlange warten.	*You have to wait in the queue.*
Man soll nicht gleich nach dem Essen schwimmen.	*You shouldn't go swimming straight after a meal.*
Kann man hier Briefmarken kaufen?	*Can you buy stamps here?*

Practice

EXERCISE A

In the youth hostel

You have arrived in a youth hostel with a group of teenagers and are being told the house rules by the warden (Herbergsvater). Read the passage and answer the questions.

Ihr dürft bis 22 Uhr fernsehen und bis 20 Uhr die Waschmaschine benutzen. Es kann sein, dass jemand von euch Klavier spielen kann. Wenn ja, dürft ihr gern das Klavier bis 21 Uhr im Aufenthaltsraum benutzen. Zwischen 20 und 22 Uhr darf man in der kleinen Küche Tee, Kaffee, usw. kochen aber bitte, niemand darf die große Küche benutzen. Frühstück gibt es von 6 bis 8 Uhr morgens. Darf ich euch jetzt bitten, eure Rucksäcke in eure Schlafzimmer zu bringen.

1 What four things are you allowed to do in the evening?
2 What is nobody allowed to do?
3 What final request does the youth hostel warden make?

EXERCISE B

Excursion

Tante Inge has a young godchild, Renate. While Renate's mother is in hospital, she takes her and her friend Anna to the zoo for the day. In the following excited conversation, fill in each gap with the appropriate form of either **dürfen** or **können**:

Anna	__ wir die Tiere füttern? (dürfen)
Tante Inge	Ihr __ sicher einige Tiere füttern aber nicht alle. (dürfen)
Renate	__ ich ein Eis haben, bitte? (dürfen)
Anna (aufgeregt)	Oh, ich __ einen Elefanten sehen! (können) __ du ihn auch sehen, Renate? (können)
Renate	__ der Elefant unser Brot essen? (dürfen)
Tante Inge	Wie bitte? Ach, es ist hier so laut! Ich __ dich nicht hören, Renate! (können) Ich frage den Zoowärter. Entschuldigen Sie, __ Sie uns sagen (können), ob wir den Elefanten füttern __? (dürfen)
Zoowärter	Selbstverständlich.
Renate	Tante Inge, __ ich bitte Mutti anrufen und ihr alles erzählen? (dürfen)

QUICK VOCAB

die Tiere *animals*
füttern *to feed*
einige *some*
ein Eis *an ice cream*
aufgeregt *excitedly*
der Elefant *elephant (accusative* **den Elefanten**, *weak noun, see Reference grammar 2.4)*
so laut *so loud, so noisy*
fragen *to ask*
der Zoowärter *zoo keeper*
entschuldigen *to excuse*
selbstverständlich *but of course*
an/rufen *to telephone*
erzählen *to tell, relate*

Ten things to remember

1 The verb **dürfen** is normally translated as *to be allowed to* or *to be permitted to*.

2 It belongs to the same group of six modal verbs as **mögen** and **wollen**, which we learned in Units 6 and 7. As with **mögen** and **wollen**, the first and third person singular forms of the verb are the same: **darf**.

3 Being a modal verb, **dürfen** is often followed by an infinitive at the end of the clause, but in practice the infinitive is often merely implied and not spoken in full.

4 The question form **Darf ich?** (*May I?*) is used very often in polite requests.

5 In German, the verb **bringen** (*to bring*) is used where English uses *to take*, e.g. **Bringst du mich bitte zum Arzt?** (*Will you take me to the doctor's, please?*)

6 The verb **können** (*to be able to*) is also a modal verb.

7 It expresses permission or ability, as in the English *I can*.

8 When making a request, **Darf ich?** (*May I?*) is more polite than **Kann ich?** (*Can I?*).

9 The indefinite pronoun **man** is translated as *one* or *you*. It takes the third person singular form of the verb.

10 Never confuse this indefinite pronoun **man** (*one, you*) with the masculine noun **der Mann** (*the man, the husband*).

9

Expressing obligation and necessity

In this unit you will learn how to
- *Make statements about obligation and need*
- *Ask questions about obligation and need*

Language points
- *The verbs* sollen, müssen *and* brauchen
- *The negative use of* dürfen
- *Phrases expressing obligation and need*

The verb **sollen** can be translated into English in many different ways, but its main use is to express moral obligation in the sense of *I am obliged to, I should, I am supposed to, I am expected to, I am to.*

Insight
It is interesting to note that the Ten Commandments are expressed by means of **sollen: Du sollst nicht töten** can be translated as *Thou shalt not kill, You ought not to kill, You are obliged not to kill, You shouldn't kill* or *You are not supposed to kill.* This verb strongly expresses moral obligation but it still allows you to decide whether to obey or not.

Look at the following examples and their translations:

Ich soll schöne Grüße von Antje bestellen.   *I am to pass on Antje's best wishes.*

Sie soll zum Arzt gehen.	*She should go to the doctor.*
Wir sollen nicht zu lange bleiben.	*We oughtn't to stay too late.*

Insight
To obey or not to obey, that is the question!

In fact, German uses two forms of **sollen** to show how
obedient you really are! Look at the following sentences
using the two forms of **sollen** and their English translations,
and see if you can work out the difference in their meanings.

Ich soll keine Schokolade essen.	*I am not supposed to eat any chocolate (and so I wouldn't dream of it).*
Ich sollte nicht so viel Schokolade essen.	*I ought not to eat so much chocolate (but I like it so much, so who cares!).*
Der Hund soll draußen warten.	*The dog should wait outside (so I'll tie him up outside).*
Der Hund sollte aber draußen warten.	*The dog ought to wait outside. (It's unhygienic to bring him in here, but he's been brought in anyway.)*
Sie sollen schon um acht Uhr da sein.	*They're supposed to be there by eight o'clock (and I expect they will be).*
Sie sollten um acht Uhr da sein.	*They were supposed to be there at eight o'clock (so where on earth are they?).*

In some situations these two forms can be interchangeable, as in
the following example:

Sie soll(te) zum Arzt gehen.	*She ought to go to the doctor's.*

Some of the examples above used the subjunctive version of **sollen,**
i.e. **sollten.** For more examples, see Unit 21.

Insight
Did you manage to work out the difference in the meanings
of **soll** and **sollte**? **Ich soll** suggests that you intend to do
what you are supposed to, whereas **ich sollte** implies that you
know what you should do but have no intention of doing it.

Grammar summary

Now look at the full verb form of **sollen**. (You will notice that, unlike the other modal verbs we have come across, **sollen** has the same vowel in the singular as in the plural. It is, however, similar to the other five modal verbs in that the first and the third person singular have no ending.)

Singular		Plural	
ich soll	*I ought to/am obliged to/should*	**wir sollen**	*we ought to, etc.*
du sollst	*you ought to, etc.*	**ihr sollt**	*you ought to, etc.*
er soll	*he ought to, etc.*	**Sie sollen**	*you ought to, etc.*
sie soll	*she ought to, etc.*	**sie sollen**	*they ought to, etc.*
es soll	*it ought to, etc.*		

EXPRESSING COMPULSION OR NECESSITY: MÜSSEN

To a certain extent there is an overlap in the usage of the verbs **müssen** and **sollen**, in that **müssen** can sometimes express obligation in the sense of *I must, I have to*; but **müssen** is normally used to express compulsion or necessity rather than obligation. Look at the following examples using **müssen** to work out the possible meanings of the verb:

Ich muss mal zum Klo gehen (colloquial).	*I must go/I've got to go to the loo.*
Du musst fleißig arbeiten.	*You must/you've got to work hard.*
Er muss jeden Tag zwölf Tabletten nehmen.	*He has to take twelve pills every day.*

You can use this verb in questions in the same way we have learned in previous units:

Was muss ich jetzt machen?	*What do I have to do now?*
Müssen wir noch einkaufen?	*Do we still have to go shopping?*
Warum müssen Sie so früh gehen?	*Why do you have to go so early?*

EXPRESSING LACK OF NECESSITY USING **MÜSSEN**

When used with a negative, **müssen** expresses the idea of lack of necessity, as the following examples show:

Ich muss nicht abnehmen.	*I don't need to lose weight.*
Sie muss heute nicht in die Schule gehen.	*She doesn't have to go to school today.*
Sie müssen nicht länger bleiben.	*You don't have to stay any longer.*

Here is the full form of the verb **müssen**:

Singular		Plural	
ich muss	*I must/I have to/I've got to*	**wir müssen**	*we must, etc.*
du musst	*you must, etc.*	**ihr müsst**	*you must, etc.*
er muss	*he must, etc.*	**Sie müssen**	*you must, etc.*
sie muss	*she must, etc.*	**sie müssen**	*they must, etc.*
es muss	*it must, etc.*		

Insight
It is very easy to overlook the difference in vowel between the singular and plural forms of the verb **müssen**:

▶ The singular is **ich muss** (with no umlaut).
▶ The plural is **wir müssen** (with an umlaut over the **u**).

In context

ENQUIRING ABOUT A VISA TO GO TO RUSSIA

Beamter	Grüß Gott! Wie kann ich Ihnen helfen?
Reisende	Muss ich ein Visum für diese Reise nach Russland haben, bitte?

(Contd)

Beamter	Ja. Sie brauchen nur dieses Formular auszufüllen, und Sie müssen es an die russische Botschaft schicken. Sie können dann einen Monat da bleiben. Sie dürfen aber nicht länger bleiben. Wann wollen Sie dorthin fahren?
Reisende	Im Juni. Soll ich das Formular hier ausfüllen?
Beamter	Nein. Ich darf das nicht abfertigen. Man muss das in der Botschaft stempeln lassen. Übrigens brauchen Sie drei Fotos und einen Scheck. Sie sollen das alles wegschicken. Aber Sie dürfen nicht zu lange warten. Es dauert sehr lange, ein Visum zu bekommen.
Reisende	Vielen Dank für Ihre Hilfe.
Beamter	Gern geschehen.

Insight
Erste Hilfe (*First Aid*)

Did you notice that the verb **helfen** (*to help*) is followed by a dative personal pronoun: **Wie kann ich Ihnen helfen?** This is because the verb **helfen** takes the dative case. It is an irregular verb, so you should look up all its forms in the verb list (Reference grammar 10.7).

If you need help, you say **Helfen Sie mir bitte!** or **Hilf mir bitte!** (*Please help me!*). But in an absolute emergency you would shout only the feminine noun **Hilfe!** (*Help!*).

QUICK VOCAB

helfen *to help*
das Visum *visa*
diese Reise *this journey, trip*
das Formular ausfüllen *to fill in the form*
die russische Botschaft *the Russian Embassy*
schicken *to send*
der Monat *month*
da *there*
bleiben *to stay*
nicht länger *not any longer*

im Juni *in June*
hier *here*
ab/fertigen *to process, clear*
stempeln lassen *to have something stamped*
übrigens *by the way, incidentally*
das Foto *photo*
der Scheck *cheque*
das alles *all that*
weg/schicken *to send away*
zu lange *too long*
es dauert *it takes (time)*
Vielen Dank für Ihre Hilfe. *Many thanks for your help.*
Gern geschehen. *You're welcome/It's a pleasure.*

Taking it further

NICHT DÜRFEN *IN THE SENSE OF MUST NOT*

We have already learned that the verb **dürfen** expresses permission. However, when it is used in the negative, it means *must not*, expressing a prohibition.

Compare the examples above using **müssen** with the examples below, which use the negative form of **dürfen**:

Ich darf nicht zu viel essen.	*I must not eat too much.*
Man darf im Restaurant nicht rauchen.	*You mustn't smoke in the restaurant.*
Sie dürfen nichts sagen.	*You mustn't say anything.*

The verb **brauchen** (*to need to*)

....
Insight
Brauchen (*to need (to)*) is a regular verb and its forms follow the pattern of **spielen** and **kochen**.

(Contd)

It can be used in a simple structure, e.g.

Er braucht viel mehr Geld.   *He needs a lot more money.*

Or it can also be used in a similar way to a modal verb, in that it can be followed by an infinitive at the end of the clause, with or without the preposition **zu**:

Du brauchst es nur zu sagen!   *You only have to say!*

Compare the following sentences with the last example from the Insight box:

Ich brauche nicht länger (zu) warten.	*I don't need to wait any longer.*
Das brauchst du nicht (zu) wiederholen.	*You don't need to repeat that.*
Er braucht nicht nach Prag (zu) fahren.	*He doesn't need to go to Prague.*
Das brauchen Sie nicht (zu) machen!	*You don't need to do that!*

Insight

You will have noticed the **zu** in brackets in the examples above. Unlike the traditional modal verbs, **brauchen** really needs the word **zu** to express the idea 'I don't need to'. In modern usage, particularly colloquial speech, it has been influenced by the modal verbs and so the **zu** is often omitted:

Er braucht nicht zur Bank gehen.	*He doesn't need to go to the bank.*
Man braucht einen gültigen Pass aber kein Visum.	*You need a valid passport but no visa.*

In this respect, **brauchen** can be considered to be an honorary modal verb. But remember that it also has other usages, for example when it simply means *'to need'* or *'to require'*.

Practice

EXERCISE A

(See Reference grammar 9.2)

You are visiting a relative in hospital. An incomplete version
of what she says is given below. Can you reconstruct the sentences
by incorporating the correct form of the modal verb in brackets?
Remember you will also have to put the finite verb into the
infinitive.

1	Ich sehe nicht gut. (**können**)	*I cannot see well.*
2	Ich stehe nicht alleine. (**können**)	*I cannot stand on my own.*
3	Ich bleibe im Bett. (**müssen**)	*I have to stay in bed.*
4	Ich nehme diese Tabletten dreimal am Tag. (**müssen**)	*I have to take these tablets three times daily.*
5	Ich rauche nicht. (**dürfen**)	*I'm not allowed to smoke.*
6	Ich trinke keinen Alkohol. (**dürfen**)	*I am not allowed to drink alcohol.*
7	Ich esse nicht so viel Schokolade. (**sollen**)	*I am not supposed to eat so much chocolate.*
8	Ich mache jeden Tag Krankengymnastik. (**sollen**)	*I ought to do physiotherapy every day.*
9	Ich gehe sofort nach Hause. (**wollen**)	*I want to go home straight away.*
10	Ich schlafe jetzt. (**wollen**)	*I want to sleep now.*

EXERCISE B

Careers advice

You are looking for a job and need to tell the careers adviser what
your expectations are. Complete the following sentences by filling
the gaps with the appropriate part of the modal verb given in
brackets at the end of the sentence.

1 Ich __ im Freien arbeiten. (**wollen**)
2 Die Arbeit __ interessant sein. (**sollen**)
3 Ich __ jeden Tag arbeiten. (**können**)
4 Ich __ nichts Schweres heben. (**dürfen**)
5 Ich __ Geld verdienen. (**müssen**)

Ten things to remember

1 The verb **sollen** is a modal verb which expresses moral obligation, e.g. *I should, I am supposed to.* It is normally followed by a verb (infinitive) at the end of the clause.

2 Remember the shades of meaning in the different forms **ich soll** and **ich sollte**. **Ich soll** suggests that you intend to do what you are supposed to, whereas **ich sollte** implies that you know what you should do but have no intention of doing it.

3 The verb **sollen** is similar to the five other modal verbs in that the first and third person singular forms are the same.

4 Remember that the vowels in the singular and plural forms of **sollen** stay the same.

5 **Müssen** is the sixth modal verb we come across and it expresses compulsion or necessity, as in *I must.*

6 Remember that there is no umlaut in the singular forms of the verb **müssen** (**ich muss**, etc.) but there is an umlaut over each **u** in the plural forms (**wir müssen**, etc.).

7 The verb **helfen** (*to help*) takes the dative case. This means that any noun or pronoun which comes after **helfen** must be in the dative case, e.g. **Wir helfen dem Kind.** (*We are helping the child.*)

8 When the modal verb **dürfen** is used in the negative, it expresses the idea of prohibition or 'must not', e.g. **Hier darf man nicht rauchen.** (*You're not allowed to smoke here.*)

9 The verb **brauchen** (*to need*) can also be used as a sort of modal verb, e.g. **Du brauchst nicht (zu) kommen.** (*You don't need to come.*)

10 Unlike modal verbs, **brauchen** sometimes uses **zu** (*to*) before the infinitive.

Asking for and giving opinions

In this unit you will learn how to
- **Ask for opinions**
- **Give opinions**

Language points
- **The verbs finden, glauben, denken, meinen**
- **Phrases using Meinung**
- **The conjunction dass**
- **Forms like dazu, etc.**

The aim of this unit is to teach you how to ask people what they think about something or somebody and to give opinions regarding what you or others think.

Asking for and giving opinions

Using the verb *finden*

> **Insight**
>
> The irregular verb **finden** means *to find* and is often used in its literal sense:
>
> **Er kann seinen Hut nicht finden.**   *He cannot find his hat.*
>
> But the same verb is also used with other shades of meaning:

> **Wie findest du das?** *What do you think of that?/What is your opinion or judgement about that?*
>
> This is the simplest way to ask for and give opinions.

Look at the following questions and answers:

Wie findest du seinen Sohn?	*What do you think of his son?* (literally 'How do you find his son?')
Sehr frech!	*Very cheeky!*
Wie finden Sie Augsburg?	*What do you think of Augsburg?*
Sehr interessant!	*Very interesting.*
Nicht schlecht.	*Not bad.*

Using the verb *glauben* (to believe)

Insight

The regular verb **glauben** means *to think* in the sense of 'to believe', 'to hold the personal conviction about'. **Ich glaube nicht** means *I don't think so/I don't believe so*. The noun **der Glaube** or **der Glauben** is used for religious, political or ideological belief.

Glaubst du, dass er das machen kann?	*Do you believe/think that he can do it?*
Ich glaube schon.	*I believe so/I think so.*
Glauben Sie, dass er heute kommt?	*Do you think that he will come today?*
Ich glaube kaum.	*I scarcely think so.*

Using the verb *denken* (to think)

Insight

Although the irregular verb **denken** means *to think*, it is used much less frequently than its English counterpart, and is often replaced by **glauben** or **meinen**. In German, **denken** is mostly used in the cerebral sense of what you have in mind.

Ich denke nicht, dass er mich vermisst.	I don't think he's missing me.
Sollen wir bleiben? Was denken Sie?	Should we stay? What do you think?
Sie denkt, ich habe genug Geld dazu.	She thinks I have enough money for it.

Using the verb *meinen*

Was meinen Sie zu diesem Vorschlag?	What do you think of this suggestion?
Was meint sie zu dieser Sache?	What does she think about this matter?
Was meinst du (dazu)?	What do you think (about it)?
Meint ihr, dass das vernünftig ist?	Do you think that's sensible?

There are many possible answers to the above questions but the following are frequently used:

Ich meine ja.	I think so.
Ich meine nein.	I don't think so.
Ich meine nicht.	I think not.
Ich meine, wir sollen ihn annehmen.	I think we ought to accept it.

Using the noun *Meinung*

The noun **die Meinung** is closely connected to the verb **meinen**, and is used very often to ask for or express opinions. **Die Meinungsumfrage** is a *(public) opinion poll*.

Was ist Ihre Meinung dazu?	*What's your opinion about that?*
Welche Meinung haben Sie dazu?	*What opinion do you have on the matter?*
Meiner Meinung nach sollten wir weitermachen.	*In my opinion we ought to continue.*
Ich bin der Meinung, dass wir weitermachen sollten.	*I am of the opinion that we ought to continue.*
Das ist auch meine Meinung!	*That's just what I think!*

Insight

Sind Sie ein Jeinsager?

If you are asked for an opinion and prefer to sit on the fence rather than commit yourself, you could jokingly be called **ein Jeinsager. Jein** is a combination of **ja** (*yes*) and **nein** (*no*). It is used in informal speech and translates as 'yes and no' or the hesitant 'sort of'. **Fettes Brot,** the hip-hop band from Hamburg, had a big hit with their single entitled 'Jein'.

Grammar summary

CONSTRUCTING MORE COMPLEX SENTENCES USING *DASS*

A sentence can consist of one or more clauses and a conjunction. The latter is a linking word that joins two clauses together to form one sentence. **Dass** is an example of a so-called subordinating conjunction and is very similar to the English word *that* in a sentence such as 'I think *that* dangerous dogs should wear a muzzle', 'He firmly believes *that* she should resign'. (Note that in colloquial English usage *that* is often left out.) You will notice in the following examples that **dass** sends the verb to the end of the clause and that there is a comma in front of it:

Glauben Sie, *dass* **er** *kommt*?   *Do you think that he will come?*

Ich meine, *dass* **wir gleich**   *I think we ought to set off straight*
  abfahren *sollten.*   *away.*

Sie denkt, *dass* **wir das**   *She thinks that we will manage*
  leicht *schaffen.*   *it easily.*

Insight

In speech, it is easy to confuse the conjunction **dass** and the neuter definite article **das**. Make sure you never confuse them in writing!

Dass is preceded by a comma and sends the verb to the end of the clause which it introduces:

Ich hoffe, dass er kommt.   *I hope he comes.*

Das comes before a neuter noun, e.g. **das Haus** (*the house*), sometimes with an adjective (or adjectives) between it and the noun, e.g. **das rote Haus** (*the red house*).

Other conjunctions follow this same pattern, for example:

weil	*because*
wenn	*if, when, whenever*
ob	*whether*
obwohl	*although*
als	*when* (when talking about the past)
Ich kaufe das Auto doch nicht, weil es zu teuer ist.	*I won't buy the car because it's too expensive.*
Er kommt nicht, wenn es regnet.	*He won't come if it's raining.*
Sie möchte wissen, ob es morgen schneit.	*She would like to know whether it will snow tomorrow.*
Sie wollen Ski fahren, obwohl es wenig Schnee gibt.	*They want to ski, even though there's little snow.*
Wir bestiegen den Eiffelturm, als wir in Paris waren.	*We climbed the Eiffel Tower when we were in Paris.*

(For further details on subordinating conjunctions, see Reference grammar 15.)

USE OF **DIE MEINUNG** AND **DIE ÜBERZEUGUNG**

In the examples shown in this unit we see the noun **die Meinung** used in various cases:

▶ In the example **Das ist meine Meinung** (*That's my opinion*), the nominative case is used because it follows the verb **sein**.

▶ **Meiner Meinung nach ist das ungerecht** (*In my opinion that is unjust* – literally 'according to my opinion'): the preposition **nach** puts **Meinung** into the dative case (even though it occurs after the noun in this example).

▶ The genitive case is used in this example: **Ich bin der Meinung, dass wir weitermachen sollen.** (*I am of the opinion that we should continue.*)

Die Überzeugung (conviction) can be used in the same way, e.g. **Meiner Überzeugung nach soll man Atomkraft verbieten.** (*I am convinced that nuclear power should be banned.*)

OTHER WAYS OF EXPRESSING STRONGLY HELD OPINIONS

überzeugt sein (*to be convinced*)

Ich bin davon überzeugt, dass Kinder schon mit fünf Jahren in die Schule gehen sollen.	*I'm convinced that children ought to go to school at five (years of age).*
Er ist fest davon überzeugt, dass man vegetarisch essen soll.	*He's firmly convinced that one ought to eat a vegetarian diet.*

halten von (*to think about*)

Was halten Sie von dem neuen Direktor?	*What do you think of/make of the new head teacher?*
Ich halte nicht sehr viel von Frau Schmidt, aber ich schätze ihren Mann sehr.	*I don't think much of Mrs Smith but I value/regard her husband highly.*

auf dem Standpunkt stehen *(to take the view that)*

Er steht auf dem Standpunkt, dass Kinder unter 16 Jahren spätestens um zehn Uhr zu Hause sein sollten.	*He takes the view that children under 16 should be home by 10 o'clock at the latest.*

In context

Read the following interview with an author who specializes in writing **Jugendliteratur** *(literature for young people)*.

Interviewer	Also, Frau Asbach, warum schreiben Sie für Jugendliche und nicht für Erwachsene?
F.A.	Ich bin der festen Meinung, dass unsere Jugend über ihre Geschichte Bescheid wissen sollte, und auch dass sie Verständnis für die heutigen Probleme haben soll. Dann wird sie, glaube ich, nicht die gleichen Fehler wie ihre Eltern machen.
Interviewer	Wie finden Sie unsere Jugend?
F.A.	Im Allgemeinen, durchaus nett. Aber ich meine, dass alle jungen Leute ein Ziel brauchen. Leider haben viele kein Ziel. Das ist das Problem.
Interviewer	Sie haben sicher Recht. Herzlichen Dank!

QUICK VOCAB

Jugendliche *young people, youth*
Erwachsene *adults*
die Jugend *youth*
Bescheid wissen *to know about*
die Geschichte *history*
das Verständnis *understanding, sympathy*
heutig *today's, of today*
das Problem *the problem*
die gleichen Fehler machen *to make the same mistakes*
im Allgemeinen *in general*
durchaus nett *thoroughly/perfectly nice*

das Ziel *goal*
brauchen *to need*
Recht haben *to be right*
Herzlichen Dank! *Many thanks!*

Taking it further

THE USE OF *DAZU, DARÜBER, DAFÜR, DAGEGEN,* **ETC.**

Insight

In some of the examples in this unit, we come across **da-** (or **dar-**) words such as **dazu, darüber, dafür** and **dagegen** in the sense of *with it, about it, for it, against it.* These are prepositional compounds, and are normally used when referring to a thing rather than a person. (When referring to a person, personal pronouns are used: see Reference grammar 4.)

This compound form is made up of the preposition you wish to use, e.g. **in, an, mit, über,** preceded by **da.** If the preposition starts with a vowel, e.g. **über,** a linking r is required in the middle: **darüber, darin** (*in it*), **daran** (*on it*), **darunter** (*under it*) for ease of pronunciation. In the spoken language, these can be shortened to **drüber, drin, dran, drunter.** This is similar to the old-fashioned English usage of *thereafter, thereupon.*

Look at the following examples:

Ich bin *dazu* **bereit.**	*I am prepared* **for that** *(for it).*
Er ist *damit* **einverstanden.**	*He is in agreement* **with it.**
Sie ist *davon* **nicht überzeugt.**	*She is not convinced* **about it.**
Wir wollen lieber nicht *daran* **denken.**	*Let's (preferably) not think* **about it.**

NB A question form of this compound can be constructed by substituting **wo-** (or **wor-** before a preposition beginning with a vowel) for **da**, giving, for example:

Woran **denken Sie?**	**What** *are you thinking* **about?**
Womit **schreibst du?**	**What** *are you writing* **with?**
Wovon (Worüber) **redet ihr?**	**What** *are you talking* **about?**

NB In German the **wo-** or **wor-** can never be separated from the preposition – something which is possible in English.

Practice

EXERCISE A

Rewrite the following sentences, replacing the bold phrases with a compound beginning with **da(r)-**:

1 Er fährt immer **mit dem Fahrrad**. *He always goes by bike.*
Er fährt immer __.

2 Ich denke ungern **an den Unfall**. *I don't like thinking about the accident.*
Ich denke ungern __.

3 Die Lampe steht dicht **neben dem Fernseher**. *The lamp is right next to the television.*
Die Lampe steht dicht __.

4 Der Kellner stellt das Glas Wasser **auf den Tisch**. *The waiter puts the glass of water onto the table.*
Der Kellner stellt das Glas Wasser __.

5 Meine Tante findet ihr Sparbuch **unter dem Bett**. *My aunt finds her savings book under the bed.*
Meine Tante findet ihr Sparbuch __.

6 Die Mülltonne ist **hinter der Garage**. *The dustbin is behind the garage.*
Die Mülltonne ist __.

7 Der Gärtner pflanzt Frühlingsblumen **zwischen den Bäumen.**
The gardener plants spring flowers between the trees.
Der Gärtner pflanzt Frühlingsblumen ___.

8 Wir essen Pizza **nach dem Film.** *We are going to eat some pizza after the film.*
Wir essen Pizza ___.

9 Er spricht gar nicht **über sein Problem.** *He doesn't talk about his problem at all.*
Er spricht gar nicht ___.

10 Es ist ein Fünfzigeuroschein **in dem Umschlag.** *There is a €50 note in the envelope.*
Es gibt einen Fünfzigeuroschein ___.

EXERCISE B

True love

Jutta is telling Jürgen some home truths. Take the part of the long-suffering Jürgen, who replies that he already knows. For example:

Jutta	Du bist sehr faul! *You're very lazy!*	
Jürgen	Ich weiß, dass ich sehr faul bin. *I know that I am very lazy.*	

1 Jutta   Du bist zu dick! *You're too fat!*
Jürgen   _____

2 Jutta   Deine ganze Kleidung ist altmodisch! *Your clothes are all old-fashioned!*
Jürgen   _____

3 Jutta   Du hast keine Hobbys! *You have no hobbies!*
Jürgen   _____

4 Jutta   Du machst nichts Vernünftiges! *You don't do anything sensible!*
Jürgen   _____

5 Jutta   Ich liebe dich sehr! *I love you very much!*
Jürgen   _____

Ten things to remember

1 The irregular verb **finden** (*to find*) is sometimes used to ask for or express an opinion, e.g. **Wie findest du den Film?** (*What do you think of the film?*)

2 The regular verb **glauben** (*to believe*) is sometimes used to enquire about belief or personal conviction.

3 The irregular verb **denken** (*to think*) is used less frequently than its equivalent in English to express or enquire about opinions.

4 The regular verb **meinen** (*to think*) is also used to ask for and give opinions.

5 A conjunction is a word which is used to link two clauses to form one sentence.

6 In earlier units, we have come across the coordinating conjunctions **und** (*and*), **aber** (*but*) and **oder** (*or*). These join phrases or clauses together without affecting the word order in any way.

7 **Dass** is a subordinating conjunction, which means that it sends the verb to the end of the clause which it introduces, and is also preceded by a comma, e.g. **Ich fürchte, dass er nicht alt genug ist.** (*I fear that he is not old enough.*)

8 Other frequently used subordinating conjunctions include **weil** (*because*), **wenn** (*if, whenever*) and **ob** (*whether*). They are each preceded by a comma and send the verb to the end of the clause which they introduce, e.g. **Ich kann nicht kommen, weil ich krank bin.** (*I cannot come because I am ill.*)

9 Prepositional compounds such as **dazu, darüber, dafür** and **dagegen** are used in the sense of *with it, about it, for it, against it*, when referring to things. They are formed by preceding the required preposition with **da-** or, if the preposition begins with a vowel, **dar-**.

10 A question form of this compound can be constructed by substituting **wo-** (or **wor-** before a preposition beginning with a vowel) for **da**, e.g. **Womit schreiben Sie?** (*What do you write with?* – literally 'With what do you write?')

11

Talking about habitual actions

In this unit you will learn how to
- *Ask for and give information about personal habits and routine actions*
- *Ask and state the exact time at which certain actions are performed*
- *Say how often you or others do certain things*
- *Ask for and give information about modes of transport used*
- *Relate a sequence of habitual actions*

Language points
- *Reflexive verbs with accusative and dative reflexive pronouns*
- *Adverbs and adverbial phrases*

Insight

When talking about personal body care and hygiene, a reflexive verb is often used in German, where sometimes none would be used in English, e.g. *I'm getting washed/I'm having a wash, she is getting dressed, he is getting shaved/he is shaving.* The equivalent verbs in German involve the use of a reflexive pronoun after the verb: **mich** (*myself*), **dich** (*yourself*), **sich** (*himself, herself, itself, oneself*), **uns** (*ourselves*), **euch** (*yourselves*), **Ihnen** (*yourself/yourselves*), **ihnen** (*themselves*):

Ich wasche mich.   *I'm getting washed/I'm having a wash.* (literally 'I wash myself')

Er rasiert sich.	*He's getting shaved/He's shaving/* *He's having a shave.* (literally 'He shaves himself')
Wir ziehen uns gerade an.	*We're just getting dressed.* (literally 'We are just dressing ourselves')

These verbs can be either regular or irregular, separable or inseparable.

TALKING ABOUT PERSONAL ROUTINE

Ich wiege mich einmal die Woche. *I weigh myself once a week.*
Du wäschst dich nicht oft genug! *You don't wash (yourself) often enough!*
Er rasiert sich jeden Morgen. *He shaves (himself) every morning.*

Insight

Note that these same verbs can also be used in different contexts without a reflexive pronoun:

Ich wasche das Auto.	*I'm washing the car.*
Die Krankenschwester rasiert den Patienten.	*The nurse is shaving the patient.*

When you look such a verb up in a dictionary, this non-reflexive usage will be marked tr.v (*transitive verb*), showing that the verb takes a direct object. The reflexive version of the verb is shown as **sich waschen** (*to wash oneself*).

Now look at these examples and their translations and compare them with the examples above:

Ich wasche mir täglich das Haar.	*I wash my hair daily.* (literally 'I wash to myself daily the hair.')
Am besten putzt man sich nach jeder Mahlzeit die Zähne.	*It's best to clean your teeth after every meal.* (literally 'It's best one cleans to oneself after every meal the teeth.')

ASKING AND ANSWERING QUESTIONS ABOUT ROUTINE

Stehen Sie früh auf?	*Do you get up early?*
Nein, ich stehe spät auf.	*No, I get up late.*
Was machst du normalerweise am Abend?	*What do you normally do in the evening?*
Normalerweise lese ich.	*I normally read.*
Wie oft geht ihr ins Kino?	*How often do you go to the cinema?*
Zweimal die Woche.	*Twice a week.*

RELATING A SEQUENCE OF HABITUAL ACTIONS

Zuerst wasche ich mich, dann ziehe ich mich an, esse schnell eine Scheibe Toast und gehe aus dem Haus.	*First of all I get washed, then I get dressed, quickly eat a slice of toast and leave the house.*
Zuerst grüße ich meinen Chef, dann lese ich die Post, spreche mit meiner Sekretärin und rufe meine Kunden an. Schließlich beginne ich mit der Arbeit!	*First of all I greet the boss, then I read the post, talk to my secretary and phone my clients. Finally I start work!*

ASKING FOR AND GIVING PRECISE TIME INFORMATION

Insight

In order to tell the time, you need to be sure of your numbers! Take a moment to check through Reference grammar 8.1. And remember that the 24-hour clock is used in Germany!

Notice how **eins** (*one*) changes when used before **Uhr** (*o'clock*):

Ich komme um ein Uhr.	*I'm coming at one o'clock.*
Ich komme um eins.	*I'm coming at one.*
Es ist Viertel vor eins.	*It's a quarter to one.*
Es ist Viertel nach eins.	*It's a quarter past one.*
Es ist halb eins.	*It's half past twelve.*

▶ If you wish to say at exactly what time something will happen, e.g. at six o'clock, at half past ten, at 10.25 p.m., use the word **um**:

Der letzte Zug von Saarbrücken kommt *um* **22.15 auf Gleis 3 an.**
The last train from Saarbrücken arrives at 10.15 p.m. on platform 3. (Notice that Germany uses the 24-hour clock.)

▶ If you wish to say 'from six to seven o'clock', you can use **von ... bis** (from ... till):

Dr. Müller hat *von* **neun** *bis* **zwölf Sprechstunde.**
Dr Müller's surgery (consulting hours) is from nine till twelve.

▶ Use the preposition **zwischen** to translate 'between two and four o'clock':

Die Anmeldung ist *zwischen* **zwei und vier Uhr.**
Registration is between two and four o'clock.

What time is it?

Wie spät ist es? *What time is it?* (literally 'How late is it?)
Wie viel Uhr ist es? *What time is it?* (literally 'What o'clock is it?')

Have a look at the following examples of times:

Es ist genau acht Uhr. *It's exactly eight o'clock.*
Er kommt um dreizehn Uhr an. *He's arriving at 1 p.m.*
Es ist eine Minute vor elf. *It's one minute to eleven.* (literally 'before eleven')
Es ist zwei Minuten nach sieben. *It's two minutes past seven.* (literally 'after seven')
Die Schule beginnt um Viertel vor acht. *School begins at a quarter to eight.*
Es ist Viertel nach sechs. *It's a quarter past six.*
Es war kurz vor Mittag. *It was shortly before midday.*
Es war kurz nach Mitternacht. *It was shortly after midnight.*
Ich komme um zwanzig Uhr. *I'll come at eight in the evening.*

Pay particular attention to the way German expresses half past the hour:

Es ist halb fünf. *It's half past four.* (i.e. 'halfway to five o'clock')
Es ist fast halb neun. *It's almost half past eight.*

Notice two ways of saying, 'It is 6.25':

Es ist fünfundzwanzig Minuten nach sechs or
Es ist fünf vor halb sieben.

Insight

Never forget that the Germans say 'half *before* the next hour', rather than 'half *past*' or 'half *after*'. You will have missed the boat which leaves **um halb neun** if you turn up at half past nine ... because the boat left at 8.30 a.m.!

Study the following questions and answers which give details of specific times:

Wann kommt der nächste Bus? Um elf Uhr.	*When is the next bus? At eleven o'clock.*
Wann beginnt die Tagesschau am Samstag? Um zwanzig Uhr.	*When does the TV news start on Saturday? At 8 p.m. (20.00).*
Wann beginnt die Schule am Montag? Um Viertel vor acht.	*When does school begin on Monday? At a quarter to eight.*
Wann verlasst ihr das Haus? Um zwanzig vor acht.	*When do you leave home? At twenty to eight.*
Wann kommen wir in Interlaken an? Um halb drei.	*When do we arrive in Interlaken? At half past two. (i.e. 'halfway to three o'clock')*
Wann endet die Tagung am Freitag? Um Viertel nach fünf.	*When does the conference finish on Friday? At 5.15.*
Wann esst ihr am Sonntag? Punkt zwölf!	*When do you eat on Sunday? On the dot of twelve!*

....

Insight

You will notice that **am**, the abbreviated form of **an dem** (*on the*), is used to say 'on Wednesday', etc.:

Ich fahre um halb elf am Mittwoch nach London.	*I'm going to London at 10.30 a.m. on Wednesday.*

Do you know all the days of the week?

Sonntag, Montag, Dienstag, Mittwoch, Donnerstag, Freitag ... and Saturday is either **Sonnabend** (in the north of Germany) or **Samstag** (in southern and western Germany). They are all masculine.

....

Grammar summary

REFLEXIVE VERBS

(Reference grammar 9.5)

Reflexive verbs give the idea of doing something either for oneself or to oneself, e.g. *I wash myself, He has cut himself.* Their use in German is different from that in English. Reflexive verbs can be regular or irregular verbs, separable or inseparable. The reflexive verb consists of the normal verb form plus a reflexive pronoun (*myself, yourself, herself,* etc.).

REFLEXIVE VERBS WITH AN ACCUSATIVE REFLEXIVE PRONOUN

(Reference grammar 9.5)

Many reflexive verbs use the pronoun in the accusative case, because the pronoun is the direct object of the verb. For example:

Sie wäscht sich nie mit Seife.   *She never washes herself with soap.*
Er wäscht sich im Badezimmer. *He's washing himself in the bathroom.*
Ich ziehe mich jetzt um.   *I'll change (my clothes) now.*

Notice the word order in the question form:

Rasierst du dich schon?   *Are you shaving (yourself) already?*

sich waschen *(to wash oneself)*	
Singular	*Plural*
ich wasche mich *I wash myself*	**wir waschen uns** *we wash ourselves*
du wäschst dich *you wash yourself*	**ihr wascht euch** *you wash yourselve*
er wäscht sich *he washes himself*	**Sie waschen sich** *you wash yourself*
sie wäscht sich *she washes herself*	**sie waschen sich** *they wash themselves*

REFLEXIVE VERBS WITH A DATIVE
REFLEXIVE PRONOUN

(Reference grammar 9.5)

When you wish to express an idea concerned with personal care such as *I wash my hair, He cleans his teeth, She washes her hands, They brush their teeth*, a reflexive verb with a dative reflexive pronoun is often used in German. You will notice that apart from the first and second person singular forms (**mir** and **dir**), these pronouns are the same as for **sich waschen**.

sich die Hände waschen *(to wash your hands)*
Singular

ich wasche mir die Hände	*I wash my hands*
du wäschst dir die Hände	*you wash your hands*
er wäscht sich die Hände	*he washes his hands*
sie wäscht sich die Hände	*she washes her hands*

Plural

wir waschen uns die Hände	*we wash our hands*
ihr wascht euch die Hände	*you wash your hands*
Sie waschen sich die Hände	*you wash your hands*
sie waschen sich die Hände	*they wash their hands*

You will notice that instead of the possessive adjective *my, his, her, their*, etc., German uses a definite or an indefinite article:

Er putzt sich regelmäßig die **Zähne.**	*He cleans his teeth regularly.*
Ich muss mir jetzt das **Haar waschen.**	*I've got to wash my hair now.*
Aber zuerst wäschst du dir das **Gesicht, verstehst du!**	*But, you'll wash your face first, you understand!*

ADVERBS

In the above examples about routine, notice that each sentence contains a word or phrase which shows frequency or time:

einmal die Woche	*once a week*
zuerst	*first of all*
nicht oft genug	*not often enough*
jeden Morgen	*every morning*
vor dem Abendessen	*before supper/dinner*

This is known as an adverb or adverbial phrase, because it adds to the verb by enhancing or expanding its meaning.

In context

Read this extract from a letter from Thorsten, in which he writes about his new life as a student:

Ich bin schon eine Woche hier in Heidelberg, und ich wohne mit vier anderen Studenten in einem Haus. Es ist ein bisschen eng aber es macht nichts. Ich stehe als Erster auf und zwar um halb acht. Ich wasche mich, aber ich rasiere mich nicht. Ich lasse mir einen Bart wachsen! Dann esse ich schnell eine Scheibe Brot und trinke eine Tasse Kaffee und fahre mit dem Bus zur Uni. (Ich glaube, ich kaufe mir ein Rad – dann spare ich Geld und ich bin schneller da.) Die erste Vorlesung beginnt um neun und dauert eine Stunde. Meistens habe ich zwei oder drei Vorlesungen pro Tag, aber am Freitag habe ich keine!

Zu Mittag esse ich in der Mensa und danach arbeite ich in der UB (Universitätsbibliothek). Am späten Nachmittag gehe ich im Park joggen, und nachher dusche ich mich. Am Abend koche ich manchmal eine Suppe oder Nudeln, oder ich kaufe eine Pizza und ich gehe erst spät ins Bett.

Taking it further

The use of **um ... zu + infinitive** (*in order to ...*)

Look at these two examples, which both have the same meaning:

Ich muss fleißig arbeiten,   *I must work hard in order to*
  um Deutsch zu lernen.   *learn German.*
Um Deutsch zu lernen, muss
  ich fleißig arbeiten.

Did you notice the verb–comma–verb structure (i.e. ... **lernen, muss** ...) in the second example?

Another similar construction is **ohne zu ... + infinitive** (*without + -ing*):

Er verließ das Restaurant,   *He left the restaurant without*
  ohne zu bezahlen.   *paying.*
Ohne zu bezahlen, verließ er
  das Restaurant.

Practice

For the following exercise you will need to know numbers. Full details of cardinal numbers, used for showing quantity and in counting, are to be found in Reference grammar 8.1.

EXERCISE A

At what time do the following activities take place?

For example:

1 Wann beginnt der Film?

Answer: **Um fünfundzwanzig (Minuten) nach sechs.** *At twenty-five past six.*

2 Wann beginnt die Schule?

3 Wann fährt der nächste Zug nach Tübingen?

4 Wann wollt ihr losfahren?

5 Wann essen wir?

6 Wann endet die Vorstellung (performance)?

7 Um wie viel Uhr fährt der letzte Bus nach Raisdorf?

8 Wann soll ich da sein?

> **PARTY**
> **Wann? Montag**
> **2–3 Uhr**
> **Wo? bei Effi**

9 Wann muss er sich anmelden?

10 Wann ist die Besuchszeit in der Klinik?

KINDERKLINIK
BESUCHSZEIT:
15–17 Uhr

EXERCISE B

Complete the following sentences, using the appropriate part of the relevant reflexive verb.

1 Hans _____

2 Ich _____

3 Lieselchen _____

4 Karlchen _____

5 Wir _____

6 Sie _____

7 Thomas _____

8 Oma _____

9 Dr. Meyer _____

10 Sie _____

QUICK VOCAB

sich kämmen _to comb one's hair_
sich ab/trocknen _to dry oneself_
sich rasieren _to shave oneself_
sich das Haar waschen _to wash one's hair_
sich setzen _to sit down_
sich die Zähne putzen _to clean one's teeth_
sich um/ziehen _to change one's clothes_
sich duschen _to have a shower_
sich an/ziehen _to get dressed_
sich wiegen _to weigh oneself_

Ten things to remember

1. Reflexive verbs appear in the dictionary as **sich waschen, sich duschen, sich rasieren**, etc. and are often used when talking about bodily care or hygiene.

2. Reflexive verbs use a reflexive pronoun, e.g. **Ich rasiere mich.**

3. The accusative reflexive pronouns are: **mich** (*me*, but *myself* in this context), **dich** (*you, yourself*), **sich** (*him(self), her(self), (it)self, oneself*), **uns** (*us, ourselves*), **euch** (*your/yourselves*), **Ihnen** (*you/yourself/yourselves*), **ihnen** (*(them)selves*).

4. If you are describing cleaning part of your body, the verb in German is followed by the appropriate reflexive pronoun in the dative case, to show the indirect object of the verb. This is followed by the body part in the accusative (the direct object of the verb), e.g. **ich wasche mir das Haar** (*I wash my hair*), **sie waschen sich nie die Füße** (*they never wash their feet*).

5. The dative form of the reflexive pronouns is: **mir, dir, sich, uns, euch, Ihnen, ihnen.**

6. Reflexive verbs can also be used in a non-reflexive way when followed by a simple direct object, e.g. **ich wasche den Hund** (*I'm washing the dog*).

7. If you wish to ask what time it is, you say either **Wie spät ist es?** (*How late is it?*) or **Wie viel Uhr ist es?** (*What o'clock is it?*).

8. The number **eins** drops the s when used in the phrase **es ist ein Uhr** (*it's one o'clock*).

9. The preposition **um** is used to say 'at' in time phrases, e.g. **um neun Uhr** (*at 9 p.m., at nine o'clock*), **um Viertel vor acht** (*at 7.45, at a quarter to eight*). The preposition **am** is used to say 'on' + days of the week, e.g. **am Dienstag** (*on Tuesday*), **am Sonntag** (*on Sunday*).

10. In German, you say 'half before the hour' rather than 'half past' or 'half after the hour', e.g. 9.30 (*half past nine*) in German is **halb zehn** (*half before ten*).

12

Expressing possession

In this unit you will learn how to
- *Express possession*
- *Ask questions regarding possession*

Language points
- *Possessive adjectives*
- *Preposition* **von** *to indicate possession*
- *The verb* **gehören**
- *Wem?*
- *The genitive case*

There are many ways of expressing possession in German.

▶ You may, for example, use words such as **mein** (*my*), **dein** (*your*), **sein** (*his*), **ihr** (*her*), **unser** (*our*), **Ihr** (*your*), **ihr** (*their*), as in 'my house', 'your car', 'their career prospects', etc. These words are called possessive adjectives.

▶ Phrases in English such as *Peter's friend, Anna's cat, Schubert's songs* can be expressed in a similar way in German: **Peters Freund, Annas Katze, Schuberts Lieder** (or **die Lieder Schuberts**). But note that no apostrophe is normally used in German.

Insight

As in English-speaking countries, there is a tendency to use the apostrophe in German shop signs and advertising. The most obvious examples are **Beck's Bier** and **McDonald's**. But you are also likely to see shop signs such as **Oma's Backstube** (*Grandma's Bakehouse*), **Ali's Obstladen** (*Ali's Fruit Shop*), etc.

Perhaps you might even see the incorrect use of the apostrophe in plurals such as **Pizza's** or **Mango's** or **Mofa's zu mieten** (*mopeds for hire*). This usage is incorrect in Germany just as it is in English-speaking countries!

▶ Later in this unit we shall also learn the fourth case, the genitive case, which is used to show possession, particularly in writing.
▶ German also has another way of expressing possession using the word *von*, meaning of: **der Freund *von* Anna, die Stadtmitte *von* Hamburg, die Lieder *von* Schubert.**

First of all, have a look at the following sentences and their translations before going on to the Grammar summary.

EXPRESSING POSSESSION

Hier ist mein Chef.	*Here is my boss.*
Hier ist deine Tasche.	*Here's your bag.*
Unser Haus ist ein Einfamilienhaus.	*Our house is a detached house.*
Unsere Kunden sind meistens aus Japan.	*Our customers are mostly from Japan.*
Er hat seinen Pass nicht bei sich.	*He doesn't have his passport on him.*
Es gibt sein neuestes Buch in der Bibliothek.	*His latest book is in the library.*
Die Mappe ist unter Ihrem Schreibtisch.	*The briefcase is under your desk.*
Ich koche lieber in meiner Küche.	*I prefer to cook in my own kitchen.*
Der Architekt arbeitet gerade in seinem Büro.	*The architect is just working in his office.*

Grammar summary

You will notice how the form of the possessive adjective changes, depending on the gender of the noun it precedes and also the context in which it is used, which determines whether it is in the nominative, accusative, dative or genitive case. In fact, possessive adjectives follow the same pattern in the singular form as **ein, eine, ein**. (See Unit 3 and Reference grammar 3.2.)

> ### Insight
> Be careful not to confuse the possessive adjectives with the possessive pronouns *mine, yours, his, hers, its, ours* and *theirs*, which we learn about later in this unit.

The following chart shows how possessive adjectives change their form according to the gender, number and case of the noun they describe:

	Masculine	Feminine	Neuter	Plural
Nom.	mein	meine	mein	meine
Acc.	meinen	meine	mein	meine
Dat.	meinem	meiner	meinem	meinen
Gen.	meines*	meiner	meines*	meiner

* **-s** or **-es** is added to the masculine and neuter noun in the genitive singular.

The basic forms of the possessive adjectives are:

mein	*my*
dein	*your* (singular, familiar)
sein	*his* or *its*
ihr	*her* or *their*
unser	*our*
eu(e)r	*your* (plural, familiar)
Ihr	*your* (singular or plural, formal)

In context

A young girl is describing her family and home:

Mein Vater ist Rechtsanwalt und arbeitet mit meinem Großvater in seiner Praxis. Meine Mutter ist Hausfrau und bleibt mit meinem kleinen Bruder zu Hause. Er ist drei Jahre alt und seine Lieblingsbeschäftigung ist Singen! Meine Schwester Anna ist älter als ich. Ihr Haar ist blond. Meins ist schwarz. Annas Augen sind blau. Meine sind braun. Ansonsten sind wir ähnlich. Unser Haus liegt am Waldrand, und es gibt viele Bäume in unserem Garten. Ein Teil von unserem Garten gehört der Gemeinde, aber das stört uns nicht. Es bedeutet nur, dass ein Gärtner von der Gemeinde unseren Garten mäht! Unsere Nachbarn sind alle sehr lieb.

der Rechtsanwalt *lawyer*
der Großvater *grandfather*
die Praxis *(professional) practice*
die Hausfrau *housewife*
bleiben *to stay*

QUICK VOCAB

zu Hause *at home*
der Bruder *brother*
die Lieblingsbeschäftigung *favourite occupation*
das Singen *singing*
älter als *older than*
schwarz *black*
blau *blue*
ansonsten *otherwise*
ähnlich *similar*
am Waldrand *on the edge of a wood*
der Baum *the tree*
der Teil *part*
die Gemeinde *(here) local authority; parish*
stören *to disturb, to bother*
bedeuten *to mean*
nur *only*
der Gärtner *gardener*
den Rasen mähen *to mow the lawn*
der Nachbar *the neighbour*
lieb *kind, nice*

Insight

Meine Schwester Anna ist älter als ich (*My sister Anna is older than I am*) is an example of the comparative form of the adjective. For details of this, see Reference grammar 5.3.

Taking it further

THE USE OF THE VERB **GEHÖREN** *(TO BELONG TO)*

It is possible to express possession, or the idea of *belonging to*, by using the verb **gehören** followed by either a noun or a pronoun, e.g. 'The cheque book belongs *to the man*' or 'The cheque book belongs *to him*'. The phrase *to the man* or *to him* is expressed in German by using the dative case of either the noun or the personal pronoun.

Der Koffer gehört dem Mann dort.	*The case belongs to the man there.*
Die Handtasche gehört der Dame da vorne.	*The handbag belongs to the lady at the front.*
Das Auto gehört den Eltern.	*The car belongs to the parents.*

THE USE OF PERSONAL PRONOUNS AFTER **GEHÖREN**

After the verb **gehören** the following dative forms of the personal pronouns should be used:

mir	*to me*	**uns**	*to us*
dir	*to you*	**euch**	*to you*
ihm	*to him*	**Ihnen**	*to you*
ihr	*to her*	**ihnen**	*to them*

Die spanische Villa gehört *mir* **leider nicht.**	*The Spanish villa unfortunately doesn't belong to me.*
Gehört *dir* **diese Reisetasche?**	*Does this travel bag belong to you?*
Der schwarze Mantel gehört *ihm*.	*The black coat belongs to him.*
Gehören *ihr* **diese Papiere?**	*Do these papers belong to her?*
Gehört *Ihnen* **dieser Regenschirm?**	*Does this umbrella belong to you?*

ASKING QUESTIONS ABOUT OWNERSHIP USING **WEM?**

In order to elicit any of the above answers you can simply use the question form used in the above examples or begin the question with the word **Wem?** (*To whom?*)

Wem **gehört der Koffer dort?**	*Who does the case there belong to?*
Wem **gehören diese Leinentaschen?**	*Who do these linen bags belong to?*

THE GENITIVE CASE

To express possession or ownership in a formal way, often
in writing, we use the genitive form of the definite article (see
Reference grammar 3): **des, der, des, der** (pl.) (*of the*); or of the
indefinite article: **eines, einer, eines** (of a); or of one of the possessive
adjectives, e.g. **meines, meiner, meines, meiner** (pl.) (*of my*).

Das ist das Motorrad des neuen Pfarrers*.	*That's the new vicar's motorbike.* (literally 'That's the motorbike of the new vicar.')
Am Anfang eines Migräneanfalls* gehe ich gleich ins Bett.	*At the beginning of a migraine attack I go straight to bed.*
Hier ist ein Bild der alten Kirche.	*Here's a picture of the old church.*
Das Alter des Mädchens* ist nicht wichtig.	*The girl's age is not important.*

Now look at these further examples and their translations:

Die neue Sprechstunde unseres Arztes ist am Dienstag.	*Our doctor's new consultation time is on Tuesday.*
Das Ziel seiner Reise ist Wien.	*The destination of his journey is Vienna.*
Das Landhaus ihrer Eltern ist riesengroß.	*Their parents' country house is enormous.*

▶ If there is no definite or indefinite article in the phrase showing possession, then **von** is preferred to the genitive, for example:

Der Bau von Atomkraftwerken ist sehr umstritten.	*The building of nuclear power stations is very controversial.*
Die Ankunft von noch mehr Truppen ist nicht willkommen.	*The arrival of even more troops is not welcome.*

▶ The genitive case is generally avoided in speech, for example:

Das ist der Hut von meinem Vater.	*That's my father's hat.*
Dort steht das Fahrrad von ihrem Freund.	*There's her boyfriend's bike.*

In colloquial speech, you are also likely to hear this curious structure to express possession:

Das ist dem Thomas seine Gitarre.	*That's Thomas's guitar.*
Das ist meiner Nichte ihr Taufkleid.	*That's my niece's christening robe.*

You will see that this involves the nominative case + possessive adjective after the verb **sein** with the dative case in front of it (as you would use for an indirect object).

POSSESSIVE PRONOUNS

> ### Insight
> We referred to possessive pronouns earlier in this unit with the warning not to confuse them with possessive adjectives:
>
> ▶ Possessive pronouns are translated as: *mine, yours, his, hers, its, ours, yours, theirs.*
> ▶ Possessive adjectives translate as: *my, your, his, her, its, our, your, their.*
>
> Now look at the following pairs of sentences, which contain a possessive adjective in the question form and a possessive pronoun in the answer:
>
> | | |
> |---|---|
> | **Wie teuer ist sein Buch?** | *How expensive is his book?* |
> | **Meins ist nicht so teuer.** | *Mine is not so dear/expensive.* |
> | **Hast du mein Buch gesehen?** | *Have you seen my book?* |
> | **Nein, das ist meins.** | *No, this is mine.* |

Look at the following examples of possessive pronouns.

Hast du einen Bleistift? Ich finde meinen nicht.	*Have you a pencil? I can't find mine.*
Haben Sie meine Brille gesehen? Ich habe seine aber nicht deine gesehen.	*Have you seen my glasses? I've seen his but not yours.*
Hast du Bleistifte da? Meine sind kaputt.	*Have you any pencils (there)? Mine are broken.*
Mögen Sie Ihren neuen Wohnwagen? Wir mögen unseren sehr.	*Do you like your new caravan? We like ours a lot.*

The following chart shows how the possessive pronouns change their form according to the gender and case of the noun they replace:

	Masculine singular	Feminine singular	Neuter singular	Plural
Nominative	meiner	meine	mein(e)s	meine
Accusative	meinen	meine	mein(e)s	meine
Dative	meinem	meiner	meinem	meinen

As we have already seen, the genitive is rarely used.

Practice

EXERCISE A

Insert the correct form of the possessive adjective into each of the gaps in the following sentences:

1 Wo ist _____ Tasche? *Where is my bag?*
2 Wie heißt _____ Klassenlehrer? *What is his form teacher called?*

3 _____ Auto hat eine Panne. *Our car has broken down.*

4 Ist das _____ Haus? *Is that her house?*

5 Wo sind _____ Koffer? *Where are our suitcases?*

6 _____ Schwester heißt Silke. *His sister is called Silke.*

7 _____ Betten sind ungemacht. *Their beds are unmade.*

8 Wohnt _____ Sohn in Düsseldorf? *Does your* (singular, polite) *son live in Düsseldorf?*

9 Hans, wo ist _____ Kreditkarte? *Hans, where is your* (singular, familiar) *credit card?*

10 _____ Rucksäcke stehen draußen vor der Tür. *Your* (plural, familiar) *rucksacks are outside the door.*

EXERCISE B

Replace the **von** prepositional phrases in bold type with the equivalent phrase in the genitive, e.g.

Example: Die Fenster **vom Rathaus** sind schmutzig. *The windows of the town hall are dirty.* → Die Fenster **des Rathauses** sind schmutzig.

1 Das Schlafzimmer **von dem Kind** ist klein. *The child's room is small.*

2 Das Auto **von dem Pfarrer** ist alt. *The vicar's car is old.*

3 Die Freundin **von meinem Bruder** kommt aus Österreich. *My brother's girlfriend comes from Austria.*

4 Ich nehme immer zwei Tabletten am Anfang **von einem Migräneanfall**. *I always take two tablets at the beginning of a migraine attack.*

5 Das Sprechzimmer **von unserem Arzt** ist immer kalt. *Our doctor's consulting room is always cold.*

6 Die Nachbarin **von meinen Eltern** ist verreist. *My parents' neighbour has gone away.*

7 Der Direktor **von dieser Schule** ist weltberühmt. *This school's head teacher is world famous.*

Ten things to remember

1 The possessive adjectives are: **mein** (*my*), **dein** (*your* – singular, familiar), **sein** (*his* or *its*), **ihr** (*her*), **unser** (*our*), **euer** (*your* – plural, familiar), **Ihr** (*your* – singular or plural, polite), **ihr** (*their*).

2 Remember that the three forms **ihr** (*her*), **Ihr** (*your* – singular or plural, polite) and **ihr** (*their*) all sound alike. You need to work out from the context which one is being used.

3 The possessive adjective always stands before a noun and takes its gender, number and case from this noun.

4 Whenever you add an ending to the possessive adjective **euer**, the internal **e** disappears, e.g. **euer Vater ist sehr geduldig** (your father is very patient), **eure Eltern sind sehr lieb** (*your parents are very kind*).

5 **Wer?** (*Who?*) is the nominative form of the interrogative pronoun.
Wen? (*Who(m)?*) is the accusative form.
Wem? (*To whom?*) is the dative form.
Wessen? (*Whose?*) is the rarely used genitive form.

6 The genitive case is used to show possession or ownership.

7 The genitive is not frequently used, being regarded as fairly formal.

8 Remember that in the genitive case, the ending **-s** or **-es** (depending on which is easier to pronounce) is added to singular masculine and neuter nouns, e.g. **der Lehrer** (*the teacher*), **das Kind** (*the child*). As a general rule, monosyllabic words add **-es**, and polysyllabic words add **-s**, e.g. **der Name des Kindes ist noch nicht bekannt** (*the child's name is not yet* *known*), **der Name des Vaters ist nicht bekannt** (*the father's name is not known*).

9 The preposition **von** (*from*), which is followed by the dative case, is often used to show possession or ownership.

10 The possessive pronouns translate as: *mine, yours, his, hers, its, ours, yours, theirs*. Do not confuse them with the more frequently used possessive adjectives: *my, your, his, her, its, our, your, their*.

13

Giving directions and instructions

In this unit you will learn how to
- *Ask for and give directions*
- *Ask for and give instructions*

Language points
- *Imperative mood*
- *Use of the infinitive, the verb* lassen *and the passive as alternatives to the imperative*

ASKING FOR DIRECTIONS

There are many ways of asking for directions. You will see from the following examples that most of them contain vocabulary and structures we have already come across.

Insight: Traveller's tip

Once you have stepped off the plane, out of the train or off the bus in a German-speaking country, the questions and answers in this unit may well be the most important structures you will need. So it is worth taking the time to learn the question **Wie komme ich am besten zum/zur ...?** (*What's the best way to ...?*). And, of course, you also need to be able to understand the directions you are given in the answer!

Entschuldigen Sie bitte, wie komme ich am besten zum Bahnhof?	*Excuse me, please, what's the best way to the railway station?*
Wie kommen wir am besten zur Post, bitte?	*How do we best get to the post office, please?*
Wo komme ich am besten in die Stadtmitte?	*What's the best way to the town centre?*
Sind wir hier richtig zur Sparkasse?	*Are we on the right way to the savings bank?*
Wir suchen die Sohststraße. Wissen Sie, wo sie ist?	*We're looking for Sohst Street. Do you know where it is?*
Wo ist die elektrische Abteilung, bitte?	*Where is the electrical department, please?*
Wo ist die Toilette, bitte?	*Where's the toilet, please?*
In welcher Richtung ist Flugsteig 28?	*(In) which direction is Gate 28?*

GIVING DIRECTIONS

Insight

You will notice from the examples that instructions are often given by using the imperative or command form. Because the instructions are being given to strangers, the polite form **Sie** is used. As you would expect, there are three main forms of the imperative, corresponding to the **du, ihr** and **Sie** forms of the verb.

Gehen Sie hier geradeaus und an der Ampel nach links. Die Bank ist auf der rechten Seite.	*Go straight ahead and left at the traffic lights. The bank is on the right.*
Fahren Sie die Hauptstraße entlang bis zur Kaserne und dann biegen Sie nach links ab.	*Drive along the main street as far as the barracks and then turn left.*
Fahren Sie über die Kreuzung, und dann nehmen Sie die erste Straße rechts.	*Go over the crossing and then take the first street on the right.*
Fahren Sie mit dem Aufzug hoch bis zum zehnten Stock. Da befindet sich die Dachterrassenbar.	*Go up by lift to the tenth floor. That's where the rooftop bar is situated.*

Gehen Sie nach unten, und Sie finden das Fitnesscenter im Keller.
Go downstairs and you will find the health club in the basement.

Gehen Sie über die Brücke, und Sie finden den Zug nach Ulm auf Gleis 2.
Go over the bridge and you'll find the Ulm train on platform 2.

ASKING FOR INSTRUCTIONS

Was muss ich machen?	What do I have to do?
Wann muss man das machen?	When do you have to do that?
Soll ich das gleich machen?	Should I do it straight away?
Wo muss ich drücken?	Where do I have to press?

GIVING INSTRUCTIONS

Münzen zuerst einwerfen, Knopf drücken und warten!
Put the coins in first, press the button and wait!

Prüfen Sie zuerst den Reifendruck!
First, check the tyre pressure!

Benutzen Sie den ersten. Gang nur zum Anfahren.
Only use first gear to get going.

Grammar summary

THE IMPERATIVE MOOD

(Reference grammar 12)

....

Insight

The imperative mood is also known as the command form because it is used to tell somebody what to do:

Biegen Sie hier nach links ab!
Turn left here!

Nehmen Sie die erste Straße rechts!
Take the first road on the right!

Iss nicht so schnell!
Don't eat so quickly!

(Contd)

You will notice that the command form normally ends with an exclamation mark, but there is a modern tendency to use only a full stop for more polite German commands:

Ich bin gleich da. Setzen Sie   *I'll be straight there. Please*
sich, bitte.   *take a seat.*

*THE **DU** IMPERATIVE FORM*

▶ The familiar singular imperative is formed by dropping both the pronoun **du** and the ending from the **du** form of the verb, e.g. **du fragst → frag.**

Frag **deine Lehrerin zuerst!**	*Ask your teacher first!*
Komm **sofort hierher!**	*Come here immediately!*
Trink **bitte keinen Alkohol!**	*Don't drink any alcohol, please!*
Geh **sofort ins Bett!**	*Go to bed immediately!*
Mach **schnell!**	*Do it quickly! Be quick!*

▶ If the verb adds an umlaut in the **du** form (e.g. **ich laufe, du läufst**), the same rules apply, but the umlaut is also dropped:

Lauf **nicht weg!**	*Don't run away!*
Schlaf **gut!**	*Sleep well!*
Fahr **doch langsam!**	*Drive slowly!*

▶ If the verb stem changes its vowel in the **du** form (e.g. **ich esse, du isst**), this vowel change is retained in the imperative mood:

Iss **bitte langsamer!**	*Please eat more slowly!*
Gib **mir das Kleingeld, bitte!**	*Give me the change, please!*
Sprich **nicht so viel!**	*Please don't talk so much!*

▶ If the pronoun **du** is used with the imperative, it intensifies the command:

Mach du das!   *You do it!*

▶ You will sometimes find that an **e** is added to this imperative form. It can have the effect of making it sound a bit more formal or imperious, even though it is addressed to a child or a friend.

Nenne drei Flüsse!   *Name three rivers!*
Antworte mit ja oder nein!   *Answer yes or no!*

In these examples, the extra **e** is added for ease of pronunciation, as we saw in Unit 5.

*THE **IHR** IMPERATIVE FORM*

The familiar plural imperative form is simply the appropriate **ihr-**form of the verb, minus the pronoun **ihr**:

Raucht **bitte nicht!**   *Please don't smoke!*
Bleibt **da!**   *Stay there!*
Schwimmt **rüber!** (colloquial)   *Swim across!*
Setzt **euch!**   *Sit down!*

*THE **SIE** IMPERATIVE FORM*

Insight

As we have already seen, the polite singular and plural imperative form consists of the inverted form of the verb. You will realize that this is the same as the question form (see Unit 1), e.g.

Fahren Sie mit dem Bus?   *Are you going by bus?*
Fahren Sie mit dem Bus!   *Go by bus!*

In speech, the intonation never leaves us in doubt as to whether the sentence is a question or a command. In the written language, a question ends in a question mark and a command with an exclamation mark or, occasionally, a full stop.

Kommen Sie wieder nach Österreich!   *Come to Austria again!*
Setzen Sie sich!   *Take a seat!*
Nehmen Sie bitte im Wartezimmer Platz.   *Please sit down in the waiting room!*

Wiederholen Sie das, bitte!	*Please repeat that!*
Essen Sie doch!	*Do eat!*
Sprechen Sie bitte langsamer!	*Please speak more slowly!*
Tun Sie das bitte nicht!	*Please don't do that!*
Verzeihen Sie!	*Forgive (me)! Excuse (me)!*

THE VERBS **SEIN** *AND* **HABEN** *IN THE IMPERATIVE FORM*

Both of these verbs have an irregular imperative form:

sein	haben
du: **sei** ruhig!	du: **hab** keine Angst!
ihr: **seid** ruhig! ⎫ *Be quiet!*	ihr: **habt** keine Angst! ⎫ *Don't be*
Sie: **seien** Sie ruhig! ⎭	Sie: **haben** Sie keine ⎭ *afraid!*
	Angst

Insight

Take care not to confuse the imperative **du** form of **essen** (*to eat*) with the imperative **du** form of **sein** (*to be*)!

▶ **Essen:**

Iss doch auf!	*Eat (your food) up!*
Iss nicht so schnell!	*Don't eat so quickly!*

▶ **Sein:**

Sei doch brav!	*Be good!*
Sei nicht böse!	*Don't be cross!*

In context

Look at this memo from the boss, which a city worker finds on his desk when he returns from a lunch break:

Würden Sie bitte morgen spätestens um 10 Uhr in meinem Büro sein? Bringen Sie den Bericht mit, der wohl bis dann fertig sein wird. Eine weitere Bitte: Fertigen Sie auch die Dokumente über Projekt A47 an, die ich gern mit Ihnen diskutieren möchte!

morgen *tomorrow*
spätestens *at the latest*
der Bericht *report*
der wohl bis dann fertig sein wird *which will presumably be ready by then*
eine weitere Bitte *a further request*
die Dokumente an/fertigen *to prepare the documentation*
über *(here) about*
das Projekt *project*
diskutieren *to discuss*

QUICK VOCAB

Read through the following recipe:

> **Glühwein**
> **Zutaten:** *Ein Achtelliter Wasser, eine Flasche Rotwein, ein Teelöffel Zimt, fünf Nelken, 150 g (Gramm) Zucker, Schale einer Zitrone.*
>
> Wasser mit Zucker, Gewürzen und Zitronenschale aufkochen, Rotwein dazugeben und bis zum Sieden erhitzen.

der Glühwein *mulled wine*
die Zutaten *ingredientsw*
das Achtel *one eighth*
die Flasche *bottle*
der Teelöffel *teaspoon*
der Zimt *cinnamon*
die Nelke *(here) clove (also carnation)*
der Zucker *sugar*
das Gewürz *spice*
die Zitronenschale *lemon peel*
auf/kochen *to bring to the boil*
das Sieden *simmering*
erhitzen *to heat*

QUICK VOCAB

Taking it further

If the speaker is involved in the projected action, a **wir** imperative form can be used by inverting the normal verb form. In this usage the pronoun **wir** is retained as follows:

Fangen wir an!	*Let's begin!*
Gehen wir!	*Let's go!*
Essen wir zuerst!	*Let's eat first!*
Schlafen wir lieber!	*Let's rather sleep!*

THE IMPERATIVE USING THE VERB **LASSEN**

Insight

The verb **lassen** (in the sense of *to let*) can be used with an infinitive at the end of the sentence to express the imperative, as in the old usage in the church liturgy:

Lass(e)t uns beten!	*Let us pray!*

Lass **uns gehen!**	*Let's go!*
Lasst **uns alles vergessen!**	*Let's forget it all!*
Lass **ihn weitersprechen!**	*Let him carry on speaking!*
Lassen **Sie mich bitte ausreden!**	*Let me finish (speaking), please!*

More general commands can be expressed by simply putting the infinitive of the verb at the end of the sentence:

Endstation. Alle aussteigen!	*Terminus. Everyone get out!*
Vorne einsteigen!	*Get in at the front!*
Bitte von links anstellen!	*Form a queue from the left, please!*
Leise sprechen!	*Talk quietly!*
Handys bitte ausschalten!	*Please turn off your mobile phones!*
Festhalten!	*Hold on tight!*
Aufmachen!	*Open (it) up!*

Hier öffnen!   *Open here!*
Nicht anfassen!   *Don't touch!*

USING THE PASSIVE TO EXPRESS THE IMPERATIVE

Insight

In spoken, colloquial speech the passive voice is also sometimes used to issue an energetic command:

Jetzt wird gearbeitet!   *Down to work now! Let's get to work!*

There is no need to look this up at the moment as it is used idiomatically here – but, for those who would like to, you can find more details in Unit 19. The passive cannot be translated directly into English in this imperative usage, as can be seen in the following examples.

Es wird hier nicht geraucht!   *No smoking here!*
Es wird hier geblieben!   *Stay here!*
Es wird jetzt geschlafen!   *Now get to sleep!*
Zuerst wird aber gegessen!   *Eat first!*
Es wird jetzt getanzt!   *Let's dance now!*

From these examples you will see that the passive is formed by using the **es** form of the verb **werden**, plus a past participle at the end of the clause. This is a very limited use of the passive. For fuller details see Unit 19.

Practice

EXERCISE A

Read through the following conversation between a tourist and a local inhabitant and then decide if the statements that follow are **richtig** (*true*) or **falsch** (*false*):

Tourist	Entschuldigen Sie! Wissen Sie bitte, wo die Wechselstelle ist?
Einwohner	Jawohl. Sie ist am Bahnhof.
Tourist	Oha! Wie komme ich bitte am besten zum Bahnhof?
Einwohner	Gehen Sie hier geradeaus bis zur Ampel. Nehmen Sie die erste Straße rechts und nach 100 Metern kommen Sie zur U-Bahnunterführung. Gehen Sie dort nach unten (entweder auf der Treppe oder mit der Rolltreppe) durch die Unterführung und dann die Treppe wieder hoch. Sie müssen dann die Kochstraße überqueren, über den Bahnhofsplatz gehen und die Wechselstelle steht gleich an der Ecke neben dem Haupteingang. Aber beeilen Sie sich. Sie macht um 18 Uhr zu. Sie brauchen höchstens fünf Minuten dorthin.

QUICK VOCAB

Entschuldigen Sie! *Excuse me!*
die Wechselstelle *bureau de change*
oha! *oh! (North German)*
der Bahnhof *railway station*
die Ampel *traffic lights*
nehmen *to take*
die U-Bahn *underground (railway)*
die Unterführung *underpass*
nach unten gehen *to go down*
entweder ... oder *either ... or*
die Treppe *steps*
die Rolltreppe *escalator*
hoch/gehen *to go up*
überqueren *to cross*
gleich an der Ecke *just at the corner*
der Haupteingang *the main entrance*
sich beeilen *to hurry*
zu/machen *to close*
brauchen *to need*
höchstens *at the most*

Sind die folgenden Sätze richtig oder falsch?

	R	F
1 Der Tourist will wissen, wo die Wechselstelle ist.	☐	☐
2 Der Einwohner weiß es nicht.	☐	☐
3 Der Tourist fragt dann nach dem Weg dorthin.	☐	☐
4 Er muss an der Ampel nach rechts abbiegen.	☐	☐
5 Die U-Bahnunterführung ist 100 Meter von der Ampel entfernt.	☐	☐
6 Er kann nur mit der Treppe nach unten gehen.	☐	☐
7 Er muss dann nur die Kochstraße überqueren.	☐	☐
8 Die Wechselstelle befindet sich an der Ecke.	☐	☐
9 Die Wechselstelle schließt um 8 Uhr abends.	☐	☐
10 Man braucht fünfzehn Minuten, um die Wechselstelle zu erreichen.	☐	☐

EXERCISE B

Respond to each of these requests with an appropriate imperative form,.

Darf ich bitte meine Mutter anrufen? *Please may I telephone my mother?*

(Du) Ruf mal an! *Do phone!*

1 Darf ich bitte ein Fax schicken? *Please may I send a fax?* (**Du**)

2 Darf ich bitte rauchen? *Please may I smoke?* (**Du**)

3 Dürfen wir bitte hier bleiben? *Please may we stay here?* (**Ihr**)

4 Dürfen wir bitte hier warten? *Please may we wait here?* (**Ihr**)

5 Dürfen wir bitte eine Tasse Tee trinken? *Please may we have a cup of tea?* (**Ihr**)

6 Darf ich bitte schon beginnen? *Please may I begin?* (**Sie**)

7 Darf ich mich bitte hinsetzen? *Please may I sit down?* (**Sie**)

8 Darf ich bitte noch ein Glas Wein einschenken? *Please may I pour another glass of wine?* (**Sie**)

Ten things to remember

1 The phrase **Wie komme ich am besten zum/zur …?** (*What's the best way to …?*) is a particularly useful phrase. The answer will normally be given in the imperative mood.

2 The imperative mood is also known as the command form because it is used to tell somebody what to do, e.g. **Biegen Sie hier nach rechts ab!** (*Turn left here!*), **Iss doch nicht so schnell!** (*Don't eat so quickly!*)

3 The polite singular and plural imperative form consists of the inverted form of the verb. This is the same as the question form, but the intonation in speech never leaves us in doubt as to whether the sentence is a question or a command. In the written language, the question ends in a question mark and the command with an exclamation mark or occasionally with a full stop.

4 For regular verbs, the familiar singular imperative is formed by dropping both the pronoun **du** and the ending from the **du** form of the verb, e.g. **du machst** (*you do*) becomes **Mach das bitte nicht!** (*Please don't do that!*)

5 If an irregular verb adds an umlaut in the **du** form (e.g. **ich laufe, du läufst**), the umlaut is dropped in the imperative: **Lauf nicht so schnell!** (*Don't run so quickly!*)

6 Take care not to confuse the imperative **du** form of **essen** (*to eat*) with the imperative **du** form of **sein** (*to be*), e.g. **Iss doch auf!** (*Eat (your food) up!*), **Sei doch ruhig!** (*Be quiet! Calm down!*)

7 If the speaker is involved in the projected action, a **wir** (*we*) imperative form can be used by inverting the normal verb form, e.g. **Gehen wir gleich!** (*Let's go straight away!*)

8 In spoken, colloquial German, the passive voice is also sometimes used to issue an energetic command, but the structure cannot be translated directly into English, e.g. **Jetzt wird geschlafen!** (*Go to sleep now! Let's go to sleep!*)

9 The verb **lassen** (in the sense of *to let*) can be used with an infinitive at the end of the sentence to express the imperative, e.g. **Lass(e)t uns anfangen!** (*Let's begin!*)

10 More general commands can be expressed simply by putting the infinitive of the verb at the end of the sentence, e.g. **Handys bitte ausschalten!** (*Please turn your mobiles off!*)

14

Making requests and offers

In this unit you will learn how to
- **Make requests**
- **Reply to a request**
- **Make offers**
- **Reply to offers**
- **Issue and accept invitations**

Language points
- **Direct and indirect objects**
- **Word order**

Look at the following examples and their translations.

PREFACING REQUESTS

You could preface your request in one of the following ways:

Ich habe eine (große) Bitte (an Sie): Können Sie mich mitnehmen?	*I have a (big) request (of you). Can you take me with you?*
Ich hätte eine Bitte: Kannst du heute das Fax schicken?	*I have a request. Can you send the fax today?*
Ich möchte Sie etwas fragen: Können Sie mich mitnehmen?	*I'd like to ask you something. Can you take me with you?*
Ich möchte/wollte/muss Sie um etwas bitten. Könnt ihr mir bitte helfen?	*I should like to/wanted to/must ask something of you. Could you help me please?*

MAKING REQUESTS

Requests can be made by using some of the question forms which we came across in previous units, or the imperative form (see Unit 13), or the verb **bitten:**

Using questions

Holst du mich von der Bushaltestelle ab?	*Will you pick me up from the bus stop?*
Darf ich bitte sprechen?	*May I speak, please?*
Können Sie das bitte buchstabieren?	*Can you spell that, please?*

....

Insight

Compare the last example above with the first example below. Both examples use the verb **können** (*to be able to*).

In the example above (**Können Sie ...?**), the verb is in the indicative mood. This is the normal form of the verb and is translated as *Can you ....?*

(Contd)

The example below uses **Könnten Sie ...?** (*Could you ...?*) in the subjunctive mood. This has the effect of making it sound more polite.

Wäre es ...? (*Would it ...?*) is another example of the subjunctive mood, as is **Ich hätte eine Bitte** (*I have a request*), used in one of the examples above.

At this stage, you can simply learn these as examples rather than trying to understand the use of the subjunctive. Wait until Units 20 and 21 for that!

Könnten Sie das ins Englische übersetzen?	*Could you translate that into English?*
Wäre es möglich, dass ich meinen Hund mitbringe?	*Would it be possible for me to bring my dog with me?*

Using the imperative

Bitte, bleib bei mir!	*Please stay with me!*
Sei lieb zu mir!	*Be kind to me!*
Rufen Sie mich bitte an!	*Please phone me!*
Sprechen Sie langsamer, bitte!	*Please speak more slowly!*
Bringen Sie eine Flasche Wein mit!	*Bring a bottle of wine with you!*
Reservieren Sie bitte vier Plätze!	*Please reserve four seats!*

Using the verb **bitten**

Insight

You will probably have noticed how frequently the word **bitte** (*please*) occurs in requests to show politeness. This is not surprising, as it is connected with the verb **bitten** (*to ask, beg, plead, beseech, invite*) and the noun **die Bitte** (*the request, plea*). Do make sure that you do not confuse this irregular verb **bitten** (*to ask*) with either the regular verb **beten** (*to pray*) or the irregular verb **bieten** (*to offer*). They are confused more often than you think, so do check the verb list in Reference grammar 10.7!

Look at the following examples:

The irregular verb **bitten** tends to be used in more formal requests.

Darf ich zu Tisch bitten?	*May I ask (invite) you to come to the table?*
Wir möchten euch zum Abendessen bitten.	*We would like to ask (invite) you to supper.*
Ich möchte dich auf ein Glas Wein bitten.	*I'd like to ask (invite) you over for a glass of wine.*
Darf ich um Verständnis bitten?	*May I ask for understanding?*
Darf ich Sie um Ihren Namen bitten?	*May I ask you for your name?*

REPLYING TO A REQUEST OR AN OFFER

The following words and phrases can be used to accept requests and offers:

(aber) ja! *yes, that's fine!*
ja gern *yes, with pleasure!*
ja (na) klar! *sure! of course!*
ja gut *yes, fine*
ja, ist gut *yes, that's fine*
ja natürlich *yes, of course*
ja gewiss *yes, of course*
selbstverständlich! *of course, that goes without saying*
freilich *of course*
sicher *certainly*
jawohl! *certainly!*
okay! *OK!*
(Das) mache ich. *I'll do it.*
(na) klar! *of course!*
Das versteht sich (von selbst). *That goes without saying.*
logo! *sure!*

REFUSING REQUESTS AND OFFERS

nein *no*
leider nicht *unfortunately not*
bestimmt nicht *certainly not*
natürlich nicht *of course not*
Leider geht das nicht. *Unfortunately that is not possible.*
Es tut mir Leid, aber heute passt es nicht. *I am sorry but today it is not convenient.*
auf keinen Fall *on no account, no way*
Das kommt nicht in Frage! *That's out of the question!*
niemals! *never!*

MAKING OFFERS USING **AN/BIETEN** (TO OFFER) AND **EIN/SCHENKEN** (TO POUR OUT)

an/bieten *(to offer)*

Darf ich Ihnen eine Tasse Kaffee anbieten?	May I offer you a cup of coffee?
Er bietet uns nur €2 500 für unser Auto an.	He is offering us only €2,500 for our car.

ein/schenken *(to pour out)*

Insight

Similarly, if you look up **einschenken** in the dictionary, you will find **jemandem etwas einschenken** (*to pour something out for somebody, to fill up someone's glass*). As shown in the examples, **jemandem** (*someone, somebody*) is in the dative case and **etwas** (*something*) is in the accusative case.

Darf ich dir noch ein Glas Wein einschenken?	May I pour you some more wine?
Ich schenke Ihnen noch eine Tasse Tee ein, oder?	I'll pour you another cup of tea, shall I?

Grammar summary

WORD ORDER OF DIRECT AND INDIRECT OBJECT

(Reference grammar 14.2)

subject pronoun	verb	indirect object in dative case	direct object in accusative case	prefix of verb
Ich	**schenke**	**Ihnen**	**noch eine Tasse Tee**	**ein.**
I (I'll)	*pour*	*you*	*another cup of tea*	*(out.)*

You will see that in the last example there are two objects after the verb: first the indirect object (**Ihnen**), and then the direct object (**eine Tasse Tee**).

- To find the direct object, ask the question *who/what undergoes the action of the verb,* i.e. here, what is being poured out? The answer to this question is the direct object of the sentence, and we know that this requires the accusative case.
- To identify what is the indirect object, check by preceding the noun or pronoun with 'to' or 'for', i.e. 'I'll pour a cup of tea for *you*'.

Here are some other examples of verbs which can have both a direct and an indirect object:

Darf ich *Ihnen einen Scheck* **im Wert von €500 überreichen?**	*May I present you with a cheque for €500?*
Können Sie *mir ein gutes Restaurant* **empfehlen?**	*Can you recommend me a good restaurant?*
Der Chef schenkt *seiner Sekretärin* **immer** *Tulpen* **zu Ostern.**	*The boss always gives his secretary tulips at Easter.*

There are certain rules for word order when there is both a direct and an indirect object after the verb:

- If both the direct and the indirect object are nouns, *the dative (indirect object) comes before the accusative (direct object),* as in the last example.
- If there is a combination of noun and pronoun, the *pronoun comes before the noun,* regardless of case, e.g.

Der Chef schenkt *ihr Tulpen.*	*The boss gives her flowers.*
Der Chef schenkt *sie der Sekretärin.*	*The boss gives them to the secretary.*

- If both the direct and indirect objects are pronouns, *the accusative pronoun comes before the dative pronoun*:

Der Chef schenkt *sie ihr.*	*The boss gives them to her.*

REQUESTS AND OFFERS

The *subjunctive* is often used to give a request a more polite ring, as the following examples show. (For further details, see Unit 21.)

Könnten Sie mir einen Gefallen tun? Könnten Sie diesen Scheck einzahlen?

Could you do me a favour? Could you pay in this cheque?

Ich wäre sehr froh, wenn Sie mich morgen anrufen könnten/würden.

I'd be very happy if you could/ would phone me tomorrow.

Wäre es möglich, dass Sie gleich hinfahren?

Would it be possible for you to go there straight away?

Hätten Sie gern etwas zu trinken?

Would you like something to drink?

Würden Sie gern mit nach Japan fahren?

Would you like to come to Japan (with me/us)?

Möchten Sie, dass ich den Rasen mähe?

Would you like me to mow the lawn?

Dürfte ich hier rauchen?

May I (possibly) smoke here?

In context

A plea for help

Liebe Silke!

Kannst du mir einen riesigen Gefallen tun? Holst du bitte Günther heute Nachmittag um 3 Uhr vom Kindergarten ab? Aber bitte gib ihm nichts zu essen. (Wenn er Hunger hat, darf er die Karotten essen, die im Kühlschrank sind!) Oh, und noch eine Bitte! Kannst du den Wellensittich füttern? Heute Morgen habe ich das vergessen. Ich bin dir sehr dankbar,

Gruß und Kuss,

dein Julius!

P.S. Ich bin um 5 Uhr wieder da!

QUICK VOCAB

einen Gefallen tun *to do a favour*
riesig *enormous*
heute Nachmittag *this afternoon*
ab/holen *to collect, pick up*
nichts *nothing*
Hunger haben *to be hungry*
die Karotte *carrot*
der Kühlschrank *fridge*
der Wellensittich *budgerigar*
füttern *to feed*
heute Morgen *this morning*
dankbar *grateful*
Gruß und Kuss, dein Julius *a jocular ending to a letter to a very close friend*
der Gruß *greeting*
der Kuss *kiss*

Taking it further

Other examples of requests:

Kaufst du mir das Kleid?	*Will you buy me the dress?*
Holst du mich bitte vom Bahnhof ab?	*Will you pick me up from the railway station, please?*
Kann ich deinen alten Rasenmäher haben?	*Can I have your old lawn mower?*
Können Sie ihn bitte besuchen?	*Please could you visit him?*

The command form can also be used as a form of request:

| Nehmen Sie mich bitte mit in die Karibik. | Please take me with you to the Caribbean. |
| Rauchen Sie doch lieber nicht. | Please don't smoke. |

Other examples of making offers:

Wollen Sie heute Abend ins Theater gehen?	Do you want to go to the theatre tonight?
Brauchen Sie sonst noch etwas?	Do you need anything else?
Trinkst du etwas?	Will you have something to drink?
Wollen wir zusammen ins Kino gehen?	Shall we go to the cinema together?
Sollen wir lieber bis morgen warten?	Would it be better for us to wait until tomorrow?
Kann ich Ihnen helfen?	Can I help you?
Brauchen Sie (meine) Hilfe?	Do you need (my) help?
Darf ich Sie in die Oper einladen?	May I invite you to the opera?
Nimmst du auch noch ein Glas?	Will you also have another glass?

Practice

EXERCISE A

You have just had an operation and are impatient to resume your normal activities. Using the appropriate form of the modal verb **dürfen**, ask if you may do the following things:

May I please get up? Darf ich bitte aufstehen?

1 Ask if you may watch the television.
2 Ask when you may drink a glass of beer.

3 Ask if you may eat a piece of cake.
4 Ask if you may go home tomorrow.
5 Ask what you may do!

EXERCISE B

Can you replace the nouns in **bold type** in the following sentences with pronouns? Remember: the word order varies if pronouns are used. (For help, see the chart in this unit's Grammar summary.)

1 **Der Kellner** schenkt **meinem Vater ein Glas Wein** ein.

The waiter pours my father a glass of wine.

2 **Der Nachbar** empfiehlt **meinem Sohn ein gutes Restaurant.**

Our neighbour recommends a good restaurant to my son.

3 Jeden Tag zeigt **der Schüler der Lehrerin seine Hausaufgaben.**

The pupil shows his homework to the teacher every day.

4 **Der Arzt** gibt **der Frau eine Spritze.**

The doctor gives the woman an injection.

5 **Das Kindermädchen** liest **dem Kind eine Gutenachtgeschichte** vor.

The nanny reads the child a bedtime story.

Ten things to remember

1 There are as many ways of making a request in German as there are in English, ranging from a straight question to a peremptory command.

2 The subjunctive forms **Könnten Sie ...?** (*Could you ...?*), **Wären sie ...?** (*Would you ...?*) and **Hätten Sie ...?** (*Would you have ...?*) are often used in polite requests.

3 Some verbs, such as **an/bieten** (*to offer*), **ein/schenken** (*to pour out*) and **geben** (*to give*) are often followed by both a direct object (in the accusative case) and an indirect object (in the dative case).

4 If you look up **an/bieten** and **ein/schenken** in a dictionary, you will find them written as **jemandem etwas anbieten** (*to offer somebody something*) and **jemandem etwas einschenken** (*to pour something out for someone*). If you look up *to shake someone's hand*, you will find **jemandem die Hand geben**. In these examples, **jemandem** (*somebody*) is in the dative case, whereas **etwas** (*something*) and **die Hand** (*the hand*) are in the accusative case.

5 To find the direct object, ask the question *who/what undergoes the action of the verb*, e.g. in the sentence **Ich schenke Ihnen eine Tasse ein** (*I'll pour you a cup of tea out*), what is being poured out? The answer to this question (**eine Tasse Tee**) is the direct object of the sentence, and we know that this requires the accusative case.

6 A simple way to check what is the indirect object is to try to rephrase it by preceding the noun or pronoun with 'to' or 'for', i.e. 'I'll pour a cup of tea for you' instead of 'I'll pour you a cup of tea'. 'You' is the indirect object.

7 Word order in German is very important. There are some rules you should learn about the position of the direct and indirect objects when they both come after the verb.

8 If both the direct and the indirect object are nouns, the dative (indirect object) comes before the accusative (direct object), e.g. **die Krankenschwester gibt der Patientin eine Spritze** (*the nurse is giving the patient an injection*).

9 If there is a combination of noun and pronoun, the pronoun comes before the noun, regardless of case, e.g. **die Krankenschwester gibt sie der Patientin** (*the nurse is giving it to the patient*), **die Krankenschwester gibt ihr die Spritze** (*the nurse is giving her the injection*).

10 If both the direct and indirect objects are pronouns, the accusative pronoun comes before the dative pronoun, e.g. **die Krankenschwester gibt sie ihr** (*the nurse is giving her it, the nurse is giving it to her*).

15

Describing people, places and things

In this unit you will learn how to
- *Ask questions leading to the description of people, places and things*
- *Describe people, places and things*
- *Describe the weather*

Language points
- *Adjectives standing alone and in the noun phrase*
- *Adjectives and verbs to describe the weather*

Insight

To describe people, places or things in general terms, German normally uses a verb such as **sein** (*to be*) followed by a word which describes the noun or pronoun, e.g. **Hans ist groß** (*Hans is tall*), **Berlin ist groß** (*Berlin is big*), **sie ist nett** (*she is nice*). This describing word is called an adjective.

It is also possible to put an adjective before a noun, resulting in a noun phrase such as **das rote Auto** (*the red car*), **unser altes Haus** (*our old house*).

ASKING FOR A DESCRIPTION OF PEOPLE, PLACES AND THINGS

To ask questions such as *What is he like?* or *What is it like in Berlin?*, use the word **wie?** (literally 'how?') followed by a verb such as **sein** or **aus/sehen** (*to look like*):

Wie ist das Wetter?	*What is the weather like?*
Was für ein Mensch ist Christoph?	*What is Christoph like? (literally 'What sort of a person is Christoph?')*
Wie sieht Inge aus?	*What does Inge look like?*

DESCRIBING PEOPLE, PLACES AND THINGS

Using an adjective after the noun and verb

Insight

Please notice at this early stage that if the adjective comes after the noun and verb, the adjective is exactly the one you will find in a dictionary, i.e. without any additional ending:

Das Auto ist neu. *The car is new.*

Inge ist groß und blond.	*Inge is tall and blond.*
Der Verkäufer sieht krank aus.	*The salesman looks ill.*
Die Kuchen sehen sehr süß aus.	*The cakes look very sweet.*

Using an adjective before the noun

Insight

An adjective can also be used immediately before the noun in a noun phrase, e.g. **das neue Auto** (*the new car*). In this case, you will need to add an ending to show that it agrees with the noun (i.e. in the appropriate gender, number and case).

Christoph ist ein sympathischer Mann.	*Christoph is a kind man.*
Neumünster ist eine große Stadt.	*Neumünster is a large town.*
Der Mercedes ist ein schnelles Auto.	*The Mercedes is a fast car.*

The examples above illustrate a masculine, a feminine and a neuter noun and adjective in the nominative case.

Now look at the following examples very carefully:

Inge hat einen **sehr sympathisch**en **Mann.**	*Inge has a very kind husband.*
Die Regierung plant eine **neue Stadt.**	*The Government is planning a new town.*
Sein Lehrer hat ein **alt**es **Auto.**	*His teacher has an old car.*

The last three examples illustrate each of the genders using a noun (with the indefinite article) and adjective in the accusative case.

Grammar summary

ADJECTIVAL ENDINGS

(Reference grammar 5.1)

....

Insight

You will have noticed from these examples that when the adjective is used immediately in front of a noun, the ending changes according to the gender, number and case of the noun. This is not as difficult as it looks (providing, of course, that you know the correct gender of the noun you are using) because there are rules to decide which ending to add on every occasion. These rules are given in charts in this unit. If you learn these charts, you will soon become confident about the use of adjectival endings.

....

Look at some examples of adjectival endings in the dative case:

Der Chef schreibt immer mit einem **schwarz**en **Füller.**	*The boss always writes with a black fountain pen.*
Das Kindermädchen kommt von einer **gut**en **Familie.**	*The nanny comes from a good family.*

| **Wir essen am liebsten in ein**em **italienischen Restaurant.** | *Most of all we like eating in an Italian restaurant.* |

Finally, look at these examples in the genitive case (for further details about the genitive case see Unit 12):

Die Hilfe eines **starken Mannes beim Wohnungsumzug ist sehr viel wert.**	*The help of a strong man when moving house is worth a lot.*
Der Preis einer **möblierten Wohnung ist sehr hoch.**	*The price of a furnished flat is very high.*
Vor dem Schlafengehen wirkt das Lesen eines **guten Buches sehr entspannend.**	*Reading a good book before going to sleep has a very relaxing effect.*

Insight

You will remember that the genitive case is not used very frequently, but it is worth noticing that the adjectival endings after the definite article (**der, die, das**) and indefinite article (**ein, eine, ein**) in the genitive case are always the same! Look for the **-en** endings in the genitive examples above.

The following chart shows the adjectival endings which are used after **ein, eine, ein**:

	M	F	N
Nominative	-er	-e	-es
Accusative	-en	-e	-es
Dative	-en	-en	-en
Genitive	-en	-en	-en

These endings are also used after **mein, dein, sein, ihr,** etc. in the singular. For example:

Montag ist *ihr* **erst**er **Schultag.**	*Monday is her first day at school.*
Meine **neu**e **Brille ist kaputt.**	*My new glasses are broken.*
Unser **zweit**es **Haus ist im Schwarzwald.**	*Our second home is in the Black Forest.*

The same endings are used after **kein, keine, kein** (*not a*). For example:

Otto ist *kein* **sympathischer Mann.** *Otto is not a kind man.*
Liebburg ist *keine* **schöne Stadt.** *Liebburg is not a nice town.*
Es gibt *keine* **gute Konditorei in** *There's no good cake shop in*
Heikendorf. *Heikendorf.*
Wir erwarten *kein* **gutes Wetter.** *We're not expecting good weather.*

There are two more sets of adjectival endings. Have a look at the next two charts before reading the remaining examples, and try to work out why each adjective ends as it does.

Adjectival endings after **der/die/das, dieser/-e/-es** (*this*), **welcher/-e/-es** (*which*):

| | Singular | | | Plural |
	M	F	N	
Nominative	-e	-e	-e	-en
Accusative	-en	-e	-e	-en
Dative	-en	-en	-en	-en
Genitive	-en	-en	-en	-en

Der **graue Schlafsack ist leider zu** *The grey sleeping bag is*
klein. *unfortunately too small.*
Die **weiße Bluse ist zu teuer.** *The white blouse is too expensive.*
Das **grüne Kleid passt dir am besten.** *The green dress suits you best.*
Die **bunten Schlipse sind im** *The brightly coloured ties are*
Moment modisch. *fashionable at the moment.*
Ich möchte *den* **schwarzen** *I'd like to buy the black coat,*
Mantel kaufen, bitte. *please.*
Er mag *die* **blaue Hose sehr.** *He likes the blue trousers very*
much.

Ich kaufe lieber *das* **rote Hemd.** *I'd prefer to buy the red shirt.*
Diese Jacke passt gut zu *dem* *This jacket goes well with the*
braunen Rock. *brown skirt.*
Ich nehme *die* **gelben Nelken.** *I'll take the yellow carnations.*

Adjectival endings used when the adjective stands alone before the noun (*black coffee revives you*) or after numbers (*three red buses*):

	Singular			Plural
	M	F	N	
Nominative	-er	-e	-es	-e
Accusative	-en	-e	-es	-e
Dative	-em	-er	-em	-en
Genitive	-en	-er	-en	-er

Schwarze*r* Kaffee schmeckt gut mit braune*m* Zucker.	*Black coffee tastes good with brown sugar.*
Schnel*le* Züge verbinden Hamburg und München.	*Fast trains connect Hamburg and Munich.*
Zwei dänisc*he* Vertreter kommen morgen an.	*Two Danish sales reps are arriving tomorrow.*
Die Deutsc*he* Bahn AG baut noch mehr schnel*le* Züge.	*The German Federal Railways are building even more fast trains.*

Insight

For the English speaker, adjectival endings are possibly the most challenging aspect of German grammar. But it is really worth devoting time to learning the various charts, as all the adjectival endings operate according to rules, never simply according to **Sprachgefühl** (*an intuitive feeling for language*). Never be tempted to agree with the Californian student, quoted by Mark Twain, who said he:

„would rather decline two drinks than one German adjective".

Mark Twain 'The Awful German Language', in
A Tramp Abroad (Hartford: American Publishing Company, 1880)

In context

DESCRIBING SOMEONE

A	Wer ist der Herr da drüben?
B	Er ist der neue Deutschlehrer.
A	Was für ein Mensch ist er?
B	Er ist sehr sympathisch, aber auch sehr streng.
A	Ist er aber ein guter Lehrer?
B	Oh ja! Er ist ein ausgezeichneter Lehrer.

aber *but*
auch *also*
streng *strict*
ausgezeichnet *excellent*

QUICK VOCAB

Taking it further

DESCRIBING THE WEATHER

There are various replies to the simple question **Wie ist das Wetter?** (*What is the weather like?* – literally 'How is the weather'?). The simplest answer uses **sein** plus an appropriate adjective:

Das Wetter ist schön.	*The weather is nice.*
Es ist sehr warm heute.	*It is very warm today.*
Im Sommer ist es sehr heiß.	*In summer it's very hot.*
Der Wind ist kalt.	*The wind is cold.*
Es ist furchtbar windig.	*It's terribly windy.*
Heute ist es bedeckt.	*It's overcast today.*
In London ist es neblig.	*It's foggy in London.*

You can also use the phrase **es gibt** (*there is, there are*). See Unit 3.

Es gibt jetzt wenig Schnee in Bayern.	*There is little snow in Bavaria just now.*
Es gibt viel Sonne in Spanien.	*There's a lot of sun in Spain.*
Es gibt oft Nebel in Hamburg.	*There's often fog in Hamburg.*
Es gibt heute Gewitter am Mittelmeer.	*There are thunderstorms in the Mediterranean today.*
Es gibt keinen Regen in Bonn.	*There's no rain in Bonn.*
Es gibt Sprühregen in Osnabrück.	*There's drizzle in Osnabrück.*

It is also possible to describe the weather by using a more specific verb:

Es friert, aber die Sonne scheint.	*It's freezing but the sun is shining.*
Es regnet oft im November.	*It often rains in November.*
Es blitzt und donnert im Norden.	*It's thundering and lightning in the north.*

(**NB** 'Thunder and lightning' appear in the reverse order in German.)

Es hagelt im Rheinland.	*It's hailing in the Rhineland.*
Es schneit noch nicht.	*It's not snowing yet.*
Die Temperatur liegt bei 26 Grad in der Schweiz.	*It's 26°C in Switzerland.*
Das Klima an der Ostsee tut gut.	*The climate on the Baltic does (you) good.*

Insight

A good way to become familiar with different weather descriptions is to look at the key to a weather chart in a local or national newspaper, or online, e.g. *Kieler Nachrichten* (www.kn-online.de), or *Die Süddeutsche Zeitung* (www.sueddeutschezeitung.de). You will probably find more details in the printed versions than online.

Practice

EXERCISE A

What's the weather like in Europe?

Write a sentence describing the weather in each of the towns marked. For example:

In Paris scheint die Sonne.

Do you remember that the verb must be the second idea in a normal sentence? That's why the verb comes before the subject (**die Sonne**) when the sentence begins *In Paris ...*

Wie ist das Wetter in Europa?

1 In London

....

2 In Madrid

....

3 In Oslo

....

4 In Porto

....

5 In Berlin

....

6 In München

....

7 In Wien

....

8 In Zürich

....

9 In Rom

....

10 In Athen

....

EXERCISE B

The amateur detective

There has recently been a spate of burglaries in your area, and from your window you see two people acting suspiciously. You phone the police to give a description of them. Use the following words to help you. Check that you are using the correct gender and case, and don't forget the adjectival ending if the adjective comes just before a noun!

Der erste Verdächtige (*The first suspect*)

He's tall and thin and is wearing a black raincoat, small sunglasses and a big hat. He is carrying an old, brown briefcase. His hair is long and blond. He looks young.

groß *tall, big*	**alt** *old*
dünn *thin*	**braun** *brown*
er trägt *he's wearing*	**die Aktentasche** *briefcase*
schwarz *black*	**das Haar** *hair*
der Regenmantel *raincoat*	**lang** *long*
klein *small*	**blond** *blond*
die Sonnenbrille *sunglasses*	**jung** *young*
der Hut *hat*	

QUICK VOCAB

Er ist ....

Er trägt ....

Er sieht .... aus.

Die zweite Verdächtige (*the second suspect*)

She's short and fat and is wearing a red blouse, a green skirt and a blue hat, and is carrying a big, white handbag. Her hair is dark and curly. She looks very old and dirty.

klein *short*
dick *fat*
die Bluse *blouse*
der Rock *skirt*
rot *red*
grün *green*
blau *blue*

weiß *white*
die Handtasche *handbag*
lockig *curly*
dunkel *dark*
alt *old*
schmutzig *dirty*

Sie ist ....

Sie trägt ....

Sie sieht .... aus.

Ten things to remember

1 Adjectives are used to describe people, places, things or situations.

2 The use of adjectives is more complex in German than in English, but you can master it by learning the rules.

3 Start by knowing the correct gender of the noun you are using, so if you are not sure, do look it up in a dictionary.

4 If the adjective comes after the noun and verb, it is exactly the one you will find in a dictionary, i.e. without any additional ending, e.g. **das Buch ist langweilig** (*the book is boring*).

5 An adjective can also be used immediately before the noun in a noun phrase, e.g. **das langweilige Buch** (*the boring book*). In this case, you will need to add an ending to the adjective to show that it agrees with the noun (i.e. in the appropriate gender, number and case).

6 As you start to use adjectival endings, it is always worth checking the three charts (Group 1, Group 2 and Group 3) in Reference grammar 5.1. With practice, you will learn to use these endings with confidence.

7 Group 1 adjectival endings (see Reference grammar 5.1) are used after the definite article **der** in all its forms, and also after **dieser, jener, jeder** and **welcher.**

8 Group 2 adjectival endings are used in the singular after the indefinite article **ein** in all its forms, and in both the singular and the plural after **kein** and possessive adjectives **mein, dein, sein,** etc.

9 Group 3 adjectival endings are used when the adjective stands alone in front of the noun, and also after numbers (**zwei, drei,** etc.), **einige, ein paar, viele, mehrere** and **wenige.**

10 Although the genitive case is rarely used, the adjectival endings after the definite and indefinite article in the genitive are easy to remember: they are always **-en.**

16

Referring to future plans and events

In this unit you will learn how to
- *Ask for and give information about future plans*
- *Ask and answer questions about future events*

Language points
- *Present tense with future meaning*
- *The future tense*
- *Verbs expressing future intent*

Insight

The future tense shows future plans, e.g. *We're going to buy a new house, They're going to get married, The party will be on Tuesday at nine o'clock, My mother-in-law will arrive on Friday.* As you will see in the following examples, the future can be expressed in German by using the present tense with an adverb of time such as **morgen** (*tomorrow*) or an adverbial phrase such as **am Abend** (*in the evening*).

ASKING QUESTIONS ABOUT FUTURE PLANS USING THE PRESENT TENSE

Fahren Sie nächstes Jahr nach Kanada?	*Are you (will you be going) to Canada next year?*
Kaufen sie im August ein neues Auto?	*Are they buying a new car in August?*
Hat Hans morgen Geburtstag?	*Is it Hans' birthday tomorrow?*

Insight

In Unit 2, we learned the greeting **Guten Morgen!** (*Good morning!*), which uses the noun **der Morgen**. Be careful not to confuse this noun with the adverb of time **morgen** (*tomorrow*), which is written with a small **m** unless it starts a sentence. Just in case you are wondering how to say *tomorrow morning* in German, it is **morgen früh** (literally 'tomorrow early').

ASKING QUESTIONS ABOUT THE FUTURE USING THE IRREGULAR VERB **WERDEN**

Insight

The future tense proper is not used nearly so much in German as in English. It is formed by using the appropriate part of the verb **werden** followed by an infinitive at the end of the clause.

Wann wird er wieder zu Hause sein?	*When will he be home again?*
Wann wird die Konferenz beginnen?	*When will the conference start?*
Werden Sie noch mehr Seide aus Thailand importieren?	*Will you be importing more silk from Thailand?*
Wo werden wir eine so gute Raumpflegerin finden?	*Where will we find such a good cleaner?*

Insight

The verb **werden** has a threefold use in German:

▶ As we have seen above, it is used as an auxiliary verb in the formation of the future tense.
▶ It is used in a similar way to form the passive voice (see Unit 19).
▶ It is also frequently used as a normal verb with the meaning *to become, e.g.* **Wann wird es dunkel?** *(When does it get/ become dark?)*.

(Contd)

Never confuse **werden** (*to become, to get*) with its false friend, the verb **bekommen** (which means *to get* in the sense of 'receive'), e.g. **Wann bekomme ich mein Hähnchen mit Pommes?** (*When are my chicken and chips coming?* – literally 'When do I get my chicken and chips?').

GIVING INFORMATION ABOUT FUTURE PLANS USING THE PRESENT TENSE

Look first at these examples which use the present tense to express the future, before starting the Grammar summary:

Heute Abend geht er in die Kneipe.   *He's going to the pub tonight.*
Ich komme nächsten Donnerstag.   *I'll come next Thursday.*

Grammar summary

USE OF THE PRESENT TENSE TO REFER TO A FUTURE EVENT

Whenever it is clear that you are referring to things to come, the present tense can be used to express the idea of the future. In each of the following sentences you can see an expression of time, e.g. **morgen, nächsten Dienstag, nächstes Jahr,** or **bald,** which clearly sets the context in the future, or **zu Weihnachten, im August,** which could be referring to the future, depending on the context.

Ich gehe morgen ins Kino.   *I shall go to the cinema tomorrow.*
Bald sind wir zu Hause!   *We'll be home soon!*
Wir fahren nächstes Jahr nach Kanada.   *We're going to Canada next year.*

THE FUTURE TENSE

The future tense is simply formed by using the appropriate part of the verb **werden** (used here as an auxiliary verb) plus an infinitive at the end of the clause. Werden is an irregular verb, and it is worth learning it in full:

Singular	Plural
ich	werde
du	wirst
er	wird
sie	wird
es	wird
wir	werden
ihr	werdet
Sie	werden
sie	werden

The future tense is frequently used in the following situations:

▶ when there is no adverb or adverbial phrase to make a clear reference to the future:

| **Er wird hinfahren.** | *He'll go (there).* |
| **Wir werden weitermachen.** | *We'll continue.* |

▶ for more formal information, such as the timing of a function:

| **Die Trauung wird in der Nikolaikirche stattfinden.** | *The wedding will take place in St. Nicholas' Church.* |
| **Der Bundeskanzler wird die Sitzung eröffnen.** | *The Federal Chancellor will open the meeting.* |

▶ to express a prediction:

| **Du wirst dick werden!** | *You'll get fat!* |

Insight

Did you notice that the verb **werden** is used twice in the above example? First, the **du** singular form of the verb **wirst** is used as an auxiliary verb to form the future tense (*You will ...*), then the infinitive **werden** is used in the sense of its full meaning to *become, to get*.

Wir werden sehen.	*We shall see.*

▶ to express determination or intention:

Ich werde mitmachen.	*I'll join in.*
Er wird abnehmen.	*He will lose weight.*

In context

Read the following press release:

Die Prinzessin wird schon morgen mit dem Hubschrauber ankommen. Ihre Kinder werden erst übermorgen ankommen. Die königliche Kapelle und der Posaunenchor werden sie begrüßen, und es ist erwartet, dass die Prinzessin eine Rede halten wird. Am Abend werden sich ungefähr 100 eingeladene Gäste in dem Schloss versammeln, wo ein Festessen stattfinden wird. Übermorgen werden die Schulkinder der Stadt für die Prinzessin auf dem Marktplatz tanzen.

QUICK VOCAB

die Prinzessin *princess*
mit dem Hubschrauber *by helicopter*
erst übermorgen *not until the day after tomorrow*
königlich *royal*
die Kapelle *band (also chapel)*
der Posaunenchor *brass band*
begrüßen *to welcome, to greet*
erwartet *expected*
eine Rede halten *to make a speech*
ungefähr *approximately*

ein/laden to invite
der Gast guest
sich versammeln to gather
das Festessen banquet
tanzen to dance

Taking it further

More verbs which express future intention:

planen (to plan)

Sie planen, nach Berlin umzuziehen. They're planning to move to Berlin.

vor/haben (to intend)

Was haben Sie (für) morgen vor? What are your plans for tomorrow?
What do you intend doing tomorrow?

Ich habe morgen nichts vor. I've nothing planned for tomorrow.

die Absicht haben (to intend)

Ich habe die Absicht, diese I intend marrying this lady.
Dame zu heiraten.

wollen (to want to)

Die Regierung will in Zukunft The Government intends to/
mehr Krankenhäuser bauen. wants to build more hospitals
in the future.

Insight
Never be tempted to translate the German verb forms **ich will**
and **er/sie/es will** as the future tense, even though they might
imply some future intention! They come from the verb
(Contd)

wollen (*to want to*) which we learned in Unit 7. Compare the meanings of the following two examples:

Ich will nächsten Donnerstag nach Potsdam fahren. *I want to go to Potsdam next Thursday.*
Ich werde nächsten Donnerstag nach Potsdam fahren. *I shall go to Potsdam next Thursday.*

Adverbs or adverbial phrases which express the future:

bald *soon*
demnächst *soon*
gleich *at once, immediately, in a minute*
morgen *tomorrow*
morgen früh *tomorrow morning*
morgen Abend *tomorrow evening*
übermorgen *the day after tomorrow*
sofort *immediately*
nächste Woche *next week*
nächsten Monat *next month*
nächstes Jahr *next year*
in Zukunft *in future*
in der nahen Zukunft *in the near future*
zukünftig *in future, from now on*

Practice

EXERCISE A

New Year resolutions

Make a list of your New Year resolutions using the notes you have made on your pinboard. Can you translate each full sentence into English?

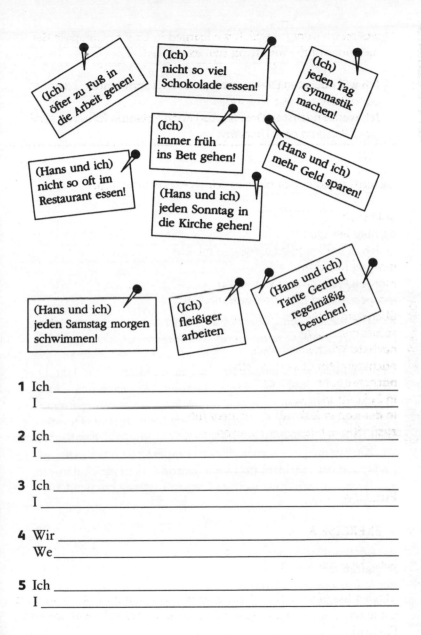

1 Ich _____

I _____

2 Ich _____

I _____

3 Ich _____

I _____

4 Wir _____

We _____

5 Ich _____

I _____

6 Wir _____
We _____

7 Wir _____
We _____

8 Wir _____
We _____

9 Ich _____
I _____

10 Wir _____
We _____

EXERCISE B

Rewrite the following notes in the future tense so that you can issue a press release with details of a foreign president's visit:

Der Präsident und seine Berater kommen um 20 Uhr in Hamburg an und fahren direkt zum Hotel Atlantik. Sie ziehen sich schnell um, und der deutsche Botschafter begleitet sie in den Speisesaal. Nach dem Essen hält der Präsident eine Rede über die Dritte Welt. Anschließend gibt es einen Empfang im Goldenen Saal für alle Angestellten der Botschaft. Der Empfang ist um 24 Uhr zu Ende, und der Präsident und seine Gattin fahren gleich danach zum Hotel zurück. Eine weitere Pressemitteilung erscheint am Mittwoch.

der Berater *adviser*
der Botschafter *ambassador*
begleiten *to accompany*
der Speisesaal *dining room*
eine Rede halten *to make a speech*
die Dritte Welt *the Third World*
anschließend *afterwards, subsequently*

der Empfang *reception*
der Goldene Saal *the Gold Room*
die Angestellten *employees*
die Botschaft *embassy*
die Gattin *wife (more formal than* **Frau***)*
die Pressemitteilung *press release*
erscheinen *to appear*

Ten things to remember

1 At its simplest, the future tense is used to express plans which have not happened yet but are still expected to happen.

2 The future tense in English is expressed by *I will, I shall* or *I am going to*, e.g. *I will not be at home on Friday, I'm going to get married on Saturday.*

3 Future plans are mostly expressed in German by using the present tense with an adverb of time or an adverbial phrase of time, e.g. **ich komme morgen** (*I will come tomorrow, I am going to come tomorrow*).

4 Be careful not to confuse the adverb **morgen** (*tomorrow*) with the noun **der Morgen** (*the morning*).

5 *Tomorrow morning* is translated as **morgen früh**.

6 The future tense proper is used very rarely in German.

7 When you do want to use the future tense in German, you need to use the appropriate form of the irregular verb **werden** in its normal place in the clause, followed by an infinitive at the end of the clause, e.g. **Wir werden im September umziehen.** (*We're going to move in September, We will move in September.*)

8 The verb **werden** has three different usages:
  ▶ as an auxiliary verb to form the future tense
  ▶ as an auxiliary verb to form the passive voice (see Unit 19)
  ▶ in its basic meaning *to become, to get*.

9 Take care not to confuse the verb **werden** (*to become*) with the German verb **bekommen** (*to receive, to get*).

10 Resist the temptation to translate **ich will** as the future tense. It comes from the verb **wollen** (*to want to*): **ich will** (*I want to*).

17

....

Describing the past

In this unit you will learn how to
- **Describe states or actions which were habitual in the past**
- **Describe events or activities which indisputably belong to the past from the narrator's point of view**
- **Turn direct into reported speech**
- **Describe states or actions which occurred before some past event**
- **Describe a past event or activity in writing**

Language points
- **The simple past tense**
- **Adverbs frequently used in the past**
- **The pluperfect tense**

DESCRIBING PAST STATES OR HABITUAL ACTIONS

....
Insight
If you look at well-known grammar books such as *Duden* (see 'Language watchdog' in 'Only got five minutes?' at the beginning of this book), you will find detailed and sometimes complex rules about the use of this simple past tense. In practice, however, the simple past tends to be used in *writing* (newspapers, books, etc.) and is occasionally called the narrative past. But do note that it is also very widely used in spoken German in northern Germany and parts of central Germany (north of the river Main).
....

Look at the following examples of the simple past tense (often rendered in English as 'used to'), which you may well hear spoken in northern Germany, and will certainly find in written German throughout the German-speaking countries:

Er *fuhr* **jedes Jahr nach Italien.**   *He travelled to Italy every year.*
Sie *besuchten* **uns jeden Sonntag.**   *They used to visit us every Sunday.*

> ### Insight
> Did you notice the very different verb forms of **fahren** (*to travel, to go (by transport)*) and **besuchen** (*to visit*) in the simple past tense? This is because **fahren** is an irregular verb and **besuchen** is a regular verb. This is explained in detail in this unit's Grammar summary.

Unser Flugzeug *landete* **mit**   *Our plane landed seven hours late.*
sieben Stunden Verspätung.
Mein Bruder *hatte* **Glück. Er**   *My brother was lucky. He didn't*
musste nicht zum Militär.   *have to join up/do military*
                                   service.

DESCRIBING THE PAST USING ADVERBS/ADVERBIAL PHRASES

In den sechziger Jahren **wohnte**   *In the sixties I lived in Ludwig Street*
ich in der Ludwigstraße in   *in Munich.*
München.
Mein Mann studierte *eine*   *My husband studied for a time in*
Zeit lang in **Marburg.**   *Marburg.*
Abends **aßen wir immer in**   *In the evenings we always ate at*
Georgios Taverne am Strand.   *Georgio's Taverna on the beach.*

Grammar summary

The simple past (also known as the preterite, the imperfect or the narrative past) has only one form in German, for example **ich**

kaufte, which can be translated into English as *I bought, I was buying* or *I used to buy*. It comprises the verb stem plus simple past endings.

The simple past tense is often used to describe an activity or event which indisputably belongs to the past from the point of view of the narrator, for example: I *asked* her to marry me.

In the next unit, we will learn that the *perfect* tense is often used to refer to events in the recent past which are of relevance or interest in the present, for example: I *have asked* her to marry me (and now – at this present moment – I'm on tenterhooks to hear if she will accept).

This difference technically applies in German, but regional and stylistic variations mean that the simple past is often replaced by the perfect tense (see Unit 18). However, it is important to know and understand the simple past tense because it is frequently used in writing, and certain forms (especially **ich war, ich hatte, ich blieb, ich ging, ich kam, ich sah, ich stand, es gab, es wurde**) appear regularly in speech.

Insight

If you have not yet discovered the list of irregular verbs in Reference grammar 10.7, now is the time to look it up and put a bookmark in the page! It shows how every irregular verb changes its form in the various tenses by giving you the third person singular form of each tense, for example:

Infinitive	Meaning	3rd person singular present tense	3rd person singular simple past tense	3rd person singular perfect tense
geben	*to give*	**gibt**	**gab**	**hat gegeben**

The fourth column shows the simple past tense. All good dictionaries have a similar list.

THE SIMPLE PAST TENSE OF REGULAR VERBS

The simple past tense of regular verbs is formed by adding the following endings to the verb stem:

kaufen *(to buy)*	
Singular	*Plural*
ich kauf**te** *I bought, I was buying, I used to buy*	wir kauf**ten** *we bought, etc.*
du kauf**test** *you bought, etc.*	ihr kauf**tet** *you bought, etc.*
er kauf**te** *he bought, etc.*	Sie kauf**ten** *you bought, etc.*
sie kauf**te** *she bought, etc.*	sie kauf**ten** *they bought, etc.*

Als Junge *lernte* **er nicht sehr viel in der Schule.**	*As a boy he didn't learn much at school.*
Sie *verkaufte* **Töpferwaren auf dem Markt.**	*She used to sell pottery at the market.*
Sie *tanzten* **ausschließlich miteinander.**	*They danced exclusively with each other.*

The simple past of verbs with stems ending in **-d, -t, -m** *or* **-n** *preceded by a consonant*

If the stem of a regular verb ends in **-d** or **-t**, e.g. **reden** (*to speak*), **arbeiten** (*to work*), or a combination of -m or -n preceded by another consonant, e.g. **atmen** (*to breathe*), **regnen** (*to rain*), an -e is added before the following endings to form the simple past:

arbeiten *(to work)*	
Singular	*Plural*
ich arbeit**ete** *I worked, I was working, I used to work*	wir arbeit**eten** *we worked, etc.*
du arbeit**etest** *you worked, etc.*	ihr arbeit**etet** *you worked, etc.*
er arbeit**ete** *he worked, etc.*	Sie arbeit**eten** *you worked, etc.*
sie arbeit**ete** *she worked, etc.*	sie arbeit**eten** *they worked, etc.*

Look at the following examples and check the endings in the box above:

Sie blutete stark nach der Operation.	*She bled heavily after the operation.*
Es regnete den ganzen Tag.	*It was raining the whole day.*
Meine Frau begegnete dem Dieb im Flur.	*My wife met the thief in the hall.*
Sie antworteten immer mit nein.	*Their answer was always no.*

THE SIMPLE PAST OF IRREGULAR VERBS

Unlike with regular verbs, it is not possible to work out what the simple past form of an irregular verb is. For the sake of simplicity, no further subdivisions of verbs are named. All good dictionaries and coursebooks include a verb list, which you should consult to find out the correct form. For guidance, there are now approximately 170 of these irregular verbs.

This is how such a verb list works:

Infinitive	Meaning	3rd person sing. present	3rd person simple past	3rd person perfect tense
bleiben	to stay	bleibt	blieb	ist geblieben
essen	to eat	isst	aß	hat gegessen
fahren	to travel	fährt	fuhr	ist gefahren
geben	to give	gibt	gab	hat gegeben
gehen	to go	geht	ging	ist gegangen

Insight

This verb list shows the verbs in all their tenses. Don't worry about the fifth column at this stage, which shows the perfect tense and the accompanying use of **hat** or **ist**. All is explained in Unit 18!

The third person singular form is given in the column for the simple past tense. This is, in effect, the simple past stem to which endings are added to form the simple past as follows:

trinken *(to drink)*	
Singular	*Plural*
ich trank *I drank, I was drinking, I used to drink*	wir tranken *we drank, etc.*
du trankst *you drank, etc.*	ihr trankt *you drank, etc.*
er trank *he drank, etc.*	Sie tranken *you drank, etc.*
sie trank *she drank, etc.*	sie tranken *they drank, etc.*
es trank *it drank, etc.*	

There is no ending at all on the **ich** and **er, sie, es** forms (which are identical to the one found in the verb list).

Früher *schlief* **er gern im Freien.**   *Previously he enjoyed sleeping in the open air.*

Jeden Morgen *gingen* **wir zusammen zur Schule.**   *Every morning we used to go to school together.*

Am Heiligen Abend *gab* **es immer Karpfen bei uns zu Hause.**   *At home there was always carp (to eat) on Christmas Eve.*

If necessary, refer to the complete verb list (Reference grammar 10.7) as you look at the following examples:

Wir *flogen* **nur mit Lufthansa.**   *We flew only with Lufthansa.*

Jedes Jahr *schrieben* **sie ihm einen netten Brief zum Geburtstag.**   *Every year they wrote him a nice letter on his birthday.*

Damals *hielt* **der Zug in Einfeld.**   *In those days the train stopped in Einfeld.*

Perhaps you have noticed that some verbs have unpredictable forms in the simple past. In Unit 18 we will see that the past participles are equally unpredictable.

Look at the various tense forms of the following verbs:

Infinitive	Meaning	3rd person sing. present	3rd person simple past	3rd person perfect tense
brennen	*to burn*	brennt	brannte	hat gebrannt
bringen	*to bring*	bringt	brachte	hat gebracht
denken	*to think*	denkt	dachte	hat gedacht
kennen	*to know*	kennt	kannte	hat gekannt
nennen	*to name*	nennt	nannte	hat genannt

Look at the following examples of the above verbs:

Die Fabrik *brannte* **die ganze Nacht hindurch.**	*The factory burned all through the night.*
Wolfgang *brachte* **uns Spätzle aus Schwaben.**	*Wolfgang brought us spaetzle (pasta) from Swabia.*
Ihr Schwiegersohn *dachte* **nicht daran, sie zu besuchen.**	*Their son-in-law didn't think of visiting them.*
Man *nannte* **ihn immer Fritzchen.**	*They always called him Little Fritz.*

THE VERBS **HABEN, SEIN** *AND* **WERDEN**

Infinitive	Meaning	3rd person sing. present	3rd person simple past	3rd person perfect tense
haben	*to have*	hat	hatte	hat gehabt
sein	*to be*	ist	war	ist gewesen
werden	*to become*	wird	wurde	ist geworden

Insight

It is well worth learning the simple past forms of the three verbs above, i.e. **hatte, war** and **wurde.** They are in frequent use, as are the simple past forms of the six modal auxiliary verbs: **dürfen → durfte, können → konnte, mögen → mochte, müssen → musste, sollen → sollte** and **wollen → wollte.**

In context

Now look at this account of Kurt's schooldays before comparing it with the English translation.

Kurt **war** insgesamt sieben Jahre auf dem Schillergymnasium und **ging** jeden Tag mit Begeisterung hin. Seine Lieblingsfächer **waren** Geschichte und deutsche Literatur. Er **las** leidenschaftlich gern und **besuchte** Museen so oft wie möglich. Er **arbeitete** fleißig und **half** gern in der Schulbibliothek. Seine Schulkameraden **nannten** ihn den kleinen Professor, denn er hatte nicht viele Hobbys. Sonntags **machte** er immer lange einsame Wanderungen. Er **schrieb** schon damals Kurzgeschichten und **wollte** unbedingt auf die Universität gehen. Seine Lehrer **schätzten** ihn sehr. Alles in allem **war** Kurt ein außergewöhnlicher Junge.

Kurt was at the Schiller Grammar School for seven years in all and he went there enthusiastically every day. His favourite subjects were history and German literature. He was a passionate reader and visited museums as often as possible. He worked hard and enjoyed helping in the school library. His schoolmates called him 'The Little Professor' as he didn't have many hobbies. On Sundays he used to go on long walks all by himself. Even then he was writing short stories and really wanted to go to university. His teachers held him in high regard (literally 'valued him very much'). All in all, Kurt was an extraordinary boy.

Taking it further

THE PAST SIMPLE TENSE IN REPORTED SPEECH

Sie sagte, sie liebte ihn damals nicht.	*She said she didn't love him in those days.*
Er sagte, er studierte den ganzen Tag.	*He said he was studying the whole day.*

NB As you will see in Unit 20, the following subjunctive forms may well be preferred:

Sie sagte, sie **liebe** ihn nicht.
Er sagte, er **habe** den ganzen Tag studiert.

THE PLUPERFECT TENSE

Describing states or actions occurring before a past event

Insight

The pluperfect tense is used both in English and in German to refer to events which took place before another event in the past. In fact it can only be used in connection with a more recent event, even if this is simply implied rather than stated in full, for example: *Her son* **had** *already* **told** *her about it (when the doctor finally got round to mentioning it),* **I had saved** *enough money to buy a Mercedes (when I decided to get married).*

The pluperfect tense can be translated into English as *I had (saved)* or *I had been (saving).*

The pluperfect tense is a compound tense formed by using the appropriate form of either **haben** or **sein** (see this unit's Grammar summary) plus a past participle at the end of the clause. You will not find this form given in the verb lists as you can work it out by combining the past stem of **haben** or **sein** (from the simple past column) with the past participle.

Die Studentin war todmüde, weil sie schlecht geschlafen hatte.	*The student was dead tired because she had slept badly.*
Der Zug war **schon** abgefahren, **als sie am Bahnhof ankamen.**	*The train had already left when they arrived at the station.*

There are two clauses in each of the sentences above. The pluperfect tense is used in one clause, and the simple past in the other.

MIXED USAGE OF TENSES IN THE PAST

It is common in newspaper articles to find that the first sentence
is written in the perfect tense (to arrest our attention, as it were)
and is then followed by a detailed description in the simple past.
For example:

Beim schwersten Unglück der Luftfahrtgeschichte *sind* **349 Menschen ums Leben** *gekommen.* **Die Absturzursache ist noch unklar. In etwa 4.200 Metern Höhe** *prallten* **zwei Flugzeuge zusammen und** *stürzten* **ab.**

In the worst accident in aviation history, 349 people died. The reason for the crash is still unclear. At a height of approximately 4,200 metres, two planes collided and crashed.

If you look at the fairy tales of the Brothers Grimm, you will find
that they often start with the opening formula **Es war einmal ...**
(*Once upon a time ...*), and continue in the simple past until the
closing formula:

Und wenn sie nicht gestorben sind, dann leben sie noch heute.

And they all lived happily ever after. (literally 'If they haven't died, they're still alive.')

Practice

EXERCISE A

Insert the appropriate form of the verb (given in brackets as an
infinitive) into the gaps in the following sentences:

1 In den sechziger Jahren ___ (**wohnen**) ich in Paris, wo ich an einer Universität ___ (**studieren**).

In the sixties I lived in Paris, where I was studying at a university.

2 Es ___ (**geben**) oft Demonstrationen in der Stadtmitte.

There were often demonstrations in the town centre.

3 Wir Studenten ___ (**singen**) Protestlieder, und wir ___ (**tragen**) Transparente.

We students sang protest songs and carried banners.

4 An jeder Straßenecke ___ (**warten**) Gruppen von Polizisten. Plötzlich ___ (**laufen**) sie uns entgegen.

On every street corner groups of police were waiting. Suddenly they ran towards us.

5 Ich ___ (**haben**) Glück. Ich ___ (**kommen**), Gott sei Dank, unversehrt davon.

I was lucky. Thank God, I escaped unharmed.

EXERCISE B

(N)Ostalgie (*Nostalgia for old East Germany*)

You are the secretary of an Anglo-German Society and have written to the elderly relative of a member to ask for his reminiscences about life in the former East Germany. Translate the contents of his letter into English for publication in the next newsletter:

Leipzig

Liebe Frau Lane,

Vielen Dank für Ihren Brief. Also, Sie wollten wissen, wie es damals in der DDR war.

Vor der Wende war nicht alles schlecht, wissen Sie! Wir hatten alle Arbeit und konnten immer schöne Urlaubsreisen an die Ostsee oder in die Berge machen. Eintrittskarten für die Oper und das Theater waren sehr billig (Fahrkarten und Bücher auch). Wir mussten natürlich jahrelang auf unsere lieben Trabis warten, aber das waren doch gute Autos! Und es gab so viele gute Möglichkeiten für unsere Kinder. Plätze in Kindertagesstätten hatten wir genug, und es gab wunderbare Sportmöglichkeiten und Bibliotheken für unsere Jugendlichen. Wir bekamen frisches Gemüse aus dem Schrebergarten. Im Sommer machten wir lange Radtouren und schwammen in den herrlichen Seen. Abends saßen wir gerne zusammen und erzählten. Und wir hatten überhaupt keine Angst, nachts alleine durch die dunklen Straßen zu laufen. Übrigens schmeckten die Brötchen damals viel besser als heute.

Es ist schade, dass Sie nicht die Gelegenheit hatten, die DDR selber zu erleben!

Mit bestem Gruß,

Walter Trublich

Ten things to remember

1 The past tenses are used to describe things that have already happened.

2 In German, there are two major past tenses: the simple past and the perfect, which we deal with in this unit and the next.

3 The simple past tends to be used in *writing* (newspapers, books, etc.) and is occasionally called the narrative past. But do note that it is also very widely used in spoken German in northern Germany and parts of central Germany (north of the River Main).

4 At this stage, it is most important to know whether the verb you are using is regular or irregular, so check the verb list in Reference grammar 10.7. If the verb does not appear on the list, even allowing for possible prefixes, it is a regular verb; but if it is on the list, it is irregular.

5 If the verb is regular, you can simply learn the rules as to how it is used in the simple past tense. If it is irregular, you must look it up in the verb list, where you will find the third person singular. Then add the appropriate ending to the 'stem'.

6 To find the stem of a regular verb, subtract the endings from the infinitive, e.g. **machen** → **mach**. Then add the following endings to the stem as appropriate: -te, -test, -te, -ten, -tet, -ten, -ten.

7 If the stem of a regular verb ends in -d or -t or a combination of -m or -n preceded by another consonant (e.g. **arbeiten** → **arbeit**), add the following endings to form the simple past tense: -ete, -etest, -ete, -eten, -etet, -eten, -eten.

8 To find the equivalent of the past stem of irregular verbs, look in the verb list where you will find the third person singular form, e.g. **geben** → **gab**. Gab is, in effect, the past stem of the verb, to which you must add the following endings: -, -st, -, -en, -(e)t, -en, -en. So the simple past tense of the verb **geben** is: **ich gab, du gabst, er/sie/es gab, wir gaben, ihr gabt, Sie gaben, sie gaben.**

9 The pluperfect tense is used both in English and in German to refer to events which took place before another event in the past. In fact it can only be used in connection with a more recent event, even if this is simply implied rather than stated in full, e.g. *Her son had already told her about it (when the doctor finally got round to mentioning it), I had saved enough money to buy a Mercedes (when I decided to get married).*

10 Don't worry that the pluperfect is yet another tense to be learned. It is merely a combination of the simple past tense of either **haben** or **sein** and the past participle. It is similar to the English usage, for example, e.g. **Ich hatte den Film schon gesehen.** (*I had already seen the film.*)

18

Talking about the past

In this unit you will learn how to
- *Talk about events in the past which are of relevance or interest to the present*
- *Talk about events which have happened in the recent past*

Language points
- *The perfect tense of regular and irregular verbs with* **haben** *or* **sein**
- *The use of* **seit** *and* **schon** *with the present tense*
- *Word order in the perfect tense after* **dass, weil, ob** *and* **obwohl**

Insight

It is impossible to give hard and fast rules to explain how to talk about the recent past, because usage varies both regionally and stylistically. As we noted in the last unit, the simple past tense is acceptable in speech as well as in writing, e.g. **Ich las die Zeitung spät gestern Abend** (*I read the newspaper late yesterday evening*). In southern and central Germany (south of the river Main), however, the perfect tense is preferred in speech, e.g. **Ich habe die Zeitung spät gestern Abend gelesen** (*I read the newspaper late yesterday evening*).

REFERRING TO PAST EVENTS WHICH ARE OF RELEVANCE OR INTEREST TO THE PRESENT

Ich habe ihn immer ehrlich gefunden.   *I've always found him honest. (I still do, and I recommend him for this job.)*

| Ich habe die ganze Woche für die Deutschprüfung gepaukt. | I've been swotting for the German exam all week. (That's why I haven't phoned you.) |
| Er hat das Büro gerade verlassen. | He's just left the office (so he can't take your phone call). |

Insight

You will notice that the perfect tense is composed of two parts: the appropriate part of the auxiliary verb **haben** (sometimes **sein**) plus a past participle which is placed at the end of the clause.

TALKING ABOUT EVENTS WHICH HAVE HAPPENED IN THE RECENT PAST

Look at the following examples of colloquial speech which refer to the recent past:

Sag mal, Uschi, was hast du in der Stadt gemacht?	*Tell me, Uschi, what did you do in town?*
Ich habe mir einen neuen Mantel gekauft und dann suchte ich neue Schuhe – vergebens. Ich habe Anna in der Hauptstraße getroffen, und wir sind zusammen ins Café gegangen. Sie hat Kaffee und Kuchen für uns beide bestellt. Hat das geschmeckt!	*I bought (myself) a new coat and then looked – in vain – for new shoes. I met Anna in the main street and we went to a café together. She ordered coffee and cakes for the two of us. Did that taste good!*
Was habt ihr beide gestern Abend gemacht?	*What did you two do last night?*
Wir sind ins Kino gegangen und haben den Film „Die Spinne" gesehen. (Er hat uns gut gefallen.) Dann haben wir Inge besucht und sind zusammen in die Disco gegangen. Da haben wir getanzt, Cola getrunken, ein bisschen geredet und haben Inge gegen Mitternacht nach Haus' gebracht.	*We went to the cinema and saw the film 'The Spider'. (We liked it.) Then we visited Inge and went to the disco together. There we danced, drank Coke and talked a bit. We took Inge home towards midnight.*

Grammar summary

THE PERFECT TENSE OF REGULAR VERBS

From the above examples we see that German has only one form of the perfect tense, for example **er hat ... geschrieben** which can be translated as *he wrote, he did write, he has written* (and occasionally *he was writing*) or **ich bin ... gefahren**, which can be translated into English as *I travelled, I did travel, I have travelled* (and occasionally *I was travelling*).

The perfect tense is formed by using the appropriate part of either **haben** or **sein** plus a past participle (e.g. **gekauft, getanzt**) at the end of the clause:

Ich **habe** einen neuen Mantel **gekauft**. *I bought a new coat.*

(In a different context this could be translated as *I have bought, I did buy* or *I was buying*.)

Wir **haben getanzt**. *We danced.*

(In different contexts this could be translated equally well as *we did dance* or *we have danced*.)

NB The past participle of most regular verbs is formed by first removing the -en from the infinitive (e.g. **kaufen**), giving us the stem of the verb (i.e. **kauf-**). Next, put ge- in front of the stem and -t after the stem, resulting in **gekauft** (*bought*). The past participle stands at the end of the clause.

Look at the following examples of verbs in the perfect tense, in which the past participle is formed in the same way:

Ich *habe* **gerade eine Zwiebelsuppe** *gekocht.*   *I have just made some onion soup.*

Der Schüler *hat* **seine Hausaufgaben** *gemacht.*   *The pupil has done his homework.*

Was *hast* **du** *gesagt?*   *What did you say?*

THE PAST PARTICIPLE OF SEPARABLE VERBS

Insight

We first came across separable verbs in Unit 5 and can find more information in Reference grammar 9.3. These verbs can appear in the dictionary as **ab/fahren**, **ab+fahren** or even with a dot between the prefix and the infinitive. The /, + or dot shows that the prefix separates from the finite verb in a normal sentence:

Der Zug fährt um zehn Uhr ab.   *The train sets off/departs at ten o'clock.*

To form the past participle of a separable verb, for example **ein/kaufen** (*to go shopping*), **auf/machen** (*to open*), **zu/machen** (*to close*), simply put the ge- between the two parts of the verb, forming a 'sandwich' past participle, e.g. **aufgemacht, eingekauft, zugemacht**. This is always written as one word.

Wir *haben* **gestern bei Kaufhof** *eingekauft.*   *We went shopping at Kaufhof yesterday.*

Er *hat* **das Geburtstagsgeschenk noch nicht** *aufgemacht.*   *He hasn't opened the birthday present yet.*

Die Hausfrau *hat* **die Tür gleich** *zugemacht.*   *The housewife closed the door immediately.*

You will find more examples of past participles of separable verbs in the section on irregular verbs below.

Past participles of verbs whose stem ends in -d, -t, or -m or -n preceded by a consonant

If the stem of the verb ends in -d, -t or -m or -n preceded by a consonant, an additional e is added before the final -t in the past participle for ease of pronunciation. For example:

Oma *hat* **im Toten Meer** *gebadet.*	*Grandma bathed in the Dead Sea.*
Es *hat* **gestern viel** *geregnet.*	*It rained a lot yesterday.*
Sie *hat* **nicht fleißig genug** *gearbeitet.*	*She didn't work hard enough.*

*Past participles of verbs beginning with **be-, emp-, ent-, er-, ge-, hinter-, miss-, ver-** or **zer-**, or ending with **-ieren***

If the infinitive begins with the prefixes listed above, or ends with -ieren, no ge- is required at the beginning of the past participle:

Wir *haben* **nichts** *bemerkt.*	*We didn't notice anything.*
Der Archäologe *hat* **ein Wikingerboot im Schlamm** *entdeckt.*	*The archaeologist discovered a Viking boat in the mud.*
Er *hat* **schon vier Jahre** *studiert.*	*He's already been studying for four years.*

THE PERFECT TENSE OF IRREGULAR VERBS

Many verbs do not form their past participle in the way described above.

Look at the following examples of irregular verbs used in the perfect tense:

Er *hat* **den ganzen Tag kein Wort** *gesprochen.*
He didn't speak a word all day. (**gesprochen** is the past participle of **sprechen**)

Ich *habe* **zu viel** *gegessen.*
I've eaten too much. (**gegessen** is the past participle of **essen**)

Hast **du dieses Buch schon** *gelesen?*
Have you already read this book? (**gelesen** is the past participle of **lesen**)

Insight

The past participles of most irregular verbs end in **-en,** and many also undergo a vowel change from the infinitive form. There is no reliable way to work this out, so the verb list (see Reference grammar 10.7, or any good German dictionary) should be consulted until individual forms of the various groups have been learned. I set my students the task of working through the verb list, learning all the tenses of one irregular verb every day, five days a week. This is a wonderful way to boost your confidence in the language.

Ein kleiner Scherz:
Weißt du, was Tante Herta gestern gemacht hat? Sie hat versucht, den Kanal mit meinem Taschenrechner zu wechseln!! Das hat natürlich nicht geklappt, und sie musste den ganzen Abend Fußball sehen!

A little joke:
Do you know what Aunt Herta did yesterday? She tried to change the TV channel with my pocket calculator. Of course it didn't work and so she had to watch football all evening!

VERBS WHICH FORM THEIR PERFECT TENSE USING **SEIN**

> ## Insight
>
> Nowadays, we always use the verb 'to have' plus a past participle to form the perfect tense in English, e.g. '*I have* come specially', 'You *have* ruined my reputation', 'He *has* already paid the price', 'We *haven't* seen the exhibition yet'. But in older English we can find examples of the verb 'to be' plus a past participle being used to form the perfect tense. In the King James Bible, for example, we can still read 'I *am* come' rather than 'I *have* come', but of course it sounds archaic. This is not so in German, where the verb **sein** (*to be*) is still used to form the perfect tense of certain verbs.

When to use **sein** in the perfect tense:

▶ If the verb shows motion or movement from one place to another:

Ich *bin* **mit dem Zug** *gefahren.*	*I travelled by train.*
Ihr Mann *ist* **um zwei Uhr morgens nach Hause** *gekommen.*	*Her husband came home at 2 a.m.*
Bist **du über Brüssel** *geflogen*?	*Did you fly via Brussels?*

▶ If the verb shows a change of state or condition:

Es *ist* **dunkel** *geworden.*
It has got dark. (literally 'It has become dark.')

Ich *bin* **schnell** *eingeschlafen.*
I fell asleep quickly.

Meine Tante *ist* **letzte Woche** *gestorben.*
My aunt died last week.

Die Katze *ist* **einfach** *verschwunden.*
The cat simply disappeared.

▶ Two exceptions which form the perfect tense using **sein** (and require the dative case):

folgen *(to follow)*
Der Herr hat gerufen und der Hund *ist* **ihm** *gefolgt.*
The master called and the dog followed him.

begegnen *(to meet)*
Sie *ist* **ihrem Exmann im Restaurant** *begegnet.*
She met her ex-husband in the restaurant.

▶ NB The verbs **sein** and **bleiben** also form their perfect tense using **sein**:

Sie *ist* **sehr krank** *gewesen.*   She has been very ill.
Er *ist* **in Rostock** *geblieben.*   He has stayed in Rostock.

Insight

The verb **sein** (*to be*) always forms its perfect tense with **sein**:

Ich war kurz bei Frau Knoop gewesen. *I was at Frau Knoop's for a short time/I briefly dropped in on Frau Knoop.*

Small children sometimes use the following rhyme to remember this small but important point about the perfect tense:

Whether the weather be wet or fine, **haben** takes **haben** and **sein** takes **sein**.

REGIONAL VARIATIONS

As suggested at the beginning of this unit, there are few hard and fast rules about the past tenses. For example, the verbs **sitzen, stehen** and **liegen** use **haben** to form their perfect tense in northern Germany, but in southern Germany, Austria and Switzerland **sein** is used. In theory this could result in confusion in some situations; for example, **sitzen** can mean either *to sit* or *to do time* in prison. Thus, **Er hat gesessen** could be ambiguous to someone in northern Germany, meaning either *He has been sitting* or *He has been in prison*, but to a southerner it could only mean *He has been in prison*.

A few other verbs use either **haben** or **sein,** depending on the meaning:

Er *ist* **nach Polen** *gefahren.*	*He (has) gone to Poland.*
Er *hat* **einen Mercedes** *gefahren.*	*He was driving a Mercedes.*
Er *ist* **den ganzen Nachmittag** *geschwommen.*	*He swam the whole afternoon.*
Er *hat* **1.000 Meter in der Olympiade** *geschwommen.*	*He swam the 1,000 metres in the Olympics.*

Insight

From these examples, we can see that the verb **sein** is often used to form the perfect tense of verbs which take no direct object (known as intransitive verbs). If the verb clearly takes a direct object (i.e. there is a person or thing which undergoes the action of the verb), then the perfect tense is formed with **haben.** Such verbs are known as transitive verbs.

In context

Look at the following conversation, in which a doctor and a nurse are discussing a patient's progress over the last 24 hours.

Arzt	Hat er denn gut geschlafen?
Krankenschwester	Nein, überhaupt nicht. Er ist die ganze Nacht unruhig gewesen und hat manchmal laut geschrien. Er hat gestern Fieber gehabt und hat auch starke Schmerzen erlitten.
Arzt	Hat er also nichts gegessen?
Krankenschwester	Doch, doch. Er hat eine Scheibe Toast 'runtergekriegt und hat ziemlich viel getrunken. Seine Frau hat ihm Apfelsaft gebracht.
Arzt	Haben Sie schon den Blutdruck gemessen?
Krankenschwester	Das habe ich um sechs Uhr früh gemacht, aber seither habe ich keine Zeit dazu gehabt.

QUICK VOCAB

überhaupt nicht *on no account*
unruhig *restless*
manchmal *sometimes*
laut schreien *to cry out loud*
gestern *yesterday*
Fieber haben *to have a temperature*
starke Schmerzen *severe pains*
erleiden *to suffer*
also *so, therefore*
nichts *nothing*
doch, doch (here) *oh yes, he has* ('No' was the expected answer)
die Scheibe *slice*
'runter/kriegen *to swallow, to get down* (colloquial)
ziemlich viel *rather a lot, quite a lot*
den Blutdruck messen *to take the blood pressure*
um sechs Uhr früh *at six o'clock in the morning*
seither *since then*
keine Zeit haben *to have no time*

Taking it further

USING THE PRESENT TENSE TO EXPRESS SOMETHING WHICH BEGAN IN THE PAST AND IS STILL CONTINUING

> ### Insight
>
> Sometimes German uses the present tense to express something that we would put into the perfect tense in English:
>
> ▶ In Unit 4, we learned the preposition **seit** *(since, for)* + dative:
>   **Ich übe seit drei Monaten die Trompete.** *I've been practising the trumpet for three months.*
>
> ▶ The adverb of time **schon** *(already)* can similarly be used in the present tense:
>   **Ich warte schon zwanzig Minuten auf den Bus.** *I've been waiting for the bus for twenty minutes.*
>
> Both of these usages suggest that something which began at some point in the past continues to be true. **Seit** is comparable to French *'depuis'*.

For example:

Seit wann *lernen* **Sie Deutsch?**	*How long have you been learning German?*
Enno *ist* **seit seiner Kindheit kränklich.**	*Enno has been sickly since childhood.*
Er *lernt* **Klavier seit einem Jahr.**	*He has been learning the piano for a year.*
Henning *wohnt* **seit der Wende in Koblenz.**	*Henning has been living in Koblenz since Unification.* (literally 'since the Turn', i.e. the fall of the Berlin Wall in 1989)

Mein Onkel *liegt* **seit Weihnachten im Krankenhaus.**	*My uncle has been in hospital since Christmas.*
Wie lange *warten* **Sie schon?**	*How long have you already been waiting?*
Waren **Sie schon in Leipzig?**	*Have you ever been to Leipzig?*

USING THE PERFECT TENSE FOR A COMPLETED ACTIVITY

When we want to show that an activity has been completed, rather than being in process, we use the perfect tense in German.

Look at the following pairs of sentences and see if you can understand the difference between them:

Sie nähte das Hochzeitskleid, als ich ankam.	*She was sewing her wedding dress when I arrived.* (i.e. she was in the process of sewing it)
Weißt du, sie hat das Hochzeitskleid selbst genäht.	*Do you know, she made her own wedding dress.* (i.e. it is now finished)
Er verdiente das Geld, das er für das Auto brauchte.	*He was earning the money he needed for the car.*
Er hat das Geld für das Auto verdient.	*He has earned the money he needed for the car.*

WORD ORDER IN THE PERFECT TENSE AFTER THE CONJUNCTIONS **DASS** *(THAT),* **WEIL** *(BECAUSE),* **OB** *(WHETHER) AND* **OBWOHL** *(ALTHOUGH)*

In Unit 7, we learned that these conjunctions send the verb to the end of their clause. This rule also applies in the perfect tense:

Ich weiß, dass er seine Hausaufgaben noch nicht gemacht hat.	*I know (that) he has not done his homework yet.*
Er kann nicht kommen, weil er sich das Bein gebrochen hat.	*He cannot come because he has broken his leg.*

Practice

EXERCISE A

Now look at the following sentences and see if you can work out from which verb each past participle comes. If in doubt, check the verb list (Reference grammar 10.7).

1 Die Direktorin hat an meinen Vater **geschrieben**. *The headmistress wrote to my father.*
2 Habt ihr gut **geschlafen**? *Did you sleep well?*
3 Ich habe einen Schock **bekommen**. *I got a shock.*
4 Ich habe meinen Ausweis immer noch nicht **gefunden**. *I still haven't found my identity card.*
5 Sie haben den ganzen Abend im Biergarten **getrunken**. *They were drinking the whole evening in the beer garden.*
6 Der Film hat spät **angefangen**. *The film began late.*
7 Unser Dirigent ist heute von London nach Wien **geflogen**. *Our conductor flew from London to Vienna today.*
8 Pastor Scheurich ist nach dem Mauerfall in Eisenach **geblieben**. *Reverend Scheurich remained in Eisenach after the fall of the (Berlin) Wall.*
9 Der Notarzt ist gleich zum Unfallort **gefahren**. *The doctor on emergency call immediately went to the scene of the accident.*
10 Er hat mein Deutsch sehr gut **verstanden**. *He understood my German very well.*

EXERCISE B

Would you use **haben** or **sein** to complete the following sentences?

1 Ilse ___ Käsekuchen bestellt. *Inge ordered cheesecake.*
2 Du ___ einen Fehler gemacht. *You've made a mistake.*
3 Der Zug ___ um 12.15 abgefahren. *The train set off at 12.15.*
4 Wir ___ sehr viel Deutsch gelernt. *We've learned a lot of German.*
5 Sie ___ sehr müde geworden. *She's got (become) very tired.*
6 ___ ihr ein neues Auto gekauft? *Have you bought a new car?*

7 Ich __ in Stuttgart ein Glas Wein getrunken. *I drank a glass of wine in Stuttgart.*

8 __ Sie Lotte im Krankenhaus besucht? *Have you visited Lotte in hospital?*

9 Hans __ so schnell gewachsen. *Hans has grown so quickly.*

10 Sevim __ noch nie in der Schweiz gewesen. *Sevim hasn't ever been to Switzerland.*

Ten things to remember

1 The perfect tense is more commonly used in southern and central Germany (south of the river Main) than in northern Germany.

2 The perfect tense is used for talking about recent events and for past events which are of relevance or interest to the present.

3 The perfect tense consists of two parts: an auxiliary verb (**haben** or **sein**) and a past participle which normally comes at the end of a clause.

4 If the verb is transitive (i.e. it can take a direct object), it forms the perfect tense using the auxiliary verb **haben**.

5 If the verb shows motion from one place to another, or a change of state, it forms the perfect tense using the auxiliary **sein**.

6 The past participles of regular verbs are formed by putting **ge-** before the stem of the verb and **-t** on the end of the stem. If the stem ends in **-t** or **-d**, insert an **e** between the stem and the letter **d** or **t**, e.g. **baden** → **gebadet**, **antworten** → **geantwortet**.

7 The past participle of separable verbs is written as one word, with the prefix coming before the past participle of the basic verb, e.g. **abgeholt** (*collected*), **angerufen** (*telephoned*).

8 If the verb begins with the prefix **be-, emp-, ent-, er-, ge-, hinter-, miss-, ver-** or **zer-**, no **ge-** is required at the beginning of the past participle, e.g. **bekommen, empfunden, missverstanden.**

9 Verbs which end in **-ieren** do NOT use **ge-** in their past participle, e.g. **rasieren → rasiert.**

10 The past participles of most irregular verbs end in **-en**, and many also undergo a vowel change from the infinitive form. There is no reliable way to work this out, so the irregular verb list (see Reference grammar 10.7, or any good German dictionary) should be consulted until individual forms of the various groups have been learned.

19

Describing processes and procedures

In this unit you will learn how to
- **Describe processes and procedures**
- **Ask questions regarding processes and procedures**

Language points
- **Passive and active sentences**
- **The use of man to avoid the passive**

Insight

Before we start to look at this grammar point in detail, let's stop to think about what we mean by the words *active* and *passive*:

▶ *Active* often has the sense of 'somebody being busy doing something', or 'somebody being involved in doing or carrying out some process or procedure'.
▶ On the other hand, the term **passive** (as in 'passive smoker') suggests that the person is undergoing or being subjected to the actions of another person or agent.

The passive voice is used much more often in formal writing than in speech, most probably because it lends a measured style or objective tone to the writing, as required for academic reports. Research has actually shown that more than 90 per cent of all

German sentences appear in the active voice. However, you should try to understand how the passive voice is formed, even though you will probably only need to recognize it, rather than produce it yourself.

LET'S TAKE THIS FURTHER:

To describe the various steps involved in a process such as *The grapes are picked by the students and are then taken to the storehouse. There they are immediately weighed by the foreman*, we use the passive. The passive sentence emphasizes the process involved, whereas the active equivalent *The students pick the grapes and then take them to the storehouse. The foreman weighs them*, shows us more clearly who are the agents in the process.

Insight

In previous units, we have come across many sentences in which the grammatical subject of the sentence performs the action of the verb, e.g. *A keen language student is reading this chapter*. This use of the verb is called the active voice.

But it is equally possible to say *This chapter is being read by a keen language student*. In this sentence, the direct object of the active sentence (*this chapter*) becomes the subject of the passive sentence, whereas the subject of the active sentence (*a keen language student*) has become the agent by which the process (*reading*) is being carried out in the passive sentence. This usage is known as the passive voice.

Look at the following examples and their translations before reading the further explanation in the Grammar summary:

Die Trauben *werden* **meistens von Studenten mit der Hand** *gepflückt.*	*The grapes are mostly picked by hand by students.*
Sie *werden* **gleich in Körbe** *getan* **und** *werden* **dann mit dem Trecker zum Lagerhaus** *gebracht.*	*They're immediately put into baskets and taken by tractor to the storehouse.*

Dort *werden* **die Trauben** *gewogen* **und in große Gefäße** *gekippt,* **wo sie** *gepresst werden.*	*There the grapes are weighed and put into large containers, where they are pressed.*
Am Ende der Weinernte *wird gefeiert.* **Auf dem Winzerfest** *wird* **eine Weinprinzessin** *gewählt.* **In einigen Dörfern** *wird* **der Wein manchmal kostenlos vom Dorfbrunnen** *angeboten,* **aber in anderen Gegenden** *wird* **der Wein von Privathäusern aus** *verkauft.*	*At the end of the wine harvest, there are celebrations. At the wine festival, a wine princess is chosen. In some villages, wine is sometimes offered free of charge from the village fountain, but in other areas the wine is sold from private houses.*
Die Weinreben *werden* **durch Frost oder Hagel oft** *beschädigt.*	*The vines are often damaged by frost or hail.*
Sehr viel Wein *wird exportiert.*	*A great deal of wine is exported.*

....

Insight

In English, we normally use the preposition 'by' to show the agent in the passive voice, irrespective of whether the agent is a person or a thing. But in German, the preposition **von** + dative is used for a human agent and the preposition **durch** + accusative is used for an inanimate agent:

Der Zaun wird gerade von dem Gärtner errichtet. *The fence is just being erected by the gardener.*
Der Zaun wird jeden Winter durch den Wind zerstört. *The fence is destroyed by the wind every winter.*

....

Grammar summary

THE PASSIVE VOICE

The passive is formed by using the appropriate part of the verb **werden** (see Unit 16 for other uses of this verb) plus a past participle at the end of the clause.

Let's analyse two sentences to learn more about the passive. First, let's look at an active sentence:

The students pick the grapes by hand.

- ▶ *The students* are the subject of the sentence because they are carrying out the action of the verb, i.e. picking. In German, the subject is put into the nominative case (see Units 1 and 3).
- ▶ *pick* is the verb.
- ▶ *the grapes* are the direct object of the sentence because they are undergoing the action of the verb, i.e. being picked. In German the direct object is put into the accusative case.
- ▶ *by hand* shows us the instrument used.

Now let's compare this sentence with the passive equivalent:

The grapes are picked by hand by the students.

- ▶ *The grapes*, the direct object in the active sentence, have become the subject of the passive sentence.
- ▶ *The students*, the subject of the active sentence, have become the agent by which the activity is carried out in the passive sentence.
- ▶ *by hand* still represents the instrument used.
- ▶ Now have a look at the German version of the active sentence:

Die Studenten	*pflücken*	*die Trauben*	*mit der Hand.*
subject, therefore *nominative* case	verb	direct object, therefore *accusative* case	instrument in *dative* after preposition **mit**

Compare this with the passive equivalent:

Die Trauben werden von den Studenten mit der Hand gepflückt.

- ▶ **Die Trauben,** the direct object of the active sentence, have become the subject of the passive sentence.
- ▶ **Die Studenten,** the subject of the active sentence, have become the agent by which the process is carried out in the passive

sentence. In German, the agent is expressed by using either **von** plus the *dative* case or **durch** plus the *accusative case*. Here, **von** is used, and so **die Studenten** is changed into the dative plural (**von den Studenten**).

▶ **mit der Hand**, the instrument, remains the same.

Insight

Don't confuse the grammatical term 'voice' with 'tense'. Just as we learned how to use the active voice in different tenses, so we can use the passive voice in present, future and past tenses.

Now look at the same passive sentence in different tenses:

Present tense:
Die Trauben werden von den Studenten mit der Hand gepflückt.   *The grapes are picked by hand by the students.*

Simple past tense:
Die Trauben wurden von den Studenten mit der Hand gepflückt.   *The grapes were picked by hand by the students.*

Perfect tense:
Die Trauben sind von den Studenten mit der Hand gepflückt worden.   *The grapes have been picked by hand by the students.*

Insight

When using the perfect tense in the passive voice in a normal sentence, the past participle of **werden** goes right to the end of the clause, i.e. after the normal past participle you would expect to see in a perfect tense sentence. When this happens, the past participle of **werden** (**geworden**) loses its **ge-** and appears as **worden**. This is the only situation in which you will find the word **worden**, e.g.

Der Taxifahrer hat den Mercedes schon verkauft. *The taxi driver has already sold the Mercedes.*
Der Mercedes ist von dem Taxifahrer schon verkauft worden. *The Mercedes has already been sold by the taxi driver.*

Pluperfect tense:

Die Trauben waren von den Studenten mit der Hand gepflückt worden. *The grapes had been picked by hand by the students.*

Future tense:

Die Trauben werden von den Studenten mit der Hand gepflückt werden. *The grapes will be picked by hand by the students.*

Now look at these different examples of the passive and check the formation of each sentence against the rules we have just learned.

Viele Autos werden importiert. *Many cars are imported.*

Wir wurden von japanischen Kellnerinnen bedient. *We were served by Japanese waitresses.*

Sein Vater wurde durch den Brief gekränkt. *His father was hurt by the letter.*

NB When the agent is inanimate, the preposition **durch** (through) is often used instead of **von**:

Viel Zeit wird von Kindern durch Computerspiele verschwendet. *A lot of time is wasted by children on computer games.*

Sein letztes Buch wurde in Singapur gedruckt. *His latest book was printed in Singapore.*

Das Kind ist schwer verletzt worden. *The child has been badly hurt.*

Viele Flugblätter gegen das Atomkraftwerk sind gestern in der Stadtmitte verteilt worden. *Many leaflets against the nuclear power station were distributed in the town centre yesterday.*

Viele Zeitschriften werden immer noch in Hamburg veröffentlicht, aber bald werden die Verlagshäuser nach Berlin umziehen. *Many magazines are still published in Hamburg, but soon the publishing houses will move to Berlin.*

Insight

Notice the two different uses of the verb **werden** in this last sentence, firstly as an auxiliary verb to form the passive voice, secondly as an auxiliary verb to form the future tense.

In context

Now look at the following report, which a social worker is helping a client threatened with eviction to compile:

Wir werden von allen asozial genannt. Es wird behauptet, dass nachts sehr laute Musik in unserem Haus gespielt wird, dass wilde Partys gehalten werden, wo zu viel Bier getrunken wird. Die Wahrheit ist, dass nachts Steine gegen unsere Fenster geworfen worden sind – ohne Grund!

Es wird auch gesagt, dass Drogen bei uns zu finden sind. Wir werden Drogenhändler genannt. Wir werden von den Kindern vermieden und von den Erwachsenen verfolgt. Wir sind aber total unschuldig.

QUICK VOCAB

von allen by everyone
asozial antisocial
nennen to name, call
behaupten to maintain
nachts at night
wild wild
eine Party halten to hold a party
zu viel too much
die Wahrheit the truth
der Stein stone
das Fenster window
ohne without
der Grund the reason
die Droge drug
zu finden sein to be found

der Drogenhändler *drug dealer*
vermeiden *to avoid*
verfolgen *to persecute*
unschuldig *innocent*

Taking it further

The use of **man** to avoid the passive

Insight

George Orwell is credited with saying:

Never use the passive where you can use the active.

George Orwell 'Politics and the English Language', first published in *Horizon* (April 1946)

There are indeed very simple ways of avoiding the passive in both English and German, e.g.

Passive:
Die Klassiker werden heutzutage nicht oft gelesen. *The classics are not often read nowadays.*

Active:
Man liest die Klassiker nicht oft heutzutage. *People/They don't often read the classics nowadays.*

The passive can often be avoided simply by using the indefinite pronoun **man.**

Compare the following sets of sentences. The first involves the passive, the second **man**. Both sentences have the same meaning.

Es wird oft gesagt, dass Albanien landschaftlich sehr schön ist.	*It is often said that Albania is scenically very pretty.*
Man **sagt oft, dass Albanien landschaftlich sehr schön ist.**	*They often say that Albania is scenically very pretty.*

Im Moment werden sehr viele Aktien verkauft.	*A lot of shares are being sold at the moment.*
Im Moment verkauft *man* **sehr viele Aktien.**	*At the moment they're selling a lot of shares.*
Dieses Jahr ist mehr Bier denn je auf dem Oktoberfest getrunken worden.	*This year more beer than ever was drunk at the October Beer Festival.*
Dieses Jahr hat *man* **mehr Bier denn je auf dem Oktoberfest getrunken.**	*This year they drank more beer than ever at the October Beer Festival.*

You will have noticed in the examples above that the verbs which can be put into the passive voice are transitive verbs, i.e. they can take an accusative direct object.

ADVANCED USES OF THE PASSIVE (FOR THE VERY KEEN STUDENT!)

Now look at the following unusual examples of passive usage:

▶ Some intransitive verbs can be used in the passive voice when used with the impersonal pronoun **es**, e.g. **Es wird jetzt geschlafen!** There is no direct translation of this into an English passive form. It is best translated as *Let's get to sleep now*!

▶ Occasionally, you will hear the irregular verb **bekommen** (*to get, to receive*) used idiomatically in spoken language to express the passive:

Sie bekam Blumen geschenkt.	*She was given flowers.*
Ich bekomme meine Medikamente geliefert.	*I get my medications delivered.*

▶ Occasionally, verbs which are normally followed by the dative case appear in the passive voice, e.g. **an/bieten** (*to offer*), **helfen** (*to help*), **schaden** (*to damage*):

Mir ist eine neue Stelle angeboten worden.	*I have been offered a new job.*

The active equivalent of this would be:

Man hat mir eine neue Stelle angeboten.	*They offered me a new job.*
Der Gesundheit wird durch Zigaretten geschadet.	*Cigarettes damage (your) health. (literally 'Health is damaged by cigarettes.')*

The active equivalent of this would be:

Zigaretten schaden der Gesundheit.	*Cigarettes damage (your) health.*
Dem Unfallopfer wurde von Passanten auf der Stelle geholfen.	*The casualty was helped on the spot by passers-by.*

The active equivalent of this would be:

Passanten haben dem Unfallopfer auf der Stelle geholfen.	*Passers by helped the victim on the spot.*

Insight

Did you notice that the dative noun phrase in the active version does not change its case when it is changed to the passive? This is only true of these few verbs which take the dative case. Also note that the plural verb in the active sentence is replaced by a singular verb in the passive sentence.

WHEN NOT TO USE THE PASSIVE

Finally, let's look at the following examples of where the passive voice is never used:

▶ Verbs which describe the weather do NOT appear in the passive voice, e.g. **es regnet** (*it's raining*), **es schneit** (*it's snowing*), **es dämmert** (*it's getting dark*), **es donnert** (*it's thundering*).
▶ Reflexive verbs which are intransitive do NOT appear in the passive, e.g. **sich beeilen** (*to hurry up*), sich **entschuldigen** (*to apologize*), **sich bemühen** (*to make an effort*).

▶ You will NOT find the verbs **haben, sein, werden, wissen** and **kennen** in the passive voice.

Practice

EXERCISE A

Have a good evening, everyone!

You want to help with the final tasks in the office, so that you can all leave early for the weekend. Unfortunately your offers of help come too late, as others are already doing the work. Change the active sentence into the present passive.

Example: Darf ich den Brief tippen?

Der Brief **wird** schon **getippt.** *The letter is already being typed.*

1 Darf ich das Fax schicken? *May I send the fax?*

_____

2 Darf ich das Fenster zumachen? *May I close the window?*

_____

3 Darf ich den Papierkorb leeren? *May I empty the wastepaper basket?*

_____

4 Darf ich die Kaffeetassen abwaschen? *May I wash up the coffee cups?*

_____

5 Darf ich die Briefe unterschreiben? *May I sign the letters?*

_____

Another colleague comes into the office and asks the same questions (1–5). You refuse her help, saying that these tasks have just been done. You should use the perfect passive.

Example: Darf ich den Brief tippen?

Nein, der Brief **ist** schon **getippt worden.** *No, the letter has already been typed.*

1 Darf ich das Fax schicken? *May I send the fax?*

_____

2 Darf ich das Fenster zumachen? *May I close the window?*

_____

3 Darf ich den Papierkorb leeren? *May I empty the wastepaper basket?*

_____

4 Darf ich die Kaffeetassen abwaschen? *May I wash up the coffee cups?*

_____

5 Darf ich die Briefe unterschreiben? *May I sign the letters?*

_____

Just as you are about to leave, your boss comes in and asks your colleague why she hasn't done various tasks. She replies that they had already been done when she offered. In response to the question with **warum?** put the reply into the pluperfect passive:

Warum haben Sie den Brief nicht getippt?	*Why have you not typed the letter?*
Der Brief war schon getippt worden.	*The letter had already been typed (when I offered.)*

1 Warum haben Sie das Fax nicht geschickt?

_____

2 Warum haben Sie das Fenster nicht zugemacht?

_____

3 Warum haben Sie den Papierkorb nicht geleert?

_____

4 Warum haben Sie die Kaffeetassen nicht abgewaschen?

_____

5 Warum haben Sie die Briefe nicht unterschrieben?

_____

EXERCISE B

Rephrase the following passive sentences using the indefinite pronoun **man** and the active form of the verb.

1 Es wird oft gesagt, dass Zigaretten der Gesundheit schaden. _It is often said that cigarettes harm one's health._

_____

2 Auf Bierfesten wird Bier oft aus Maßkrügen getrunken. _At beer festivals beer is often drunk out of one-litre steins._

_____

3 Zu Weihnachten wird eine Gans nicht mehr so oft gegessen wie früher. _At Christmas, goose is not eaten as often as formerly._

_____

4 Zu viel wird von Kleinkindern erwartet. _Too much is expected of toddlers._

_____

5 Hier wird Deutsch gesprochen. *German is spoken here.*

---

6 Der Reifendruck wird kostenlos geprüft. *Tyre pressure is checked free of charge.*

---

7 Der Müll wird in fast jeder deutschen Küche getrennt. *Refuse is separated in almost every German kitchen.*

---

8 Das Brot wird mit einer Schneidemaschine geschnitten. *Bread is cut with a slicing machine.*

---

9 Immer mehr Geld wird bei den Sommerschlussverkäufen ausgegeben. *More and more money is being spent in the summer sales.*

---

10 In dieser Schule wird nicht sehr viel gelernt. *Not very much is learned in this school.*

Ten things to remember

1 Most sentences in German appear in the active voice, where the grammatical subject of the sentence performs the action of the verb.

2 The passive voice is found mostly in writing and lends a measured, objective tone to the writing.

3 The passive voice is formed by using the appropriate form and tense of the verb **werden** plus a past participle at the end of the clause.

4 The passive voice can be used in the present, future and past tenses.

5 **Der Lehrer korrigiert den Aufsatz** (*The teacher marks the essay*) is in the active voice.

6 **Der Aufsatz wird von dem Lehrer korrigiert** (*The essay is marked by the teacher*) is in the passive voice.

7 The teacher in point 6 above is called the agent. If the agent is a person, the preposition **von** + dative is used.

8 If the agent is inanimate, the preposition **durch** + accusative is normally used, e.g. **Die Patientin wurde durch eine Notoperation gerettet.** (*The patient was saved by an emergency operation.*)

9 When using the passive voice in the perfect tense in a normal clause, the past participle of **werden** (**geworden**) drops its **ge-** and appears right at the end of the clause, e.g. **Das ist schon erwähnt worden.** (*That has already been mentioned.*)

10 The passive voice is often avoided by using the impersonal pronoun **man** (*one, you, people, they*).

20

Reporting what was said and asked

In this unit you will learn how to
- **Report who said and asked what**

Language points
- **Subjunctive 1**

When we say or ask something directly, we call this *direct speech*, e.g. *I've no money. Have you any?* We use the normal form (or mood) of the verb, that which you have used in the book so far. This is known as the indicative mood.

If, however, we wish to report a statement or question to someone, and are not absolutely sure of the truth of the original statement, or wish in some way to distance ourselves from it, e.g. *He said he had no money and asked me whether I had any*, then a different mood of the verb is often used in German: the subjunctive. It indicates that we cannot be one hundred per cent sure that what is being reported is true.

Insight

We have now come across three moods in German:

- ▶ the indicative mood: to express certainty and facts
- ▶ the imperative mood: to express the attitude of the speaker in the form of commands

▶ the subjunctive mood: to express uncertainty, possibility, wishes and unreal conditional sentences. The subjunctive mood is also used to convey reported speech, because we only have the speaker's word as to the truth of the matter being reported.

There are very few remnants of the subjunctive left in English, mostly expressions such as *Be that as it may* or *So be it* or, in the words of Topol's song, *If I were a rich man.*

DIRECT SPEECH? INDIRECT SPEECH? WHAT'S THE DIFFERENCE?

▶ Direct speech reports the exact words spoken. These are introduced by the appropriate part of a verb such as 'to say', 'to tell', 'to explain' or 'to ask'. The exact words are marked by inverted commas, e.g. (*Fred said/I heard Fred say*) "*I am too ill to go to work.*"

▶ Indirect speech (or reported speech) requires no inverted commas but often uses a conjunction such as 'that' or 'whether'. Now notice how the first person pronoun (I) in the above example changes to the third person (*he*), and how the present tense changes to the past tense, in the following English example of reported speech: *Fred said that he was too ill to go to work.*

▶ In German, however, the verb changes into the subjunctive mood to denote indirect speech, but it remains in the tense in which it was originally said:

Direct speech: **Ich bin zu krank zum Dienst zu gehen.**
Indirect (reported) speech: **Friedrich sagte, er sei zu krank zum Dienst zu gehen.**

Note that **sei** is the third person singular subjunctive form of the verb **sein** (*to be*), the indicative equivalent being **ist**.

Now look at the following examples:

Direct speech	Indirect speech or reported speech
1 My son's exact words to my husband this morning:	This same conversation as related to me by my husband:
Vati, ich bin krank.	Er sagte, er **sei** krank.
Dad, I'm ill.	*He said he was ill.*
Ich habe Kopfschmerzen.	(Er sagte,) er **habe** Kopfschmerzen.
I've got a headache.	*(He said) he had a headache.*
Ich kann nicht für meine Prüfung lernen.	(Er sagte,) er **könne** nicht für seine Prüfung lernen.
I can't learn for my exam.	*(He said) he couldn't learn for his exam.*
Ich muss ins Bett gehen.	(Er sagte,) er **müsse** ins Bett gehen.
I've got to go to bed.	*(He said) he had to go to bed.*
Ich brauche Ruhe.	(Er sagte,) er **brauche** Ruhe.
I need (some) rest.	*(He said) he needed (some) rest.*
Ich rufe lieber den Arzt an.	(Er sagte,) er **rufe** lieber den Arzt an.
I'd better phone the doctor.	*(He said) he'd better phone the doctor.*

Insight

One of the effects of reported speech can be to convey that what is being reported is not necessarily true, or that the speaker does not believe it is true, which might be the case in the examples in box 1. But this is not always so. Indirect speech is also very often used in newspapers and television news broadcasts to report what has been said in Parliament or in the law courts.

Insight

Have another look at the subjunctive verb forms in the examples in box 1, and compare them with the corresponding indicative forms which we have learned so far:

Subjunctive	Indicative
er (or sie) sei	er/sie ist
er/sie habe	er/sie hat
er/sie könne	er/sie kann
er/sie müsse	er/sie muss
er/sie brauche	er/sie braucht
er/sie rufe ... an	er/sie ruft ... an

In the examples in box 1, the subjunctive forms are in the present tense in indirect speech, because the original statements were made in the present tense in direct speech.

Direct speech	Indirect speech or reported speech
2 Look at the comments my doctor made when she visited me this morning:	Now look at the way I pass these comments on to my boss:
Sie sehen nicht gut aus!	Die Ärztin sagte mir, ich **sähe** nicht gut aus.
You don't look well!	*The doctor told me I didn't look well.*
Aha! Sie haben Fieber!	(Sie sagte,) ich **hätte** Fieber.
Well! You've got a temperature.	*(She told me) I had a temperature.*
Sie sollen im Bett bleiben!	(Sie sagte,) ich **solle** im Bett bleiben.
You should stay in bed.	*(She told me) I should stay in bed.*
Sie müssen viel trinken.	(Sie sagte,) ich **müsse** viel trinken.
You must drink a lot.	*(She said) I had to drink a lot.*
Sie dürfen nichts essen.	(Sie sagte,) ich **dürfe** nichts essen.
You're not allowed to eat anything.	*(She said) I'm not allowed to eat anything.*

Sie sind wirklich krank.	(Sie sagte,) ich **sei** wirklich krank.
You are really ill.	*(She said) I was really ill.*
Ich komme morgen wieder vorbei.	(Sie sagte,) sie **komme** morgen wieder vorbei.
I'll call round again tomorrow.	*(She said) she would call round again tomorrow.*

Insight: Punctuation for direct speech

You may well come across direct speech in modern novels, where the action is described in the present tense for dramatic effect. The actual words said are contained within speech marks or inverted commas.

In German, these punctuation marks are officially called **Anführungszeichen** but are also informally known as **Gänsefüßchen** (*little geese feet*)! They differ from English speech marks in that the introductory marks appear on the base line at the start of the quotation, and the final marks are placed on a level with the top of the last letter. The first are in the shape of 99 and the last are in the shape of 66, e.g.
„Ich komme morgen", sagte sie. *'I'll come tomorrow', she said.*

Sometimes you will find these inverted commas written as:
»Ich komme morgen«, sagte sie.

Direct speech	Indirect speech or reported speech
3 Look at the questions a policeman asks two little children who are lost in town:	Now study the way the children later report these questions to their parents:
Wie heißt ihr?	Er fragte uns, wie wir **hießen**.
What are you called?	*He asked us what we were called.*
Wie alt seid ihr?	Er fragte uns, wie alt wir **seien**.
How old are you?	*He asked us how old we were.*
Wo wohnt ihr?	Er fragte uns, wo wir **wohnten**.
Where do you live?	*He asked us where we lived.*

Sind eure Eltern zu Hause?	Er fragte uns, ob unsere Eltern zu Hause **seien**.
Are your parents at home?	*He asked us whether our parents were at home.*
Kommt ihr oft allein in die Stadt?	Er fragte uns, ob wir oft allein in die Stadt **kämen**.
Do you often come to town alone?	*He asked us whether we often came to town alone.*
Habt ihr Geld für den Bus?	Er fragte, ob wir Geld für den Bus **hätten**.
Have you money for the bus?	*He asked us whether we had money for the bus.*

Insight: ob

The subordinating conjunction **ob** (*whether*) often occurs in reported questions. We came across it in Unit 10. Remember that it is preceded by a comma and sends the verb to the end of the clause.

Grammar summary

Insight

The use of the subjunctive in German is very different from other languages, so please forget any rules that you might have already learned for French or Spanish grammar!

THE SUBJUNCTIVE

▶ There are two forms of the subjunctive in German, sometimes described as the present subjunctive and imperfect subjunctive. This can be misleading in that the subjunctive does not directly correspond to the tenses referred to, and so we shall use the terms Subjunctive 1 for the so-called present subjunctive and Subjunctive 2 for the so-called imperfect subjunctive.
▶ The two forms are sometimes interchangeable, and there is a trend in speech to avoid the subjunctive altogether by using the indicative.

▶ Although one can very often avoid using it oneself, the subjunctive is still frequently used in newspapers and television news reports when reporting proceedings in Parliament or details of negotiations, etc. (e.g. in the **Tageschau**, which is broadcast at 8 p.m. every evening). So you should at least be able to recognize how it is formed, even if you restrict your own usage to a few common forms.

THE FORMATION OF SUBJUNCTIVE 1

By the very nature of reported speech, the third person singular and plural forms (*he said that ...*, *she told me that ...*, *they related that ...*) are most frequently used. In fact, you are unlikely to come across some of the other forms – but you may well be interested to see what they are.

Subjunctive 1 is formed by adding the following endings to the stem of the verb:

haben Singular	Plural
ich hab**e**	wir hab**en**
du hab**est**	ihr hab**et**
er hab**e**	Sie hab**en**
sie hab**e**	sie hab**en**
es hab**e**	

Insight

You will notice that the **ich, wir, Sie** and **sie** forms are the same in the subjunctive as in the indicative present tense for **haben**.

In practice, the Subjunctive 2 form is often substituted to make the use of the subjunctive more obvious (see Unit 21):

Er sagte, wir hätten nicht genug Zeit. *He said we didn't have enough time.*

| **können** | |
Singular	Plural
ich könn**e**	wir könn**en**
du könn**est**	ihr könn**et**
er könn**e**	Sie könn**e**
sie könn**e**	sie könn**en**
es könn**e**	

The verb **sein** is an exception in that it forms its present subjunctive as follows, without -e in the singular:

| **sein** | |
Singular	Plural
ich **sei**	wir **seien**
du **seiest**	ihr **seiet**
er **sei**	Sie **seien**
sie **sei**	sie **seien**
es **sei**	

This form will be familiar to you, as it is the same as the imperative mood of sein (see Unit 13).

THE USE OF **DASS** IN REPORTED SPEECH

Insight

You may be interested to learn that the German word for the subjunctive is **der Konjunktiv**. Some people think that this is because many subjunctive clauses begin with a *conjunction*, such as **dass** (*that*), **ob** (*whether*) and **wenn** (*if*).

The conjunction **dass** (*that*) is sometimes used in reported speech in the same way as in English. For example: *She told me she was hoping to change her job* or *She told me **that** she was hoping to change her job*. This tends to be a little more formal, and the subjunctive is normally used in reported speech which involves **dass**. See also Unit 10.

Sie sagte, *dass* sie krank sei.	She said that she was ill.
Er behauptete, *dass* er kein Geld habe.	He maintained that he had no money.
Sie erzählten uns, *dass* sie in Dresden *wohne*.	They told us that she lived in Dresden.

THE USE OF **OB** IN REPORTED QUESTIONS

Ob means whether or if, and is frequently used in reported questions. It follows the same pattern as **dass** (see Unit 10):

| Er fragte mich, *ob* ich kommen *könne*. | He asked me if I could come. |
| Sie wollte wissen, *ob* ich genügend Geld *habe*. | She wanted to know if I had enough money. |

Similarly, **ob** can also be used in indicative sentences, as follows:

| Ich frage mich, *ob* es sich *lohnt*. | I ask myself whether it's worth it. |
| Er will wissen, *ob* der Anorak regendicht *ist*. | He wants to know if the anorak is waterproof. |

In context

Read the following newspaper account of yesterday in Parliament:

Der Finanzminister versicherte, diese Sparmaßnahmen seien unvermeidlich. Er denke nur an die Zukunft und wolle alles Erdenkliche für Kinder machen. Er müsse also neue Geldquellen finden, um seine Pläne zu finanzieren. Er werde daher nächste Woche den Preis von Zigaretten und Alkohol erhöhen, und ab Mitternacht werde Benzin 8 Cent pro Liter mehr kosten. Ab sofort sei jedoch mehr Kindergeld für Eltern erhältlich, und es gebe ein zinsloses Darlehen für Studenten.

der Finanzminister *Minister of Finance*
versichern *to assure, affirm*
die Sparmaßnahme *economy measure*
denken an + *accusative to think of*
die Zukunft *the future*
alles Erdenkliche *everything conceivable, imaginable*
die Geldquelle *source of money*
der Plan *plan*
finanzieren *to finance*
daher *that is why*
nächste Woche *next week*
der Preis *price (also prize)*
erhöhen *to raise, increase*
ab *from*
das Benzin *petrol*
pro Liter *per litre*
ab sofort *with immediate effect*
jedoch *however*
das Kindergeld *child allowance*
die Eltern *parents*
erhältlich *available, obtainable*
ein zinsloses Darlehen *an interest-free loan*
der Student *student*

Taking it further

You can further combine the Subjunctive 1 form of either **haben** or **sein** with a past participle to produce a perfect form such as:

Er sagte, er *habe* **nichts getrunken.**   *He said he had drunk nothing.*
Sie sagte, sie *sei* **allein gekommen.**   *She said she had come alone.*

Practice

EXERCISE A

Study the following examples of reported speech, and then write out what was actually said in the original conversation:

For example:

Mein Chef sagte, er sei müde. *My boss said he was tired.*

Der Chef sagt: „Ich bin müde." *The boss says: I am tired.*

1 Das Mädchen meinte, sie habe Hunger. *The girl said she was hungry.*

Das Mädchen sagt: „Ich __ "

2 Der Politiker meinte, er könne nichts mehr machen. *The politician said he couldn't do any more.*

Der Politiker sagt: „Ich __ "

3 Der Arzt fragte, ob ich Tabletten habe. *The doctor asked whether I had any tablets.*

Der Arzt fragt: „Haben Sie __ "

4 Sein Freund fragte, was im Kino laufe. *His friend asked what was on at the cinema.*

Sein Freund fragt: „Was __ "

5 Der Schaffner fragte den Schüler, ob er seinen Ausweis sehen dürfe. *The bus/tram conductor asked the schoolboy if he might see his identity card.*

Der Schaffner fragt: „Darf __ "

EXERCISE B

Look at the report of a recent study on sleep, and then write out what you think was actually said in the original findings of the report:

Laut einer Studie schliefen die Deutschen jetzt weniger als vor zwanzig Jahren. Heutzutage brauche man eine halbe Stunde weniger Schlaf als damals, aber dafür nähmen mindestens 30% aller Erwachsenen Schlafmittel. Stress am Arbeitsplatz sei der Grund dafür.

laut + *dative according to*
die Studie *study*
weniger als *less than*
vor zwanzig Jahren *twenty years ago*
heutzutage *nowadays*
brauchen *to need*
eine halbe Stunde *half an hour*
der Schlaf *sleep*
damals *then*
dafür *to make up for that, for all that*
nähmen *(Subjunctive 2 of* **nehmen***) to take*
die Erwachsenen *adults*
Schlafmittel nehmen *to take sleeping pills*
mindestens *at least*
am Arbeitsplatz *in the workplace*
der Grund dafür *the reason for it*

QUICK VOCAB

Ten things to remember

1 The indicative mood is the normal form we have learned to express or ask about facts and statements. This is also used for direct speech and direct questions.

2 The subjunctive mood is used to report a statement or question to someone, if we are not absolutely sure of the truth of the original statement, or if we wish in some way to distance ourselves from it.

3 The subjunctive mood is used rarely in English and is becoming less frequent in spoken German.

4 You will come across the subjunctive in written reports in newspapers and magazines, or when, for example, reporting the proceedings in Parliament.

5 The subjunctive mood is used for indirect speech. The same tense of the verb is used as in the direct speech version.

6 Speech marks are different in German, either appearing as „ ... " or as » ... «.

7 The conjunctions **ob** (*whether*), **wenn** (*if*) and less frequently **dass** (*that*) are often used at the start of a subjunctive clause. Each conjunction is preceded by a comma and sends the verb to the end of the clause.

8 There are two forms of the subjunctive, which are sometimes described as the present subjunctive and the imperfect subjunctive. However, these terms are not always helpful, so ...

9 ... we refer to the present subjunctive as Subjunctive 1 and to the imperfect subjunctive as Subjunctive 2.

10 The **ich, wir, Sie** and **sie** forms of the verb **haben** are the same in Subjunctive 1 as in the indicative present tense, so the Subjunctive 2 form is often substituted to make the use of the subjunctive more obvious.

21

Expressing conditions

In this unit you will learn how to
- **Express open conditions**
- **Express remote conditions**
- **Express unfulfilled conditions**

Language points
- **Wenn** *followed by the indicative*
- **Wenn** *followed by Subjunctive 2*
- *More ways of expressing conditions*
- *Other uses of Subjunctive 2 (indirect speech,* **als ob,** **das wär's***)*

To express conditions in German, we normally use the word **wenn** (*if, whenever, when*).

Insight

We have already come across the conjunction **wenn** in several contexts. In Unit 5, we used it in the sense of *whenever, each time when*, e.g.

Wenn ich ankomme, freuen sich alle. *Whenever/each time I arrive, everyone is delighted.*

Wenn is often used in Subjunctive 2, but never in this sense of *whenever*. Here, **wenn** is used in the sense of *if*.

- If we are talking about a real condition (i.e. if it is really likely to happen), for example: *If it stays fine, I shall play tennis this afternoon*, follow **wenn** with the indicative mood. This is called an open condition.
- If you are talking about an unreal or hypothetical condition, for example: *If I were a rich man* or *If I were you*, follow **wenn** with Subjunctive 2. This is called a 'remote' condition. (It is one of the few examples of the subjunctive still heard in English, although some people replace it by the indicative.)
- If we are reflecting on something which could have happened if circumstances had been different, for example: *If I had known in time, I would have gone to meet him (but I didn't know, so I didn't go, and now it is too late)*, this is an 'unfulfilled' condition. It is expressed by Subjunctive 2 in the pluperfect.

Have a look at the following examples:

EXPRESSING REAL CONDITIONS

Ich gebe ihr das Buch, wenn ich sie sehe.
I'll give her the book when/if I see her.

Insight

We see above that the conjunction **wenn** is preceded by a comma and sends the verb to the end of the clause. If **wenn** comes at the start of the sentence, it still sends the verb to the end of the clause. This verb is followed by a comma and then the verb from the next clause is inverted, giving us a 'verb–comma–verb' structure, as in the following examples.

Wenn es morgen regnet, bleibe ich zu Hause.
If it rains tomorrow, I'll stay at home.
Wenn ich Zeit habe, rufe ich ihn an.
If I have time I'll phone him.

EXPRESSING HYPOTHETICAL CONDITIONS

Wenn ich mehr Platz hätte, würde ich euch alle einladen.	*If I had more room, I'd invite you all.*
Wenn er reich wäre, würde er sich ein Haus kaufen.	*If he were rich, he'd buy himself a house.*
Wenn ich das gewusst hätte, hätte ich nichts gesagt.	*If I had known that, I would have said nothing.*

Grammar summary

Insight

You have already come across Subjunctive 2, even though you didn't realize it. We have already learned the set phrases **Ich möchte** (the Subjunctive 2 form of **mögen**) and **Hätten Sie ...?** (the Subjunctive 2 form of **haben**), which are used as polite requests:

Ich möchte den schwarzen Mantel kaufen, bitte.	*I should like to buy the black coat, please.*
Hätten Sie gern etwas zu trinken?	*Would you like something to drink?*

Now let's look at it in more detail.

THE FORMATION OF SUBJUNCTIVE 2

Regular verbs
The Subjunctive 2 form of regular verbs is the same as the imperfect indicative, for example **kaufte** in the sentence:

Wenn ich das kaufte, würde mein Mann lachen.	*If I bought that, my husband would laugh.*

Irregular verbs

To form the Subjunctive 2 of irregular verbs, the following endings are added to the imperfect indicative (found in the verb list, Reference grammar 10.7). In addition to these endings, an umlaut must be added to the vowels **a, o** or **u** in the stem.

sein (to be)	**haben** (to have)
The imperfect indicative stem is **war**.	The imperfect indicative stem is **hatte**.
Singular	Singular
ich **wäre**	ich **hätte**
du **wärest**	du **hättest**
er **wäre**	er **hätte**
sie **wäre**	sie **hätte**
es **ware**	es **hätte**
Plural	Plural
wir **wären**	wir **hätten**
ihr **wäret**	ihr **hättet**
Sie **wären**	Sie **hätten**
sie **wären**	sie **hätten**

gehen (to go)	
The imperfect indicative stem is **ging**.	
Singular	Plural
ich **ginge**	wir **gingen**
du **gingest**	ihr **ginget**
er **ginge**	Sie **gingen**
sie **ginge**	sie **gingen**
es **ginge**	

You can further combine the Subjunctive 2 form of **haben** or **sein** with a past participle to produce a pluperfect form expressing unfulfilled conditions, as follows:

Wenn er das gewusst hätte, wäre er weggelaufen.	*If he had known that, he would have run away.*
Wenn ich das gehört hätte, hätte ich laut gelacht.	*If I had heard that, I would have laughed out loud.*
Wenn sein Chef das gesehen hätte, hätte er ihm gekündigt.	*If his boss had seen that, he would have given him the sack.*
Hätte er uns rechtzeitig geschrieben, wäre dies nie passiert.	*Had he written to us in time, this would have never happened.*

Insight

As we mentioned in Unit 20, there is a trend either to simplify or to avoid the subjunctive in modern spoken German. In situations where a subjunctive is clearly needed, the useful and simple formula **Ich würde** (*I would*) + infinitive is often used:

Ich würde sagen, dass es unbedingt nötig ist. *I would say that it's absolutely necessary.*
Ich würde gerne mitmachen, aber ich habe keine Zeit. *I'd love to join in but I have no time.*

This formula (**ich würde** + infinitive) is not used with **sein, haben** or the modal verbs. The forms **wäre, hätte, könnte,** etc. are preferred:

Ich wäre sehr dankbar, wenn Sie das nicht weitersagen würden.	*I'd be most grateful if you wouldn't pass this on.*

As we have already seen, **wenn** sends the verb to the end of the clause. If **wenn** starts the sentence, it still sends the verb to the end of the clause, but the verb in the next clause is inverted, resulting in a so-called verb–comma–verb structure:

Wenn du *willst,* **fahre ich gerne mit.**	*If you want, I'll gladly come (with you).*

It is also possible to omit **wenn** and still express a conditional sentence in the same way as in the following English examples:

▶ *Had I known that, I would never have consented to it.* Although the word *if* does not appear in this sentence, it clearly has the meaning of: *If I had known that, I would never have consented to it.*

▶ *Were I able to start again, I would do it differently.* Again, the word *if* doesn't appear in this sentence, but the meaning is clearly: *If I could start again, I would do it differently.*

Now look at the following German examples of this.

Hätte ich das gewusst, *so* **hätte ich nie ja gesagt.**	*Had I known that, I would never have said yes.*
Wäre Norbert hier gewesen, *dann* **hätte er uns sicher geholfen.**	*Had Norbert been here, then he would certainly have helped us.*

You will notice from these examples that **so** (*so*) or **dann** (*then*) is added in mid-sentence if **wenn** is omitted. This can also happen in examples using the indicative:

Regnet es weiter, *dann* **spiele ich nicht Tennis.**	*If it continues raining, I'll not play tennis.*
Sollte es schön sein, *dann* **bringe ich meine Mutter mit.**	*Should it be nice (weather), I'll bring my mother.*

In context

Look at the following conversation in which two friends fantasize about winning the lottery.

TRÄUMEREI (DAYDREAMING)

Jürgen	Sag mal, Udo, was würdest du machen, wenn du in der Lotterie gewinnen würdest?
Udo	Ich würde nie wieder zum Dienst gehen. Ich würde mir ein großes Haus an der See kaufen und würde jeden Tag segeln. Das wäre was! Und du?
Jürgen	Wenn ich über Nacht Millionär würde, würde ich alle meine Freunde zu einer Party in der Karibik einladen. Aber sollte der Gewinn nicht so groß sein, dann lade ich dich ein! Egal, wie wäre es, wenn wir jetzt ein Bier trinken würden? Wir könnten eins trinken, ohne in der Lotterie gewonnen zu haben!

in der Lotterie gewinnen *to win the lottery*
zum Dienst gehen *to go to work*
an der See *by the sea*
jeden Tag *every day*
segeln *to go sailing*
über Nacht *overnight*
in der Karibik *in the Caribbean*
ein/laden *to invite*
der Gewinn *the win*
egal *all the same*
ohne die Lotterie gewonnen zu haben *without having won the lottery*

QUICK VOCAB

Taking it further

More ways of expressing conditions

Ich bringe einen Regenschirm mit – im Falle eines Falles.	*I'll bring an umbrella – just in case.*
Hier ist die Adresse des Hotels, falls du dich verläufst.	*Here is the hotel address, **in case** you get lost.*

Er muss fleißig lernen, *sonst* **besteht er die Aufnahmeprüfung nicht.**	*He's got to study hard,* **otherwise** *he won't pass the entrance exam.*
Bei Regen fällt die Theateraufführung im Freien aus.	*In the event of rain the open-air performance will be cancelled.*
Was? Du willst nicht hinfahren? Dann fahre ich auch nicht hin!	*What? You don't want to go (there)? Then I shan't either.*
Ohne seinen Klassenlehrer hätte er das Abitur nicht schaffen können.	*Without (the help of) his form teacher he would not have been able to manage the Abitur (A-levels).*

OTHER USES OF SUBJUNCTIVE 2

▶ Indirect speech

We have so far concentrated on the use of **wenn** in Subjunctive 2. But do you remember that in Unit 20 we learned how Subjunctive 2 is also used sometimes for indirect speech? Whenever the present tense indicative form of the verb is the same as the Subjunctive 1 form, we replace Subjunctive 1 with Subjunctive 2. The reason for this is so that we can be sure to recognize that the verb is in the subjunctive mood, e.g.

Er sagte, wir hätten nicht genug Zeit.	*He said we didn't have enough time.*
Sie sagten, sie hätten das Schlafzimmer schon aufgeräumt.	*They said they had already tidied the room up.*

▶ **als ob** *(as if, as though)*

This unusual conjunction is normally followed by Subjunctive 2. It is preceded by a comma and sends the verb to the end of the clause. Its use is sometimes called 'unreal comparison'.

Sie sah aus, als ob sie die ganze Nacht nicht geschlafen hätte.	*She looked as if she hadn't slept all night.*
Er rannte, als ob es um sein Leben ginge.	*He ran as if his life depended on it.*

Die Studentin redet, als ob sie alles wüsste. — *The student talks as if she knows everything.*

Sometimes you will come across this **als ob** structure using only the **als** without the **ob**. In this usage, the verb is not sent to the end of the clause:

Es sieht aus, als würde es bald schneien. — *It looks as though it will snow soon.*

▶ **Das wär's!** (*That's all! That's it!*)

And finally, there is a common idiomatic expression in Subjunctive 2 which is often used by a customer at the end of an order in a shop or in a restaurant. It is a shortened form of **Das wäre es!** and means *That would be all! That's it!*

▶ **Das wär's!** (*That's all folks!*)

Practice

EXERCISE A

Link up each clause from the left column, beginning with a number, with one from the right column, beginning with a letter, to form sentences which make sense:

1 Wenn ich genug Geld habe, **A** werde ich alles erklären.

2 Wenn ich Millionär wäre, **B** hätte ich ihm keine Schokolade gegeben.

3 Wenn ich von seiner Zuckerkrankheit gewusst hätte, **C** kaufe ich mir ein neues Auto.

4 Wenn wir mehr Platz hätten, **D** können wir in den Bergen wandern.

5 Ich wäre Ihnen sehr dankbar, **E** würde ich nicht mehr arbeiten.

6 Wenn du willst,	**F** würden wir euch alle zu Silvester einladen.
7 Wenn das Wetter morgen schön ist,	**G** wenn Sie das nicht weitersagen würden.
8 Wenn ich sie sehe,	**H** besuche ich dich.
9 Wenn es weiter regnet,	**I** würde ich die Samstagsschule abschaffen.
10 Wenn ich Direktor dieser Schule wäre,	**J** können wir nicht mehr im Garten arbeiten.

EXERCISE B

You have been asked to give advice as to what you would do in someone else's position. Rephrase each recommendation, using the construction **ich würde** plus the appropriate infinitive, e.g.

Du solltest zum Arzt gehen. *You ought to go to the doctor's.*
An deiner Stelle würde ich zum *If I were you I would go to the*
 Arzt gehen.   *doctor's.*

1 Du solltest ein neues Hobby finden. *You ought to find a new hobby.*

2 Du solltest früher ins Bett gehen. *You ought to go to bed earlier.*

3 Du solltest Diät machen. *You ought to go on a diet.*

4 Du solltest nicht so viel Geld ausgeben. *You ought not to spend so much money.*

5 Du solltest nicht rauchen. *You ought not to smoke.*

6 Du solltest fleißiger arbeiten. *You ought to work more diligently.*

7 Du solltest viel mehr lesen. *You ought to read far more.*

8 Du solltest den Rasen öfter mähen. *You ought to mow the lawn more often.*

9 Du solltest eine Ferienreise buchen. *You ought to book a holiday trip.*

10 Du solltest weniger Alkohol trinken. *You ought to drink less alcohol.*

EXERCISE C

Schlussworte ... *(And finally ...)*

Now that you have worked your way through the fundamentals of German grammar, can you discover the secret of happiness from this passage which was written by Johann Wolfgang von Goethe's mother? Use a dictionary to try to work out what it means and look out for examples of Subjunctive 1, the passive, dative plurals and much more. You can find the translation in the answers key.

Altes Kochrezept für Glücklichkeit *(Old Recipe for Happiness)*

Man nehme: 12 Monate, putze sie ganz sauber von Bitterkeit, Geiz, Pedanterie und Angst und zerlege jeden Monat in 30 oder 31 Teile, so dass der Vorrat genau für ein Jahr reicht.

Es wird jeden Tag einzeln angerichtet aus: 1 Teil Arbeit und 2 Teilen Frohsinn und Humor.

Man füge 3 gehäufte Esslöffel Optimismus hinzu, 1 Teelöffel Toleranz, 1 Körnchen Ironie und 1 Prise Takt. Dann wird die Masse sehr reichlich mit Liebe übergossen.

Das fertige Gericht schmücke man mit Sträußchen kleiner Aufmerksamkeiten und serviere es täglich mit Heiterkeit und mit einer guten erquickenden Tasse Tee ...

Katharina Elisabeth Goethe (1731–1808)

Ten things to remember

1 The indicative mood is used for real conditions, e.g. **Ich komme morgen, wenn es nicht regnet.** (*I'll come tomorrow if it doesn't rain.*)

2 Subjunctive 2 is used for unreal or hypothetical conditions, e.g. **Wenn ich reich wäre, ...** (*If I were rich, ...*).

3 Unless it starts a sentence, **wenn** is preceded by a comma and sends the verb to the end of the clause.

4 If the conjunction **wenn** starts the sentence, it sends the verb to the end of the clause. This verb is followed by a comma and the verb in the next clause is inverted, e.g. **Wenn ich vorher mit ihm gesprochen hätte, hätte ich das nicht gemacht.** (*If I had spoken to him beforehand, I wouldn't have done that.*)

5 Subjunctive 2 also has the effect of giving a more polite tone to a request, e.g. **ich möchte lieber Kaffee** (*I'd prefer coffee*).

6 The Subjunctive 2 form of **haben** or **sein** can be combined with a past participle to form the pluperfect tense in the subjunctive mood.

7 There is a trend in German to either simplify or avoid the subjunctive.

8 **Ich würde, er würde,** etc. + an infinitive is a particularly useful phrase, but never use this with **haben, sein** or modal verbs.

9 **Wenn** can be omitted from conditional sentences in the same way as it is omitted in English. In this situation, the word order is different in that the clause starts with a verb and the next clause can be introduced by the word so, e.g. **Hätte ich**

das gewusst, so wäre ich nicht gekommen. (*If I had known that, I would not have come.*)

10 **Als ob** (*as if, as though*) is preceded by a comma and is followed by the imperfect subjunctive (Subjunctive 2) at the end of the clause, e.g. **Sie sah aus, als ob sie schliefe.** (*She looked as if she were asleep.*)

Reference grammar

1 Pronunciation

1.1 THE GERMAN ALPHABET

For those readers who need only to spell their name or give details of their car number plate or postal code, the names of the letters shown in this simple alphabet will be sufficient, without the more detailed explanation which follows.

a	ah	**f**	eff	**k**	kah	**p**	pay	**u**	ooh	**x**	iks
b	bay	**g**	gay	**l**	el	**q**	kuh	**v**	fau	**y**	ypsilon
c	tsay	**h**	ha	**m**	em	**r**	err	**w**	vay	**z**	tsett
d	day	**i**	ih	**n**	en	**s**	ess				
e	ay	**j**	yot	**o**	oh	**t**	tay				

1.2 PRONUNCIATION AND SPELLING

The following information about pronunciation starts with the German spelling system, and shows how the various letters or combinations of letters are pronounced. The pronunciation is given in rough terms of comparison with English sounds and represents the standard pronunciation set out in *Duden 6 Aussprachewörterbuch* (6th edition, Mannheim 2005).

Vowels
▶ German has nine vowel letters: a, ä, e, i, o, ö, u, ü, y.
▶ These vowels can be pronounced both short and long but are always 'pure' vowels, as in Scottish English, as opposed to the 'double' or diphthongal sounds of southern English.
▶ They are usually short if they are followed by a double consonant or combination of consonants.

286

In the following examples the vowels whose pronunciation is being illustrated are in bold type.

Short vowels
R**a**tte *rat*, pronounced as in northern English 'rat'

B**e**tt *bed*, G**ä**ste *guests*, both pronounced as in English 'bet'

b**i**tte *please*, pronounced as in English 'bitter'

M**o**tte *moth*, pronounced as in English 'bottle'

G**ö**tter *gods*, pronounced as in English 'better', but with rounded lips

B**u**tter *butter*, pronounced as in northern English 'butter' (with **u** as in foot)

M**ü**tter *mothers*, pronounced as in English 'bitter', but with rounded lips

m**y**stisch *mystic*, pronounced as in English 'misty', but with rounded lips

▶ The letter **y** is only used in foreign words, usually from Latin and Greek, e.g. **Psychologie** psychology.
▶ The three umlaut vowels, **ä, ö, ü**, occur chiefly in words which are derived in turn from other words containing **a, o, u**, e.g. the plural forms **Gäste** *guests*, **Götter** *gods*, **Mütter** *mothers*, derived from the singular forms **Gast, Gott, Mutter**.
▶ Since the letters **e** and **ä** represent the same short vowel and **ü** and **y** also represent one vowel, the nine vowel letters represent seven short vowel sounds.

Long vowels
These same letters can also represent long vowels when they occur in certain positions in the word or are followed by certain letters.

1 Vowels are pronounced long when they occur before a single consonant, usually in the middle of a word:

baden to *bathe*, pronounced as in English 'rather'

Räder *wheels*, pronounced as in English 'cairn'

eben *even*, pronounced as in English 'neighbour'

Bibel *Bible*, pronounced as in English 'feeble'

oder *or*, pronounced as in English 'odour'

töten to *kill*, pronounced as in English 'patent', but with rounded lips

bluten *to bleed*, pronounced as in English 'moot'

Güte *goodness*, pronounced as in English 'beater', but with rounded lips

2 Vowels are pronounced long when they are followed by the letter **h**, and, in the case of **i**, when it is followed by **e**:

Biene *bee*, pronounced as in English 'keen'

Stuhl *chair*, pronounced as in English 'stool'

Bohne *bean*, pronounced as in English 'loner'

nahmen *took*, pronounced as in English 'calmer'

lehnen *to lean*, pronounced as in English 'gain'

Söhne *sons*, pronounced as in English 'retainer', but with rounded lips

Bühne *stage*, pronounced as in English 'bean', but with rounded lips

Mythos *myth*, pronounced as in English 'metres', but with rounded lips

3 Vowels are pronounced long when they are doubled:

Boote *boats*, pronounced as in English 'boats'

Saal *room*, pronounced as in English 'marl'

leeren *to empty*, pronounced as in English 'bearing'

▶ The vowel letters ä, ö, u, ü never occur in a double combination. For example, the plural of **Saal** (*room*) is **Säle**, and the diminutive of **Boot** (*boat*) is **Bötchenh** (*little boat*).

Diphthongs
Combinations of vowel letters represent what are called diphthongs, 'double' sounds. In German these are represented by **ai, ei, au, eu, äu**. In English, diphthongs are very often spelled with a single letter, e.g. *mine*. The German diphthongs are pronounced as follows:

Main (*river*) Main, pronounced as in English 'mine'

fein *fine*, pronounced as in English 'fine'

Maus *mouse*, pronounced as in English 'mouse'

heute *today*, pronounced as in English 'hoity-toity'

Häuser *houses*, pronounced as in English 'noises'

▶ The diphthong **ai** occurs only in a few words, e.g. **Kaiser** *emperor*, **Waise** *orphan*, **Kai** *quay*, **Saite** *string* (of an instrument).
▶ The combination **äu** occurs only in words which are derived from another word which contains **au**, e.g. **Häuser** from **Haus**, **Fräulein** from **Frau**.

Consonants
To illustrate the pronunciation of consonants in German we will take the individual consonant letters and letter combinations and treat them together, again referring to English pronunciation.

b Bad *bath*, **Abend** *evening*, pronounced as in English 'bath', 'robing'

bb Krabbe *shrimp*, pronounced as in English 'lobby' (for the pronunciation of **b** at the end of words, see **p**)

ch Loch *hole*, pronounced as in Scottish 'loch' after **a**, **o** and **u**, and as in English '**huge**' after e and i, e.g. **nicht** *not*

d Dieb *thief*, **laden** *to load*, pronounced as in English 'dove', 'laden'

dd Kladde *rough book*, pronounced as in English 'muddy' (for the pronunciation of **d** at the end of words, see **t**)

f fast *almost*, **schlafen** to *sleep*, **v** **Vogel** *bird*, pronounced as in English 'fast'

ff schaffen *manage*, pronounced as in English 'stuffy'

ph Philosphie *philosophy*, mostly in foreign words

g gehen *to go*, pronounced as in English 'get'

gg Egge *harrow*, pronounced as in English 'eggy' (for the pronunciation of **g** at the end of words, see **k**)

h Hand *hand*, pronounced as in English 'hand'

j ja yes, **Boje** *buoy*, pronounced as in English 'yam' (*never* as j in 'jam')

k Kind *child*, pronounced as in English 'kind'

ck Brücke *bridge*, **Blick** glance, pronounced as in English 'mucky', 'duck'

NB g at the end of words is also pronounced as **k**: **Tag** day

l lachen *to laugh*, pronounced as in English 'laugh' (*never* as in 'ball')

ll Wille *will*, pronounced as in English 'lid'

m man *one*, pronounced as in English 'man'

mm Lamm *lamb*, pronounced as in English 'ram', 'swimming'

n nein *no*, pronounced as in English 'no'

nn nennen *to call*, pronounced as in English 'thinning'

ng singen *to sing*, **Gesang** *song*, pronounced as in English 'singing', 'sing' (never with the **g** sound as in 'finger')

p Post *post*, pronounced as in English 'paper', 'up'

pp üppig *abundant*, pronounced as in English 'upper'

NB b at the end of words is also pronounced as **p: Staub** dust

pf Pferd *horse*, **Apfel** *apple*, **Kopf** *head*, pronounced as **p** followed by **f**, cf. English 'cupful'

qu Quelle *source*, pronounced as in English 'quick'

r reisen *to travel*, **sparen** *to save*, **rar** rare, pronounced either as in French with a trill or roll at the back of the mouth, or else as in Scottish English with a trill or roll of the tongue tip against the teeth or gums

rr irren to err, pronounced as **r** above

NB rh in foreign words is pronounced as **r: Rhythmus** *rhythm*

s sein *to be*, **lesen** *to read*, pronounced as in English 'zeal', 'busy'

s las *read* (in final position), pronounced as in English 'boss'

ss dass *that*, wissen *to know*, after a short vowel, pronounced as in English 'kiss', 'kissing'

ß aß *ate*, heiß *hot* (after a long vowel or a diphthong), pronounced as in English 'dose', 'bias'

sch schon *already*, waschen *to wash*, pronounced as in English 'shine', 'washing'

NB s before **p** and **t** at the beginning of words is also pronounced **sch: spät** *late*, stehen *to stand*

t tun *to do*, raten *to guess*, Rat *advice*, pronounced as in English 'tone', 'rating', 'rat'

tt Mitte *middle*, pronounced as in English 'written'

NB d at the end of words is also pronounced as **t: Tod** *death*

dt is also pronounced as **t** in the frequently used word **Stadt** *town*

th in foreign words, e.g. **Thema** *topic*, is pronounced as **t** (never as English th in 'thing')

tsch tschechisch *Czech*, deutsch *German*, pronounced as in English 'cheers', 'fetch'

w waschen *to wash*, Möwe *seagull*, pronounced as in English 'vast', 'even' (never as in 'wipe')

x Hexe *witch*, pronounced as in English 'six'

z Zeit *time*, heizen *to heat*, pronounced as in English 'bits'

tz sitzen *to sit*, Platz *square*, *place*, also pronounced as in English 'bits'

2 Nouns

A noun is a word used for naming a person (**der Mensch** *person*), place (**die Stadt** *town*), thing (**der Tisch** *table*) or abstract idea (**die Freiheit** *freedom*). It is normally preceded by a determiner such as **der, ein, kein,** etc. or by a preposition (in **Ordnung** *in order, all right*; in **Zukunft** *in the future*). In German a noun always starts with a capital letter, irrespective of its position in the sentence. A German noun can be masculine (**der**), feminine (**die**) or neuter (**das**).

2.1 GENDER

German nouns have three genders, usually shown by the definite article, **der** (masculine), **die** (feminine) and **das** (neuter). (See Functional grammar Unit 1.) The allocation of gender is sometimes as one would expect, in that males, male roles and professions are mostly masculine, e.g. **der Mann, der Vater, der Sohn, der Onkel, der Neffe, der Kellner,** and females, female roles and professions are mostly feminine: **die Frau, die Mutter, die Tochter, die Tante, die Nichte, die Kellnerin.** More often than not, however, gender is arbitrary. There are a few helpful rules, but remember that there are always exceptions to the rule! Here are some guidelines on gender:

▶ The following groups of nouns are masculine (**der**):

1 Nouns which end in -er and refer to a male: **der Lehrer** *teacher*, **der Pfarrer** *vicar/minister*, **der Schneider** *tailor*, **der Schweizer** *Swiss*

2 The days of the week: **der Sonntag** *Sunday*, **der Montag** *Monday*, **der Dienstag** *Tuesday*, **der Mittwoch** *Wednesday*, **der Donnerstag** *Thursday*, **der Freitag** *Friday*, **der Samstag** or **der Sonnabend** *Saturday*

3 The months of the year: **Januar** *January*, **Februar** *February*, **März** *March*, **April** *April*, **Mai** *May*, **Juni** *June*, **Juli** *July*, **August** *August*, **September** *September*, **Oktober** *October*, **November** *November*, **Dezember** *December*

4 The seasons of the year: der Frühling *spring*, der Sommer *summer*, der Herbst *autumn*, der Winter *winter*

5 Many nouns connected with the weather: der Frost *frost*, der Hagel *hail*, der Nebel *fog*, der Regen *rain*, der Schnee *snow*, der Wind *wind*

6 The points of the compass: der Norden *north*, der Süden *south*, der Osten *east*, der Westen *west*

7 Nouns which end in -ant, -eur, -ich, -ig, -ismus, -ist, -ling, -or: der Fabrikant *manufacturer*, der Ingenieur *engineer*, der Teppich *carpet*, der König *king*, der Atheismus *atheism*, der Jurist *lawyer*, der Lehrling *apprentice*, der Doktor *doctor*

▶ The following groups of nouns are feminine (**die**):

1 Nouns which end in -age, -anz, -ei, -enz, -heit, -ie, -ik, -in, -ion, -ität, -keit, -schaft, -ung, -ur: die Massage *massage*, die Toleranz *tolerance*, die Brauerei *brewery*, die Tendenz *tendency*, die Schönheit *beauty*, die Kolonie *colony*, die Politik *politics*, die Religion *religion*, die Nationalität *nationality*, die Kindheit *childhood*, die Freundschaft *friendship*, die Teilung *division*, die Natur *nature*

2 Many nouns which end in -e: die Brücke *bridge*, die Kirche *church*, die Lampe *lamp*, die Rose *rose*, die Tulpe *tulip*

NB The exceptions to these are weak nouns. See 2.4.

3 Whole numbers under a hundred such as die Eins, die Zwei, die Drei, die Vier (for example, when referring to bus numbers)

4 Many European rivers (with the exception of der Rhein *Rhine*): die Themse *Thames*, die Elbe, die Donau *Danube*, die Mosel *Moselle*, die Seine, die Oder

▶ The following groups of nouns are neuter (**das**):

1 An infinitive used as a noun: **das Essen** *food* (from the verb **essen** *to eat*), **das Schwimmen** (*swimming*), **das Singen** (*singing*)

2 Nouns which end in -chen, -ett, -ium, -lein, -ment: **das Mädchen** *girl*, **das Ballett** *ballet*, **das Studium** *course, studies*, **das Fräulein** *young lady*, **das Klima** *climate*, **das Parlament** *parliament*

2.2 COMPOUND NOUNS *(SEE FUNCTIONAL GRAMMAR UNIT 3)*

Compound nouns are formed by combining two or more nouns.

A compound noun always takes the gender of the last element, e.g.

das Atom *atom* + **die Kraft** *power* + **das Werk** *plant, works, factory* = **das Atomkraftwerk** *atomic* or *nuclear power station*

Sometimes the compound noun is formed by joining a plural and a singular noun, e.g.

die Kranken *sick people* + **der Wagen** *car* = **der Krankenwagen** *ambulance*

die Tage *days* + **das Buch** *book* = **das Tagebuch** *diary*

Sometimes a compound noun is formed by joining two nouns with a connecting -s, e.g.

der Staat + **das Examen** = **das Staatsexamen** *state examination* (often refers to the first university degree)

die Universität + **der Professor** = **der Universitätsprofessor** *university professor*

2.3 NOUN PLURALS *(SEE FUNCTIONAL GRAMMAR UNIT 1)*

There are many different ways in which nouns show that they are plural in German, and it is best to learn the plural of each noun with its gender. In dictionaries the plural is normally given in brackets after the noun, and any changes required for the plural are shown like this:

der Wagen (-) *car*, i.e. the plural is die Wagen

der Vater (¨-) *father*, i.e. the plural is die Väter

die Schwester (-n) *sister*, i.e. the plural is die Schwestern

das Kind (-er i.e. die Kinder) *child*

der Freund (-e i.e. die Freunde) *male friend*

der Wald (¨-er i.e. die Wälder) w*ood, forest*

der Autor (-en i.e. die Autoren) *author*

das Hotel (-s i.e. die Hotels) *hotel*

Some nouns change more radically in the plural:

Singular	Plural
die Firma *the firm*	die Firmen
das Bankkonto *bank account*	die Bankkonten
das Museum *museum*	die Museen
der Fachmann *expert*	die Fachleute

Some nouns are mainly used in the plural in German:

die Eltern *parents*
die Ferien *the holiday(s)*
die Lebensmittel *food, provisions*
die Leute *people*

2.4 WEAK NOUNS

This group of masculine nouns is unusual in that an -n or -en is added to the noun in every case apart from the nominative singular, e.g.

der Junge (-n, -n): Ich kenne den Jungen. *I know the boy.*

der Dirigent (-en, -en): Er sprach mit dem Dirigenten. *He spoke to* (literally 'with') *the conductor.*

In many dictionaries and coursebooks, a weak noun is signalled by showing the weak noun endings in brackets, before the plural: **der Herr** (-n, -en) *gentleman*, **der Präsident** (-en, -en) *president*.

Some masculine nouns which end in -e add an **n** to the noun in every case but the nominative singular: **der Brite** *Briton*, **der Franzose** *Frenchman*, **der Kunde** *customer*, **der Geologe** *geologist*.

Some other masculine nouns which end in a consonant add -en to the noun in every case but the nominative singular: **der Assistent** *assistant*, **der Kandidat** *candidate*, **der Philosoph** *philosopher*, **der Soldat** *soldier*, **der Christ** *the Christian*, **der Mensch** *person* (male or female), **der Kommunist** *communist*.

In dictionaries these weak noun endings are shown in brackets just before the plural: **der Kollege** (-n, -n) *colleague*, **der Student** (-en, -en).

---

3 Declension of determiners

Nouns are normally preceded by a determiner, i.e. the *definite* article, **der** *the*, the indefinite article **ein** *a/an*, or other words such as **dieser** *this*, **jeder** *each*.

The determiner declines or changes its form according to the function of the noun in the sentence.

There is no gender distinction in the plural, i.e. the nominative forms of **der, die, das** all change to **die** for the plural. The indefinite article **eine, eine, ein** disappears in the plural form, or is replaced by a higher numeral, e.g.

ein Bus *one bus*, **Busse** *buses*, **zwei Busse** *two buses*

3.1 CHANGES IN THE DEFINITE ARTICLE

This chart shows the changes in the definite article. The same pattern of changes applies to the demonstrative **dieser** *this/these*, and other determiners such as **jener** *that/those*, **jeder** *each/every*, **welcher** *which*, **mancher** *many a* and **solcher** *such a*. The plural also forms a pattern for **alle** *all*.

Masculine	Singular	Plural
Nominative:	**der** Vater	**die** Väter
Accusative:	**den** Vater	**die** Väter
Dative:	**dem** Vater	**den** Vätern*
Genitive:	**des** Vaters†	**der** Väter

Feminine	Singular	Plural
Nominative:	**die** Mutter	**die** Mütter
Accusative:	**die** Mutter	**die** Mütter
Dative:	**der** Mutter	**den** Müttern*
Genitive:	**der** Mutter	**der** Mütter

Neuter	Singular	Plural
Nominative:	**das** Kind	**die** Kinder
Accusative:	**das** Kind	**die** Kinder
Dative:	**dem** Kind	**den** Kindern*
Genitive:	**des** Kindes†	**der** Kinder

Nouns in the dative plural end in -n unless the plural is -s, for example, **das Büro (-s)** *office*, **in den Büros.**

† **-s** or **-es** is added to the end of masculine and neuter singular nouns in the genitive case

3.2 CHANGES IN THE INDEFINITE ARTICLE

This chart shows the changes in the indefinite article **ein,** which also provide the pattern for **kein** *not a* and the possessive adjectives **mein** *my,* **dein** *your,* **sein** *his.* **NB** As there is no plural for **ein,** the plural form is given using **mein** *my:*

	Masculine singular	Feminine singular	Neuter singular	Plural
Nom.	ein Mann	eine Frau	ein Kind	meine Kinder
Acc.	einen Mann	eine Frau	ein Kind	meine Kinder
Dat.	einem Mann	einer Frau	einem Kind	meinen Kindern
Gen.	eines Mannes	einer Frau	eines Kindes	meiner Kinder

4 Declension of personal pronouns

You are familiar with the nominative form of the personal pronoun from the conjugation of verbs, but these pronouns also change or inflect when used in different cases:

	Singular					Plural			
	1st	2nd	3rd			1st	2nd	2nd	3rd
Nom.	ich	du	er	sie	es	wir	ihr	Sie	sie
Acc.	mich	dich	ihn	sie	fs	uns	euch	Sie	sie
Dat.	mir	dir	ihm	ihr	ihm	uns	euch	Ihnen	ihnen
Gen.	meiner	deiner	seiner	ihrer	seiner	unser	euer	Ihrer	ihrer

NB The genitive form is rarely used. The **Sie** forms are polite singular as well as plural.

5 Adjectives

An adjective is a word which gives more information about a noun or pronoun. When an adjective is used after the noun, e.g. **das Fahrrad ist neu** *The bicycle is new*, no ending is needed, but when the adjective comes *before* the noun, e.g. **das neue Rad** *the new bicycle*, the adjective itself must decline to agree with the gender, number and case of the noun.

5.1 ADJECTIVAL ENDINGS *(SEE FUNCTIONAL GRAMMAR UNIT 15)*

Adjectival endings can be divided into three groups:

Group 1 is used after **der** and all its forms, also after **dieser, jener, jeder, welcher**:

Der **französische Koch wohnt uns gegenüber.**	*The French chef lives opposite us.*
Ich kenne *die* **beiden Ärzte gut.**	*I know both the doctors well.*
Laut *dem* **neuen Gesetz muss man das machen.**	*According to the new law one has to do that.*
Der Sohn *des* **alten Pfarrers ist der Minister für Gesundheit.**	*The son of the old vicar is the minister of health.*

	Singular			Plural
	M.	**F.**	**N.**	
Nom.	-e	-e	-e	-en
Acc.	-en	-e	-e	-en
Dat.	-en	-en	-en	-en
Gen.	-en	-en	-en	-en

Group 2 is used in the singular after **ein** and all its forms, and in both the singular and the plural after **kein** and possessive adjectives **mein, dein, sein,** etc.

	Sein neuer Chef ist sehr streng.	His new boss is very strict.
	Er hat einen sehr großen Hund.	He has a very big dog.
	Ich bleibe bei meiner altenTante.	I am staying with my old aunt.
	Er freut sich auf den Besuch eines	He is looking forward to the visit
	reichen Onkels.	of a rich uncle.

	Singular			Plural
	M.	F.	N.	
Nom.	-er	-e	-es	-en
Acc.	-en	-e	-es	-en
Dat.	-en	-en	-en	-en
Gen.	-en	-en	-en	-en

Group 3 is used when the adjective stands alone in front of the noun:

Schwarzer Kaffee tut gut!	Black coffee does you good!
Er kauft seiner Frau nur rote Rosen.	He buys only red roses for his wife.
Ich schreibe immer mit schwarzer Tinte.	I always write with black ink.
Er ist immer guter Laune.	He is always in a good mood.

The plural endings in this group are also used after numbers, e.g. **drei grüne Bleistifte** *three green pencils* and after **einige** *some*, **ein paar** *a few*, **viele** *many*, **mehrere** *several, various*, **wenige** *few*:

	Singular			Plural
	M.	F.	N.	
Nom.	-er	-e	-es	-e
Acc.	-en	-e	-es	-e
Dat.	-em	-er	-em	-en
Gen.	-en	-er	-en	-er

Be careful! Never be tempted to use these endings with **kein, mein, dein, sein**, etc.

Adjectives formed from town names

If you wish to use the name of a town as an adjective you do not need to use the charts above. Simply add -er to the town name, irrespective of the gender, case and number of the noun it is describing, e.g.

Die Frankfurter Buchmesse ist weltberühmt.	*The Frankfurt Book Fair is world famous.*
Wir wollen den Kölner Dom besuchen.	*We want to visit Cologne cathedral.*
Ich habe den Artikel in dem Hamburger Abendblatt gelesen.	*I read the article in the Hamburg evening paper.*
Während der Kieler Woche sind die Hotels voll.	*The hotels are full during Kiel Week.*

5.2 ADJECTIVAL NOUNS

In German, adjectives are frequently turned into nouns. To do this, the adjective is given a capital letter and it retains the gender and adjectival ending which is appropriate for the noun which it is replacing: **der Arme** *the poor man*, **die Arme** *the poor woman*, **die Armen** *the poor (people)*.

The following examples (meaning *the* or *a German* (man), *the* or *a German* (woman) and *the Germans* or *Germans*) form a pattern for adjectival nouns:

	Masculine	Feminine	Plural
Nom.	der Deutsche	die Deutsche	die Deutschen
Acc.	den Deutschen	die Deutsche	die Deutschen
Dat.	dem Deutschen	der Deutschen	den Deutschen
Gen.	des Deutschen	der Deutschen	der Deutschen

	Masculine	Feminine	Plural
Nom.	ein Deutscher	eine Deutsche	Deutsche
Acc.	einen Deutschen	eine Deutsche	Deutsche
Dat.	einem Deutschen	einer Deutschen	Deutschen
Gen.	eines Deutschen	einer Deutschen	Deutscher

5.3 THE COMPARATIVE AND SUPERLATIVE FORMS OF ADJECTIVES

Adjectives can be used in various degrees of intensity:

▶ the normal (sometimes called positive) form, e.g. **der Mann ist alt** *the man is old* or **der alte Mann** *the old man.*
▶ the comparative form, e.g. **der Mann ist älter** *the man is older* or **der ältere Mann** *the older man.*
▶ the superlative form, e.g. **der Mann ist der älteste** *the man is the oldest* or **der älteste Mann** *the oldest man.*

NB Where no noun is used, the form **am ältesten**, e.g. **Er ist am ältesten**, *He's the oldest*, is often used. This is in fact the superlative form of adverbs.

The formation of the comparative
In German the comparative is formed by adding **-er** to the normal adjective. Sometimes an umlaut is also added to an **a**, **o** or **u**. If the comparative adjective is used after the verb, e.g. **der Mann ist älter**, no further adjectival ending is required. If, however, the comparative degree of the adjective is used in front of the noun, normal adjectival endings must be added, e.g. **der ältere Mann**, *ein* **älterer Mann**.

The following adjectives take an umlaut in the comparative and superlative forms:

alt – älter	*old – older*
arm – ärmer	*poor – poorer*
dumm – dümmer	*stupid – more stupid*
grob – gröber	*coarse – coarser*
groß – größer	*big – bigger*
hart – härter	*hard – harder*
kalt – kälter	*cold – colder*
klug – klüger	*clever – cleverer*
krank – kränker	*ill – more ill*
kurz – kürzer	*short – shorter*

lang – länger	*long – longer*
oft – öfter	*often – more often*
scharf – schärfer	*sharp – sharper*
schwach – schwächer	*weak – weaker*
schwarz – schwärzer	*black – blacker*
stark – stärker	*strong – stronger*
warm – wärmer	*warm – warmer*

The formation of the superlative

The superlative is normally formed by adding **-st** to the adjective, and sometimes an umlaut (see list for comparative). Very occasionally, **-est** is added for ease of pronunciation, e.g. **der berühmteste Dirigent** *the most famous conductor*. If a superlative adjective is used in front of the noun, the appropriate adjectival ending must be added.

Frequently used exceptions:

gut – besser	*good-better*	der, die, das beste	*the best*
hoch – höher	*high-higher*	der, die, das höchste	*the highest*
nah(e) – näher	*near-nearer*	der, die, das nächste	*the next, nearest*

---

6 The use of the cases (see Functional grammar Unit 3)

There are four cases in German: nominative, accusative, dative and genitive.

6.1 THE NOMINATIVE CASE

The nominative case is used:

▶ for the subject of the sentence and
▶ after the verb **sein** *to be*.

It is the form of nouns found in dictionaries.

6.2 THE ACCUSATIVE CASE

The accusative case is used:

▶ to indicate the direct object of the sentence
▶ after the following prepositions:

bis	*until*	Wir bleiben bis nächsten Dienstag.	*We'll stay until next Tuesday.*
durch	*through*	Das Kind läuft durch den Eingang.	*The child runs through the entrance.*
für	*for*	Das Geschenk ist für seinen Vater.	*The present is for his father.*
gegen	*against*	Der Schüler stellt sein Fahrrad gegen den Zaun.	*The pupil puts his bicycle against the fence.*
ohne	*without*	Sie ist ohne einen Regenschirm ausgegangen.	*She went out without an umbrella.*
um	*around, round*	Der Taxifahrer fuhr schnell um die Ecke.	*The taxi driver drove quickly around the corner.*
wider	*against*	Wir heirateten wider seinen Willen.	*We got married against his will.*

Entlang can be used with either the accusative (most commonly) or the dative. In the accusative, **entlang** often comes after the noun, e.g.

Er kommt die Straße entlang.   *He comes along the street.*

▶ after the following prepositions if they are used in a context which shows motion or movement from one place to another:

in *to, into*	Wir gehen ins Kino.	*We're going to the cinema.*
an *on, onto*	Er klebt das Plakat an die Wand.	*He sticks the poster onto the wall.*
auf *on, onto*	Der Kellner stellt den Teller auf den Tisch.	*The waiter puts the plate on the table.*
über *above*	Sie hängt die Lampe über das Sofa.	*She hangs the lamp above the sofa.*

unter *under*	Sie schiebt ihren Koffer unter das Bett.	*She pushes her case under the bed.*
neben *next to*	Setzen Sie sich bitte neben den Bürgermeister!	*Please sit down next to the mayor!*
vor *in front of*	Der Polizist trat vor die Tür.	*The policeman stepped in front of the door.*
hinter *behind*	Der Junge geht hinter die Garage.	*The boy goes behind the garage.*
zwischen *between*	Der Hund läuft zwischen die Häuser und verschwindet.	*The dog runs between the houses and disappears.*

▶ for expressions of time which contain no preposition, e.g.

Er kommt nächsten Sonntag.　　*He's coming next Sunday.*
Jeden Winter fahren wir Ski.　　*We go skiing every winter.*
den vierten Juli　　*the fourth of July*

6.3 THE DATIVE CASE

The dative case is used:

▶ to indicate the indirect object of the sentence
▶ after the following prepositions:

aus *out of*	Der Dieb läuft aus dem Haus.	*The thief runs out of the house.*
bei *at, with*	Er wohnt bei seiner Freundin.	*He lives at his girlfriend's.*
laut *according to*	Laut dem Gesetz darf man den Jungen nicht nennen.	*According to the law the boy may not be named.*
mit *with*	Ich schreibe immer mit einem Kugelschreiber.	*I always write with a biro.*
nach *after*	Nach dem Film gehen wir zusammen in die Eisdiele.	*After the film we go to the ice-cream parlour together.*

seit *since*	Meine Tante wohnt seit dem Krieg in Hamburg.	*My aunt has lived in Hamburg since the war.*
von *from*	Der Brief ist von ihrem Exmann.	*The letter is from her ex-husband.*
zu *to*	Ich muss schnell zur Post gehen.	*I must quickly go to the post office.*

(sometimes used in conjunction with **bis**, e.g. **bis zum nächsten Mal** *until the next time*)

gegenüber *opposite*	Der Minister wohnt gegenüber dem Museum.	*The minister lives opposite the museum.*

(**Gegenüber** sometimes appears after the noun, e.g. **dem Museum gegenüber** *opposite the museum*.)

▶ after the following prepositions if they show position (as opposed to movement from one place to another):

in *in*	Er wohnt in einem Wohnwagen.	*He lives in a caravan.*
an *on, at*	Wir haben ein Ferienhaus an der Küste.	*We have a holiday home on the coast.*
auf *on*	Das Essen ist schon auf dem Tisch.	*The food is already on the table.*
über *above*	Der Bäcker wohnt über der Bäckerei.	*The baker lives above the bakery.*
unter *under*	Als Experiment baut man Häuser unter der Erde.	*As an experiment they are building houses underground.*
hinter *behind*	Direkt hinter ihrem Haus gibt es einen Wald.	*Directly behind their house is a wood.*
vor *in front of*	Das Taxi wartet vor dem Restaurant.	*The taxi is waiting in front of the restaurant.*

zwischen *between*   Zwischen den Bäumen *The mill is between the*
                         steht die Mühle.   *trees.*
neben *next to*   Der Pfarrer wohnt   *The vicar/minister lives*
                         neben der Kirche.   *next to the church.*

▶ after several verbs, e.g. **danken** *to thank*, **folgen** *to follow*,
   gehören *to belong to*, **gratulieren** *to congratulate*, **helfen** *to*
   help, **imponieren** *to impress*, **schaden** *to damage*.

6.4 THE GENITIVE CASE

The genitive case is used:

▶ to show possession or ownership, the equivalent of the English
   Peter's friends.
▶ It is also used after the following prepositions:

außerhalb *outside*   Seine Freunde wohnen *His friends live outside*
                          außerhalb der Stadt. *the town.*
infolge *because of* Infolge des Streiks   *Because of the strike*
                          bleibt die Fabrik   *the factory will remain*
                          heute geschlossen.   *closed today.*
(an)statt *instead of* Statt eines Briefes *Instead of a letter he*
                          schickte er mir eine *sent me a postcard.*
                          Postkarte.
trotz *in spite of*   Trotz des Regens   *In spite of the rain we*
                          spielen wir heute   *will play tennis today.*
                          Tennis.
während *during*   Während des Krieges   *During the war they*
                          wohnten sie auf dem   *lived in the country.*
                          Lande.
wegen *because of*   Wir fahren erst am   *Because of the traffic*
                          Sonntag wegen des   *we will not travel until*
                          Verkehrs.   *Sunday.*

NB In colloquial speech and some regional usage **trotz**, **wegen** and
während are sometimes followed by the dative case.

7 Adverbs

An adverb is a word or a group of words which tells us more about a verb. Adverbs do not normally inflect or change their form in any way. Very many well-known words which we learn as simple items of vocabulary, such as **auch** *also*, **heute** *today*, **hier** *here*, **gern** *with pleasure*, **bald** *soon*, *fast almost*, **jetzt** *now*, **sofort** *immediately*, **oft** *often*, **schon** *already*, **vielleicht** *perhaps* are in fact adverbs.

Some adverbs which are derived from other word classes end in -weise, e.g. **glücklicherweise** *fortunately*, **beispielsweise** *by way of example*, **teilweise** *partly*. **Stundenlang** *for hours*, **tagelang** *for days* are formed in a similar way, using **-lang** instead of -weise.

Sometimes the adverb is the same as the adjective, e.g.

Sie ist schön (adjective).	*She is beautiful.*
Sie singt schön (adverb).	*She sings beautifully.*
Seine Sicht ist nicht gut.	*His sight is not good.*
Er sieht nicht gut.	*He does not see well.*

7.1 THE FORMATION OF THE COMPARATIVE FORMS OF ADJECTIVE-ADVERBS

Those adverbs which have the same form as adjectives are sometimes called *adjective-adverbs*, e.g. **schnell, heiß, klein.**

These form their comparative in the same way as the adjective – minus, of course, any additional adjectival ending, e.g.

Gabi läuft schneller als Silke.	*Gabi runs more quickly than Silke.*
Hans singt schöner als Fritz.	*Hans sings more beautifully than Fritz.*

Notice also:

Du singst genauso gut wie ich.	*You sing just as well as I do.*
Margarine schmeckt nicht so gut wie Butter.	*Margarine doesn't taste as good as butter.*

7.2 THE FORMATION OF THE SUPERLATIVE FORMS OF ADVERBS

German uses the form **am ...-sten** to represent the superlative of adverbs, with the addition of an umlaut where necessary (as listed under the comparison of adjectives), e.g.

Er singt am schönsten.	*He sings the most beautifully.*
Wir fahren am schnellsten mit der Bahn.	*We will travel the fastest on the train.*
Am besten gehst du gleich ins Bett.	*It's best that you go to bed immediately.*

Frequently used exceptions:

gern – lieber – am liebsten	*with pleasure, rather, best of all*
gut – besser – am besten	*good, better, best*
hoch – höher – am höchsten	*high, higher, highest*
nah(e) – näher – am nächsten	*near, nearer, nearest/next*
viel – mehr – am meisten	*much, more, most*

---

8 Numbers and dates

8.1 CARDINAL NUMBERS

null (*nought, zero*)	elf (11)
ein(s) (1)	zwölf (12)
zwei (2)	dreizehn (13)
drei (3)	vierzehn (14)
vier (4)	fünfzehn (15)
fünf (5)	sechzehn (16)
sechs (6)	siebzehn (17)
sieben (7)	achtzehn (18)
acht (8)	neunzehn (19)
neun (9)	zwanzig (20)
zehn (10)	einundzwanzig (21)

zweiundzwanzig (22)
dreiundzwanzig (23)
vierundzwanzig (24)
fünfundzwanzig (25)
sechsundzwanzig (26)
siebenundzwanzig (27)
achtundzwanzig (28)
neunundzwanzig (29)
dreißig (30)
tausend *or* eintausend (1 000)
zehntausend (10 000)
eine Million (*a million*)

einunddreißig (31), etc.
vierzig (40)
fünfzig (50)
sechzig (60)
siebzig (70)
achtzig (80)
neunzig (90)
hundert or einhundert (100)
hunderteins or hundertundeins (101)
tausendeins (1 001)
eine Milliarde (*thousand million*)
eine Billion (*billion*)

- ▶ NB the unexpected spelling of **sechzehn** (no -s-), **siebzehn** (no -en-), **dreißig** (no -z-), **sechzig** (no -s-), **siebzig** (no -en-).
- ▶ Numbers under a million are normally written with a small letter. **Hundert** and **tausend**, however, can also be used as nouns, in which case they are written as **ein Hundert, ein Tausend**.
- ▶ **Eine Million, eine Milliarde** *thousand million* and **eine Billion** are only used as nouns.
- ▶ Apart from **eins** (which changes its form when used as an indefinite article before a noun or as a pronoun, e.g. eine **Katze** *a cat*) cardinal numbers are never declined.
- ▶ If cardinals under a hundred are used as a noun (e.g. referring to a mark at school) they are feminine: **die Vier, die Sechs**.
- ▶ Telephone numbers are usually given in groups of two. For example, 96 48 37 is **sechsundneunzig achtundvierzig siebenunddreißig**.
- ▶ Commas are never used between thousands and hundreds. A space is simply left between them: **10 475**.
- ▶ A comma is used instead of a decimal point in German: 0,8 – **null Komma acht**.
- ▶ The year is written simply as either 2009 (**zweitausendneun**) or **im Jahre 2009**.
- ▶ Clock times use predominantly cardinals, e.g. es ist zwei Uhr (2.00), **es ist fünf (Minuten) nach eins** (1.05), **es ist zwanzig vor zwölf** (11.40), **es ist dreiundzwanzig Uhr** (11 *p.m.*).

8.2 ORDINAL NUMBERS

These are, in effect, adjectives which are used specifically to show the order, position or arithmetical ranking of something or someone, e.g. **mein erster Schultag** *my first day at school*, **Elisabeth die Zweite** *Elizabeth the Second*, **die Dritte Welt** *the Third World*.

▶ To form ordinals for the numbers from four up to and including nineteen, add -t to the cardinal number: **viert-, fünft, sechst-** and then the appropriate adjectival ending.

NB either **siebt-** or **siebent-** is possible for seventh, and **acht** requires only the adjectival ending, with no additional -t, e.g. **seine vierte Frau** *his fourth wife*, **der fünfte Versuch** *the fifth attempt*.

▶ To form ordinals for numbers for twenty upwards, add -st to the cardinal number, and then the appropriate adjectival ending, e.g. **sein fünfzigster Geburtstag** *his fiftieth birthday*.

8.3 DATES

Obviously, one of the most frequent uses of ordinals is to express dates, e.g.

Silvester ist am einunddreißigsten Dezember.	*New Year's Eve is on December 31st.*
Mein Mann hat am dreizehnten Juni Geburtstag.	*My husband's birthday is on June 13th.*
Die Schulferien sind vom sechsten Juli bis zum ersten September.	*The school holidays are from July 6th to September 1st.*

Usually numbers are used instead of words, and are always followed by a full stop: **am 13. Juni** *on 13 June*, **vom 6. Juli bis zum 1. September** *from 6 July to 1 September*.

To ask the date you can ask: **Der wievielte ist heute?** (literally 'The how manyeth is it today?'). The reply will be in the nominative: **der erste Mai** (*1 May*), **der elfte März** (*11 March*).

You could also ask: **Den wievielten haben wir heute?** The reply will then be in the accusative because it is the direct object: **den ersten Mai** or **den 1. Mai; den elften März** or **den 11. März.** (This latter form is found at the top of letters. The trend is to omit the definite article, e.g. **1. Mai** or **11. März.**)

---

9 Verbs

A verb is a word or group of words which tells you what a person or thing is doing or being, e.g. **Ich sammle Briefmarken** *I collect stamps*, **Sie erwartete zu viel** *She expected too much*, **Es regnet viel im April** *It rains a lot in April*. A verb can be used in various tenses, e.g. *I read, I was reading, I have read, I had read, I shall read, I shall have read*. The present tense is used to talk about an activity, action, state of affairs or event which is happening just now. For further details, see Functional grammar Unit 5).

In dictionaries and coursebooks, verbs are listed in their infinitive form which comprises the stem + the ending -*en*, e.g. **kauf + en**. Endings are added to the stem according to person, number, and the tense of the verb.

There are three simple tenses in German:

1 present: **ich schreibe** *I write*
2 future: **ich werde schreiben** *I shall write*
3 past: **ich schrieb** *I wrote*

There are also three compound tenses formed with either the verb **haben** or **sein** plus a past participle:

4 perfect: **ich habe geschrieben** *I have written*
5 pluperfect: **ich hatte geschrieben** *I had written*
6 future perfect: **ich werde geschrieben haben** *I shall have written*

The last three are called compound tenses because they involve using two verbal forms, and so they do have a separate entry in the verb list.

9.1 THE PRESENT TENSE

The present tense of regular verbs
The verb **kaufen** *to buy* is a regular verb. It consists of the stem **kauf-** plus various endings, shown in bold in the following box. This provides the pattern for other verbs in the present tense.

If the stem of a regular verb ends in **d** or **t** (e.g. **reden** *to speak*, **arbeiten** *to work*), or a combination of **m** or **n** preceded by another consonant (e.g. **atmen** *to breathe*, **regnen** *to rain*), endings including an **e** are added to form the present tense of the **du, er, sie, es** and **ihr** forms, for ease of pronunciation. For example: **ihr antwortet nicht.** *You are not answering*; **er redet** *he is speaking*; **sie atmet** *she is breathing*; **du zeichnest** *you are drawing*) **es regnet** *it's raining.*

Singular	
ich kauf**e**	*I buy, I am buying, I do buy*
du kauf**st**	*you buy, etc.*
er kauf**t**	*he buys, etc.*
sie kauf**t**	*she buys, etc.*
es kauf**t**	*it buys, etc.*

Plural	
wir kauf**en**	*we buy, etc.*
ihr kauf**t**	*you buy, etc.*
Sie kauf**en**	*you buy, etc.* (polite singular and plural)
sie kauf**en**	*they buy, etc.*

The present tense of irregular verbs
Although we noticed some slight variations in the endings of the regular verbs above to ease pronunciation, the stem was always based on the infinitive form.

Some verbs, however, change their stem vowel in the second (**du**) and third (**er, sie, es**) person singular so that these forms differ from the stem and thus also from the infinitive, e.g.

geben *(to give)*:

Singular		Plural	
ich gebe	*I give*	wir geben	*we give*
du g**ib**st	*you give*	ihr gebt	*you give*
er, sie, es g**ib**t	*he, she, it gives*	Sie geben	*you (polite) give*
sie geben	*they give*		

essen – *to eat* – er **isst**
fahren – *to travel* – er **fährt**
laufen – *to run, to go* – er **läuft**
lesen – *to read* – er **liest**
schlafen – *to sleep* – er **schläft**
treffen – *to meet* – er **trifft**

We cannot predict these changes and have to refer to the verb list (Reference grammar 10.7) to be sure of the correct form.

Furthermore, some verbs do not change their stem in the present tense, but in the past: **gehen** – **geht** – **ging** – **gegangen**. Even a cursory glance at a verb list will reveal further variations, which can be described and subdivided more fully. But for the purposes of this grammar, only the distinction between regular and irregular verbs is made.

9.2 MODAL VERBS *(SEE FUNCTIONAL GRAMMAR UNITS 7, 8 AND 9)*

There are six irregular verbs:

dürfen *to be allowed to, may*
können *to be able to, can*
mögen *to like*

müssen *to have to, must*
sollen *to be supposed to, ought*
wollen *to want to*

These belong to a group of verbs known as modal verbs. They reflect the mood of the speaker in that they express a wish, sense of obligation, volition, liking, ability or possibility.

These six verbs share several common features:

- ▶ they are often followed by an infinitive at the end of the clause
- ▶ with the exception of **sollen**, the singular form has a different vowel from the plural
- ▶ the first and third person singular have no endings
- ▶ the first and third person plural and second person polite form is always the same as the infinitive.

dürfen	*können*	*mögen*
ich darf	ich kann	ich mag
du darfst	du kannst	du magst
er/sie/es darf	er/sie/es kann	er/sie/es mag
wir dürfen, etc.	wir können, etc.	wir mögen, etc.

müssen	*wollen*	*sollen*
ich muss	ich will	ich soll
du musst	du willst	du sollst
er/sie/es muss	er/sie/es will	er/sie/es soll
wir müssen, etc.	wir wollen, etc.	wir sollen, etc.

9.3 SEPARABLE AND INSEPARABLE VERBS

The infinitive of some verbs begins with a prefix such as **an-**, **ab-**, **be-**, **über-**, **zu-**, etc. If the prefix moves to the end of the clause when used as a finite verb, the verb is known as a separable verb, e.g. **an/kommen**:

Der Zug *kommt* **um neun Uhr** *an*.   *The train arrives at 9 a.m.*

If the prefix always remains in front of the verb when used as a finite verb, it is known as an inseparable verb, e.g. **bekommen:**

Wir *bekommen* **kein Kindergeld** *We do not receive the child*
mehr. *allowance any more.*

Separable verbs
▶ A prefix can be added to the infinitive of many frequently used verbs such as **fahren** *to travel, to go*, **kommen** *to come*, **machen** *to make, to do*.
▶ The addition of such a prefix has the effect of changing the meaning of the verb, e.g. *ab/*fahren *to depart*, *an/*kommen *to arrive*, *auf/*machen *to open*.
▶ The prefix is always at the front of the verb in the infinitive form.
▶ When the verb is used (in the normal second position in the main clause), the prefix separates from the verb and is placed at the end of the clause, e.g.

Der Zug *fährt* **um zwei Uhr** *The train will depart from platform*
von Gleis 5 *ab.* *5 at two o'clock.*

▶ In a subordinate clause (when a subordinating conjunction has sent the verb to the end of the clause) the prefix is reattached to the front of the verb and is written as one word:

Ich warte, bis der Zug *abfährt.* *I'll wait until the train departs.*

▶ The past participle of separable verbs is written as one word, with the prefix coming before the past participle of the basic verb, e.g. **abgeholt** *collected*, **angerufen** *telephoned*.
▶ Verbs starting with the following prefixes are separable: **ab-, an-, auf-, aus-, bei-, ein-, fest-, fort-, her-, hin-, los-, mit-, vor-, weg-, zu-, zurück-, zusammen-.**
▶ The emphasis or stress in the infinitive of a separable verb is always on the prefix, e.g. *ab/*biegen, *an/*ziehen.

▶ In this book, as in many others, the separable verb is signalled by a diagonal slash between the prefix and the verb, e.g. **zu/machen** *to shut*. In dictionaries the verb is sometimes identified as separable by *sep* written after the verb.

NB Not all verbs which start with a prefix are separable! (See next section.)

Inseparable verbs
▶ The following prefixes remain always at the beginning of inseparable verbs: **be-, emp-, ent-, er-, ge-, miss-, ver-, zer-.** For example:

Er bekommt erst nächste Woche sein Zeugnis.	*He will not receive his school report until next week.*
Mein Arzt verschreibt mir Penizillin.	*The doctor is prescribing penicillin for me.*

▶ The past participle of inseparable verbs never starts with **ge-**:

Er hat sein Zeugnis letzte Woche bekommen.	*He received his school report last week.*
Der Arzt hat mir Penizillin verschrieben.	*The doctor prescribed penicillin for me.*

▶ The emphasis or stress in inseparable verbs is always on the verb itself, never on the prefix.
▶ In dictionaries, inseparable verbs are normally shown by *insep* written after the verb.

Separable or inseparable?
Some verbs can be either separable or inseparable, depending on their meaning. This should not daunt us too much as we are used to it from such English verbs as *to overtake* and *to take over*.

▶ Verbs which start with the following prefixes can be either separable or inseparable, according to meaning: **durch-, hinter-, über-, um-, unter-, voll-, wieder-, wider-**:

übersetzen	*to translate*
über/setzen	*to take across, to ferry across*
unterhalten	*to entertain, to maintain*
unter/halten	*to hold underneath*
umfahren	*to drive around, to bypass*
um/fahren	*to run over, to knock down*

9.4 VERBS ASSOCIATED WITH PARTICULAR PREPOSITIONS

Just as some verbs are followed by a particular case, e.g. dative, so other verbs are followed by a particular preposition. This information is usually found in a good dictionary. The following are examples of some frequently used verbs and their prepositions.

Angst haben vor + dative	*to be frightened of*
an/kommen in + dative	*to arrive at, to arrive in*
bitten um + accusative	*to ask for, to request*
denken an + accusative	*to think of something or someone, to have something or someone in mind*
denken über + accusative	*to think about, to have an opinion about*
halten von + dative	*to think of, to rate*
sich erinnern an + accusative	*to remember*
fragen nach + dative	*to ask about, to enquire about*
sich freuen auf + accusative	*to look forward to*
sich freuen über + accusative	*to be happy about*
schreiben an + accusative	*to write to*
vorbei/fahren an + dative	*to go past*
warten auf + accusative	*to wait for*

9.5 REFLEXIVE VERBS *(SEE FUNCTIONAL GRAMMAR UNIT 11)*

Reflexive verbs express the idea of doing something either for oneself or to oneself, e.g. *I wash myself, I astonish myself.* Their use in German is different from that in English. Reflexive verbs can be regular or irregular verbs, separable or inseparable. The reflexive verb consists of the normal verb form plus a reflexive pronoun (*myself*, *yourself*, *herself*, etc.).

Reflexive verbs with an accusative reflexive pronoun

Many reflexive verbs use the pronoun in the accusative case, because the pronoun is the direct object of the verb. For example:

sich wiegen *to weigh oneself*	
Singular	*Plural*

ich wiege **mich** *I weigh myself*	wir wiegen **uns** *we weigh ourselves*
du wiegst **dich** *you weigh yourself*	ihr wiegt **euch** *you weigh yourselves*
er wiegt **sich** *he weighs himself*	Sie wiegen **sich** *you weigh yourself*
sie wiegt **sich** *she weighs herself*	sie wiegen **sich** *they weigh themselves*

Note the word order:

1 in the question form:

Wiegen Sie sich regelmäßig?   *Do you weigh yourself regularly?*

2 in the command form:

Wiegen Sie sich regelmäßig!   *Weigh yourself regularly!*

Other reflexive verbs with an accusative reflexive pronoun

sich an/ziehen	*to get dressed*
sich aus/ziehen	*to get undressed*
sich um/ziehen	*to get changed*
sich ärgern	*to get annoyed*
sich aus/ruhen	*to rest, to have a rest*
sich beeilen	*to hurry up*
sich entschuldigen	*to apologize*
sich erinnern an + acc.	*to remember*
sich erkälten	*to catch a cold*
sich freuen auf + acc.	*to look forward to*

sich freuen über + acc.	*to be pleased about*
sich hin/legen	*to lie down*
sich hin/setzen	*to sit down*
sich kämmen	*to comb one's hair*
sich konzentrieren	*to concentrate*
sich rasieren	*to shave*
sich verabschieden	*to take one's leave*
sich verletzen	*to hurt oneself*
sich waschen	*to have a wash, to wash oneself*

Reflexive verbs with a dative reflexive pronoun

The idea of doing something for one's own benefit, e.g. **Ich kaufe mir ein Haus** *I am buying a house (for myself)*, is often expressed with a reflexive verb. In this usage the reflexive pronoun is in the dative case, because it is the indirect object of the sentence and it is followed by the direct object in the accusative case:

Ich (*I*)	**kaufe** (*buy*)	**mir** (*myself*)	**ein Haus** (*a house*)
subject	finite verb	reflexive pronoun	direct object
pronoun		as indirect object	(accusative)
(nominative)		(dative)	

sich die Hände waschen *to wash one's hands*
Singular

ich wasche **mir** die Hände	*I wash my hands*
du wäschst **dir** die Hände	*you wash your hands*
er wäscht **sich** die Hände	*he washes his hands*
sie wäscht **sich** die Hände	*she washes her hands*

Plural

wir waschen **uns** die Hände	*we wash our hands*
ihr wäscht **euch** die Hände	*you wash your hands*
Sie waschen **sich** die Hände	*you wash your hands*
sie waschen **sich** die Hände	*they wash their hands*

Other reflexive verbs with a dative reflexive pronoun:

sich das Haar waschen   *to wash one's hair*
sich die Zähne putzen   *to clean one's teeth*

Getting something done for oneself using the verb **lassen**
The same reflexive pronouns as in the last example are also used in
the expression **sich etwas tun lassen** *to have something done* or *to
get something done*:

Ich lasse mir das Haar schneiden.   *I'm having my hair cut.*
Sie lässt sich einen Hotelprospekt   *She is having a hotel brochure*
  schicken.   *sent (to her).*
Er lässt sich einen Zahn ziehen.   *He is having a tooth out.*
Wir lassen uns ein Haus bauen.   *We're having a house built.*
Ihr müsst euch untersuchen lassen.   *You must get yourselves examined.*
Sie müssen sich operieren lassen.   *You must have an operation.*

---

10 Tenses

10.1 THE FORMATION OF THE SIMPLE PAST TENSE OF REGULAR VERBS

The simple past tense of regular verbs is formed by adding the
following endings to the verb stem:

kaufen *to buy*			
Singular		*Plural*	
ich kauf**te**	*I bought,* *I was buying,* *I used to buy*	wir kauf**ten**	*we bought, etc.*
du kauf**test**	*you bought, etc.*	ihr kauf**tet**	*you bought, etc.*
er kauf**te**	*he bought, etc.*	Sie kauf**ten**	*you bought, etc.*
sie kauf**te**	*she bought, etc.*	sie kauf**ten**	*they bought, etc.*

If the stem of a regular verb ends in **-d** or **-t**, e.g. **reden** *to speak*, **arbeiten** *to work*, or a combination of **m** or **n** preceded by another consonant, e.g. **atmen** *to breathe*, **regnen** *to rain*, an **e** is added before the past tense endings, e.g. **ich arbeitete, du arbeitetest**, etc.

10.2 THE FORMATION OF THE SIMPLE PAST OF IRREGULAR VERBS

Unlike with regular verbs, it is not possible to work out what the simple past form of an irregular verb is. All good dictionaries and coursebooks include a verb list which you should consult to find out the correct form.

You will notice that in most verb tables the third person singular form is given in the column for the simple past tense. This is in effect the simple past stem, to which endings are added to form the simple past as follows:

trinken to drink		
Singular		*Plural*
ich trank	I drank, I was drinking, I used to drink	wir trank**en** we drank, etc.
du trank**st**	you drank, etc.	ihr trank**t** you drank, etc.
er trank	he drank, etc.	Sie trank**en** you drank, etc.
sie trank	she drank, etc.	sie trank**en** they drank, etc.

There is no ending at all on the **ich** and **er, sie, es** forms, which are thus identical to the one found in the verb list.

Separable and inseparable prefixes can be added to these verbs, and change the meaning, e.g.

schreiben	*to write*	**an**kommen	*to arrive*
beschreiben	*to describe*	**aus**kommen	*to get by*
verschreiben	*to prescribe*	**um**kommen	*to die*
kommen	*to come*		

You will not find the form with the prefix in the verb list (10.7).
Always look up the basic verb and then add the prefix.

10.3 THE PERFECT TENSE *(FUNCTIONAL GRAMMAR UNIT 18)*

The formation of the perfect tense of regular verbs
The perfect tense is formed by using the appropriate part of either
the verb **haben** or **sein**, plus a past participle at the end of the
clause, e.g.

Ich *habe* **einen neuen Mantel** *gekauft.*   *I bought a new coat.*
Wir *haben getanzt.*   *We danced.*

The perfect tense in German, for example, **er hat … geschrieben,**
can be translated into English as *he wrote, he was writing, he did
write, he has written.* **Ich bin … gefahren** can be translated as
I travelled, I was travelling, I did travel and *I have travelled.*

Formation of the past participle
The past participle of most regular verbs is formed by firstly
removing the **-en** from the infinitive (e.g. **kaufen**), giving us the
stem of the verb (**kauf**). Next we put **ge-** in front of the stem and **-t**
after the stem, resulting in **gekauft** *bought.* You will have noticed
that the past participle is sent to the end of the clause.

▶ To form the past participle of a separable verb (for example
   ein/kaufen *to go shopping,* **auf/machen** *to open,* **zu/machen**
   to close) simply put the **ge-** between the two parts of the verb,
   for example:

   Wir haben gestern bei Kaufhof   *We went shopping at Kaufhof*
   eingekauft.   *yesterday.*

▶ If the stem of the verb ends in **-d, -t, -m** or **-n,** an additional
   e is added before the final **t** in the past participle for ease of
   pronunciation. For example:

   Oma hat im Toten Meer   *Grandma bathed in the Dead*
   gebad*e*t.   *Sea.*

- ▶ If the infinitive begins with **be-, ge-, ent-, er-, ver-, zer-,** or ends with **-ieren**, no **ge-** is required at the beginning of the past participle:

  Wir haben nichts bemerkt.   *We didn't notice anything*

- ▶ Many verbs do not form their past participle in the way described for regular verbs. The past participles of most irregular verbs end in -en and many undergo a vowel change from the infinitive form, e.g. **gehen – gegangen, schreiben – geschrieben, sprechen – gesprochen.** As already noted, a few verbs change the stem vowel of their infinitive in the past tense and past participle and also add **t** like regular verbs, e.g. **kennen** *to know* **– kannte, gekannt.** The verb list (10.7) or any good German dictionary should be consulted until individual forms of irregular verbs have been learned.

Verbs which form the perfect tense using sein

- ▶ If the verb shows motion or movement from one place to another the perfect tense is formed by using the appropriate part of the verb **sein** plus a past participle at the end of the clause:

fahren *to travel*
Ich *bin* **mit dem Zug gefahren.**   *I travelled by train.*

kommen *to come*
Ihr Mann *ist* **um zwei Uhr morgens**   *Her husband came home*
  nach Hause gekommen.   *at 2 a.m.*

fliegen *to fly*
Bist **du über Brüssel geflogen?**   *Did you fly via Brussels?*

ab/fahren *to depart, set off*
Mein Nachbar *ist* **gestern abgefahren.**   *My neighbour set off yesterday.*

an/kommen *to arrive*
Der Zug aus Paris *ist* **mit zwei**   *The train from Paris arrived two*
Stunden Verspätung angekommen. *hours late.*

folgen *to follow* **NB** this verb requires the dative case!
Der Herr hat gerufen und der   *The master called and the dog*
Hund *ist* **ihm gefolgt.**   *followed him.*

▶ **Sein** is also used if the verb shows a change of state or condition:

    Es *ist* **dunkel** *geworden.* *It has got (literally 'it has become') dark.*

NB The verbs **sein** and **bleiben** also form their perfect tense using **sein**:

Sie *ist* **sehr krank** *gewesen.*   *She has been very ill.*
Er *ist* **in Rostock** *geblieben.*   *He has stayed in Rostock.*

10.4 THE PLUPERFECT TENSE *(SEE FUNCTIONAL GRAMMAR UNIT 17)*

The pluperfect tense is a compound tense, formed by using the appropriate form of the simple past tense of either **haben** or **sein**, plus a past participle at the end of the clause. You will not find this form given in the verb lists as you can work it out: combine the past stem of **haben** or **sein** (from the simple past column) with the past participle:

Er *hatte* **schon zwei Liter Bier**   *He had already drunk two litres*
getrunken, **bevor er mit dem**   *of beer before he drove home*
Wagen nach Hause fuhr.   *by car.*
Vor der Hochzeit *war* **sie noch**   *She had never been in a church*
nie in einer Kirche *gewesen.*   *before the wedding.*

10.5 THE FUTURE TENSE

The future tense is another compound tense. It is formed by using the appropriate part of the present tense of the verb **werden** plus an infinitive at the end of the clause. On its own **werden** means *to become*, but when used to form the future tense, it is used merely as an auxiliary verb:

Wir werden **acht Monate in Kanada** verbringen.

We shall spend eight months in Canada.

It is an irregular verb, and its present tense is shown in Functional grammar Unit 16.

The future is also often expressed in German by the present tense plus an adverb:

Ich fahre nächste Woche nach Ulm.

I am/shall be going to Ulm next week.

10.6 THE FUTURE PERFECT TENSE

The future perfect is a compound tense formed by using the appropriate part of the present tense of the verb **werden** plus two other verbal forms: the past participle of the main verb, plus either **haben** or **sein**:

Er wird schon daran gedacht haben.

He will already have thought of that.

Sie werden **schon in Afrika** angekommen sein.

They will already have arrived in Africa.

NB The future perfect tense is very rarely used.

10.7 LIST OF IRREGULAR VERBS WITH SIMPLE PAST AND PERFECT FORMS

Infinitive	Meaning	3rd person sing. present	3rd person simple past	3rd person perfect tense
backen	to bake	backt	backte/buk	hat gebacken
befehlen	to order	befiehlt	befahl	hat befohlen
beginnen	to begin	beginnt	begann	hat begonnen
beißen	to bite	beißt	biss	hat gebissen
bergen	to save	birgt	barg	hat geborgen
bewegen	to move	bewegt	bewog	hat bewogen
biegen	to turn	biegt	bog	hat gebogen
bieten	to offer	bietet	bot	hat geboten
binden	to bind	bindet	band	hat gebunden
bitten	to ask	bittet	bat	hat gebeten
blasen	to blow	bläst	blies	hat geblasen
bleiben	to remain	bleibt	blieb	ist geblieben
braten	to fry	brät	briet	hat gebraten
brechen	to break	bricht	brach	hat gebrochen
brennen	to burn	brennt	brannte	hat gebrannt
bringen	to bring	bringt	brachte	hat gebracht
denken	to think	denkt	dachte	hat gedacht
dürfen	to be allowed to	darf	durfte	hat gedurft
empfehlen	to recommend	empfiehlt	empfahl	hat empfohlen
essen	to eat	isst	aß	hat gegessen
fahren	to travel	fährt	fuhr	ist/hat gefahren
fallen	to fall	fällt	fiel	ist gefallen
fangen	to catch	fängt	fing	hat gefangen
finden	to find	findet	fand	hat gefunden
fliegen	to fly	fliegt	flog	ist geflogen
fliehen	to flee	flieht	floh	ist geflohen
fließen	to flow	fließt	floss	ist geflossen
frieren	to freeze	friert	fror	ist gefroren
geben	to give	gibt	gab	hat gegeben
gehen	to go	geht	ging	ist gegangen
gelingen	to succeed	gelingt	gelang	ist gelungen
gelten	to be valid	gilt	galt	hat gegolten

Infinitive	Meaning	3rd person sing. present	3rd person simple past	3rd person perfect tense
genießen	*to enjoy*	genießt	genoss	hat genossen
geschehen	*to happen*	geschieht	geschah	ist geschehen
gewinnen	*to win*	gewinnt	gewann	hat gewonnen
gießen	*to pour*	gießt	goss	hat gegossen
gleiten	*to glide*	gleitet	glitt	ist geglitten
graben	*to dig*	gräbt	grub	hat gegraben
greifen	*to grab*	greift	griff	hat gegriffen
haben	*to have*	hat	hatte	hat gehabt
halten	*to hold*	hält	hielt	hat gehalten
hängen	*to hang*	hängt	hing	hat gehangen
heben	*to lift*	hebt	hob	hat gehoben
heißen	*to be called*	heißt	hieß	hat geheißen
helfen	*to help*	hilft	half	hat geholfen
kennen	*to know*	kennt	kannte	hat gekannt
kneifen	*to pinch*	kneift	kniff	hat gekniffen
kommen	*to come*	kommt	kam	ist gekommen
können	*to be able to*	kann	konnte	hat gekonnt
kriechen	*to crawl*	kriecht	kroch	ist gekrochen
laden	*to load*	lädt	lud	hat geladen
lassen	*to let, leave*	lässt	ließ	hat gelassen
laufen	*to walk, run*	läuft	lief	ist gelaufen
leiden	*to suffer*	leidet	litt	hat gelitten
leihen	*to lend*	leiht	lieh	hat geliehen
liegen	*to lie*	liegt	lag	ist/hat gelegen
lügen	*to tell a lie*	lügt	log	hat gelogen
meiden	*to avoid*	meidet	mied	hat gemieden
messen	*to measure*	misst	maß	hat gemessen
mögen	*to like*	mag	mochte	hat gemocht
nehmen	*to take*	nimmt	nahm	hat genommen
nennen	*to call*	nennt	nannte	hat gennannt
pfeifen	*to whistle*	pfeift	pfiff	hat gepfiffen
preisen	*to praise*	preist	pries	hat gepriesen
raten	*to advise*	rät	riet	hat geraten
reiben	*to rub*	reibt	rieb	hat gerieben
reißen	*to tear*	reißt	riss	hat gerissen

Infinitive	Meaning	3rd person sing. present	3rd person simple past	3rd person perfect tense
rennen	to run	rennt	rannte	hat gerannt
reiten	to ride	reitet	ritt	ist geritten
riechen	to smell	riecht	roch	hat gerochen
rufen	to call	ruft	rief	hat gerufen
schaffen	to create	schafft	schuf	hat geschaffen
scheiden	to separate	scheidet	schied	hat geschieden
scheinen	to shine	scheint	schien	hat geschienen
schieben	to push	schiebt	schob	hat geschoben
schießen	to shoot	schießt	schoss	hat geschossen
schlafen	to sleep	schläft	schlief	hat geschlafen
schlagen	to hit	schlägt	schlug	hat geschlagen
schließen	to close	schließt	schloss	hat geschlossen
schmeißen	to throw	schmeißt	schmiss	hat geschmissen
schmelzen	to melt	schmilzt	schmolz	ist geschmolzen
schneiden	to cut	schneidet	schnitt	hat geschnitten
schreiben	to write	schreibt	schrieb	hat geschrieben
schreien	to scream	schreit	schrie	hat geschrien
schreiten	to step	schreitet	schritt	ist geschritten
schweigen	to be silent	schweigt	schwieg	hat geschwiegen
schwimmen	to swim	schwimmt	schwomm	ist/hat geschwommen
sehen	to see	sieht	sah	hat gesehen
sein	to be	ist	war	ist gewesen
senden	to send	sendet	sandte	hat gesandt
singen	to sing	singt	sang	hat gesungen
sinken	to sink	sinkt	sank	ist gesunken
sitzen	to sit	sitzt	saß	ist/hat gesessen
sollen	ought to	soll	sollte	hat gesollt
sprechen	to talk	spricht	sprach	hat gesprochen
springen	to jump	springt	sprang	ist gesprungen
stechen	to sting	sticht	stach	hat gestochen
stehen	to stand	steht	stand	ist/hat gestanden
stehlen	to steal	stiehlt	stahl	hat gestohlen

Infinitive	Meaning	3rd person sing. present	3rd person simple past	3rd person perfect tense
steigen	*to climb*	steigt	stieg	ist/hat gestiegen
sterben	*to die*	stirbt	starb	ist gestorben
stinken	*to stink*	stinkt	stank	hat gestunken
stoßen	*to push*	stößt	stieß	hat gestoßen
streichen	*to stroke, paint*	streicht	strich	hat gestrichen
streiten	*to quarrel*	streitet	stritt	hat gestritten
tragen	*to carry*	trägt	trug	hat getragen
treffen	*to meet*	trifft	traf	hat getroffen
treiben	*to drive, push*	treibt	trieb	hat getrieben
treten	*to step*	tritt	trat	ist getreten
trinken	*to drink*	trinkt	trank	hat getrunken
tun	*to do*	tut	tat	hat getan
verderben	*to spoil*	verdirbt	verdarb	hat verdorben
vergessen	*to forget*	vergisst	vergaß	hat vergessen
verlieren	*to lose*	verliert	verlor	hat verloren
verschwinden	*to disappear*	verschwindet	verschwand	ist verschwunden
wachsen	*to grow*	wächst	wuchs	ist gewachsen
waschen	*to wash*	wäscht	wusch	hat gewaschen
weisen	*to point*	weist	wies	hat gewiesen
wenden	*to turn*	wendet	wandte	hat gewandt
werden	*to become*	wird	wurde	ist geworden
werfen	*to throw*	wirft	warf	hat geworfen
wiegen	*to weigh*	wiegt	wog	hat gewogen
wissen	*to know*	weiß	wusste	hat gewusst
wollen	*to want to*	will	wollte	hat gewollt
verzeihen	*to pardon*	verzeiht	verzieh	hat verziehen
ziehen	*to pull*	zieht	zog	hat gezogen
zwingen	*to force*	zwingt	zwang	hat gezwungen

11 The subjunctive

There are two forms of the subjunctive in German, which are sometimes described as the present subjunctive and imperfect subjunctive. This can be misleading in that the subjunctive does not directly correspond to the tenses referred to, and so we shall use the terms Subjunctive 1 for the so-called present subjunctive and Subjunctive 2 for the so-called imperfect subjunctive.

11.1 THE USE OF THE SUBJUNCTIVE

The subjunctive is used for a few short, set phrases, often expressing hopes or wishes:

Gott *sei* **dank!**	*Thank God!*
Es *lebe* **der König!**	*Long live the King!*
Sei **es gut, sei es schlecht**	*whether it be good or bad*
Das *wär's!*	*That's all, that's it!* (often used at the end of an order in shops)

Subjunctive 2 is used:

▶ after **als ob** *as if*:

> **Sie sah aus, als ob sie nicht geschlafen** *hätte.*   *She looked as if she had not slept.*

▶ for conditional hypothetical sentences:

> **Wenn ich reich** *wäre, würde* **ich mir ein neues Haus** *kaufen.*   *If I were rich, I would buy a new house.*
>
> **Wenn ich das** *gewusst hätte,* *wäre* **ich sofort nach Hause** *gegangen.*   *If I had known that, I would have gone home immediately.*

▶ for indirect speech. As a general rule, the subjunctive verb is put into the same tense as was used in the indicative speech, e.g. from the direct statement: Der Lehrer sagte: "Ich bin müde." *The teacher said,* 'I am tired' we can form the indirect speech: Der Lehrer sagte, dass er müde sei/Der Lehrer sagte, er sei müde. *The teacher said he was tired.*

▶ for indirect questions. From the direct question: Er fragte: "Hat das Auto eine Stereoanlage?" *He asked,* '*Does the car have a stereo system?*' we can form the indirect question: Er fragte, ob das Auto eine Stereoanlage **habe.** *He asked if the car had a stereo system.*

However, Units 20 and 21 show wide variations in usage.

11.2 THE FORMATION OF THE SUBJUNCTIVE

The formation of Subjunctive 1 (See Functional grammar Unit 20)
Subjunctive 1 is formed by adding the following endings to the stem of the verb:

The **ich, wir, Sie** and **sie** forms are the same in the subjunctive as in the indicative for this verb.

> ich kaufe, du kaufest, er kaufe, sie kaufe, es kaufe, wir kaufen, ihr kaufet, Sie kaufen, sie kaufen

By the very nature of reported speech, the third person singular and plural forms are most frequently used. In fact, you are unlikely to come across some of the other forms but we have shown them here for reference.

In practice, the Subjunctive 2 form and/or the auxiliary **würde** plus infinitive is often substituted for Subjunctive 1 in reported speech, e.g.

Sie sagten, sie *hätten* **keine Zeit.** *They said they had no time.*
Er sagte, er *würde* **sich ein neues** *He said he would buy a new car.*
Auto *kaufen.*

The Subjunctive 1 of irregular and modal verbs is formed in exactly the same way as that of the regular verbs, i.e. from the stem plus the same endings:

> ich fahre, du fahrest, er/sie/es fahre, wir fahren, ihr fahret, Sie fahren, sie fahren ich könne, du könnest, er/sie/es könne, wir können, ihr könnet, Sie können, sie können

Even **haben** (*to have*) forms its Subjunctive 1 in the same way as a regular verb:

> ich habe, du habest, er/sie/es habe, wir haben, ihr habet, Sie haben, sie haben

Sein is an exception in that it forms its present subjunctive as follows, without -e in the singular:

> ich sei, du seist, er/sie/es sei, wir seien, ihr seiet, Sie seien, sie seien

This form will be familiar to you as it is the same as the imperative mood of **sein**. (See Functional grammar Unit 13)

The formation of Subjunctive 2 (see Functional grammar Unit 21)
Regular verbs

The Subjunctive 2 form of regular verbs is the same as the imperfect indicative, for example **machte** in the sentence:

Wenn er das *machte*, **würde ich weinen.** *If he did that, I would cry.*

Irregular verbs

▶ To form the Subjunctive 2 of irregular verbs, the following endings are added to the imperfect indicative (found in the verb list, see 10.7). Using **kommen** *to come* as an example:

The imperfect stem is **kam**

> ich käm**e**, du käm**est**, er/sie/es käm**e**, wir käm**en**, ihr käm**et**, Sie
> käm**en**, sie käm**en**

- ► As you can see, in addition to these endings an umlaut must be added to the vowels **a**, **o** or **u** in the stem.
- ► If the stem vowel is not **a**, **o**, **u** then it does not change. The imperfect indicative stem from **gehen** *to go* is **ging**, and the Subjunctive 2 forms are:

> ich ging**e**, du ging**est**, er/sie/es ging**e**, wir ging**en**, ihr ging**et**, Sie
> ging**en**, sie ging**en**

- ► The Subjunctive 2 forms of **sein** *to be* and **haben** *to have* are formed in the same way.

sein	**haben**
The imperfect indicative stem is **war**	*The imperfect indicative stem is* **hatte**
ich wäre	ich hätte
du wärest	du hättest
er/sie/es wäre	er/sie/es hätte
wir wären	wir hätten
ihr wäret	ihr hättet
Sie wären	Sie hätten
sie wären	sie hätten

- ► You can further combine the Subjunctive 2 form of either **haben** or **sein** with a past participle to produce a pluperfect form expressing unfulfilled conditions, as follows:

Wenn er das *gewusst hätte,*   *If he had known that, he*
wäre **er** *weggelaufen.*   *would have run away.*

- ► There is also a trend either to simplify or to avoid the subjunctive in modern spoken German. In situations where a subjunctive is clearly needed, a useful and simple formula **Ich würde** plus an infinitive is often used, for example:

Ich *würde sagen,* **dass es unbedingt nötig ist.**	*I would say that it's absolutely necessary.*
Ich *würde* **gerne** *mitmachen,* **aber ich habe keine Zeit.**	*I'd love to join in but I have no time.*

NB This formula is not used with the verb **sein**. The form **wäre** is preferred:

Ich *wäre* **sehr dankbar, wenn Sie das nicht** *weitersagen würden.*	*I'd be most grateful if you wouldn't pass this on.*

The most commonly used forms of Subjunctive 2 are:

> ich wäre, bräuchte, dürfte, ginge, käme, könnte, möchte, müsste, sollte, wollte, wüsste

For example:

Das *wäre* **gar nicht schlecht!**	*That wouldn't be at all bad!*
Wenn ich nur *wüsste,* **was ich machen sollte.**	*If only I knew what I ought to do.*

---

12 The imperative mood

The *du* **imperative form** (Functional grammar Unit 13)

▶ The familiar singular imperative is formed by dropping both the pronoun **du** and the ending from the **du** form of the verb, e.g. **du fragst**:

Frag **deine Lehrerin zuerst!**	*Ask your teacher first!*

Note 1: You will sometimes find that an **e** is added to this form. It can have the effect of making it sound a bit more formal or imperious, even though it is addressed to a child or a friend.

Note 2: If the verb adds an umlaut in the **du** form (e.g. **ich laufe, du läufst**) the same rules as above apply, but the umlaut is dropped:

Lauf **nicht weg!**	*Don't run away!*
Schlaf **gut!**	*Sleep well!*

The *ihr* imperative form

▶ The familiar plural imperative form simply comprises the appropriate **ihr** form of the verb minus the pronoun **ihr**:

Raucht **bitte nicht!**	*Please don't smoke!*

The *Sie* imperative form

Setzen Sie **sich!**	*Take a seat!*

The imperative forms of verbs *sein* and *haben*

sein	haben
du : **Seid** ruhig! *Be quiet!*	**Hab** keine Angst! Don't be afraid!
ihr : **Sei** ruhig! *Be quiet!*	**Habt** keine Angst! *Don't be afraid!*
Sie : **Seien Sie** ruhig! Be quiet!	**Haben Sie** keine Angst *Don't be afraid!*

Commands involving the speaker

If the speaker is involved in the projected action, a **wir** imperative form can be used by inverting the normal verb form. In this usage the pronoun **wir** is retained as follows:

Fangen wir an!	*Let's begin!*
Gehen wir!	*Let's go!*

13 The passive voice (Functional grammar Unit 19)

The passive voice is used in a structure which shows the subject of an equivalent active sentence undergoing or suffering the action of the verb, e.g. The workmen are felling the tree outside the gym → **The tree** outside the gym **is being felled** by the workmen.

The passive voice is formed by using the appropriate part and tense of the verb **werden** as an auxiliary verb, plus a past participle at the end of the clause.

Compare the following two sentences, which both have the same meaning but a different emphasis:

Present active voice:

Die Gemeinde baut einen neuen Sportplatz. *The local authority is building a new sports ground.*

Present passive voice:

Ein neuer Sportplatz wird von der Gemeinde gebaut. *A new sports ground is being built by the local authority.*

▶ In the passive sentence, more emphasis is given to the process which is being carried out by the local authority (i.e. what is being built).

▶ The direct object of the active sentence has become the subject of the passive sentence, and has therefore changed from the accusative to the nominative case.

▶ The agent by whom or which the activity is carried out is expressed by **von** + dative case.

Simple past passive:

Ein neuer Sportplatz *wurde* **von**   *A new sports ground was built by*
der Gemeinde *gebaut.*   *the local authority.*

Perfect passive:

Ein neuer Sportplatz *ist* **von der**   *A new sports ground has been built*
Gemeinde *gebaut worden.*   *by the local authority.*

NB The **ge-** is dropped from the past participle of **werden** when used next to another past participle.

Pluperfect passive:

Ein neuer Sportplatz *war* **von der**   *A new sports ground had been*
Gemeinde *gebaut worden.*   *built by the local authority.*

Future passive:

Ein neuer Sportplatz *wird* **von**   *A new sports ground will be built by*
der Gemeinde *gebaut werden.*   *the local authority.*

Additional notes:

1 The means by which something is or was done is expressed by the preposition **durch** + accusative case:

Meine Sonnenblumen sind durch   *My sunflowers have been*
den Wind zerstört worden.   *destroyed by the wind.*

2 The object or instrument used to carry out an action is expressed by the preposition **mit** + dative case:

Der Brief wurde mit der Hand   *The letter was written by*
geschrieben.   *hand.*

3 If the object of the verb in the active sentence is in the dative, e.g. Der Lehrer hilft **dem Kind**. *The teacher is helping the child*, then it must remain in the dative in the passive version: **Dem Kind** wird von dem Lehrer geholfen. *The child is being helped by the teacher*. Compare:

Die Firma Braun hat ihm eine Stelle angeboten. – Ihm ist eine Stelle von der Firma Braun angeboten worden.	*Braun and Company has offered him a job. – He has been offered a job by Braun and Company.*

4 There are several ways of avoiding the passive, most notably by using the indefinite pronoun **man**:

Auf Bierfesten wird oft zu viel getrunken. – *Man* **trinkt oft zu viel auf Bierfesten.**	*Often too much is drunk at beer festivals. – People often drink too much at beer festivals.*

5 There are sometimes very close similarities between sentences with an adjective or past participle after the verb **sein** *to be* and passive sentences. Compare, for example:

Die Haustür ist nach 22 Uhr geschlossen.	*The front door is closed after 10 p.m.*

and

Die Haustür wird um 22 Uhr geschlossen.	*The front door is closed at 10 p.m.*
Das Mittagessen ist serviert.	*Lunch is served.*

and

Das Mittagessen wird serviert.	*Lunch is being served.*

14 Word order

14.1 MAIN CLAUSES

In a main clause (i.e. one which can stand independently as a sentence) which is not a question or command, the finite verb is the second element or 'idea' (see Functional grammar Unit 3). An element or idea is not necessarily only one word, as the following translations of the English sentence *I'm going to the cinema this evening* demonstrate:

1	*2*	*3*	*4*
Ich	**gehe**	**heute Abend**	**ins Kino.**
subject pronoun	finite verb	adverbial phrase	adverbial phrase

or

1	*2*	*3*	*4*
Heute Abend	**gehe**	**ich**	**ins Kino.**
adverbial phrase	finite verb	subject pronoun	adverbial phrase

This rule seems strange to an English speaker, but there are still relics of this 'verb second' practice in the English language, for example: 'Scarcely had I finished speaking', or 'Here endeth the first lesson'.

If a subordinate clause begins the sentence, it also counts as the first idea and the finite verb of the main clause comes next, i.e. in second position:

1				*2*	*3* *4*

Wenn die Sonne heute Nachmittag scheint, spiele ich Tennis.

The occurrence of the two finite verbs next to each other in the middle of the sentence, separated by only a comma, is often called a verb-comma-verb structure. This happens whenever a subordinate clause begins the sentence, as a subordinating conjunction sends the verb to the end of the clause:

Als ich jung *war, spielte* **ich die Gitarre**.　　*When I was young, I played the guitar.*

- ▶ In terms of word order, interjections are not counted as an idea or element.

  Ach, ich wollte Gabi anrufen. *Oh bother, I wanted to phone Gabi.*

- ▶ If **ja** or **nein** is used at the beginning of a sentence it is usually followed by a comma, and has no effect on subsequent word order:

  Ja, man kann nur hoffen. *Yes, you can only hope.*

- ▶ The same applies if a name or a word such as **also** *so, therefore* is followed by a comma at the beginning of a sentence:

  Also, wir können endlich essen. *Well then, we can eat at long last.*

- ▶ In questions and the imperative, the finite verb begins the sentence:

  Trinken Sie viel Tee? *Do you drink a lot of tea?*
  Trinken Sie viel Tee! *Drink a lot of tea!*

14.2 THE POSITION OF THE DIRECT AND INDIRECT OBJECT

- ▶ Sometimes the direct object appears **before** the verb in German, especially if you wish to give it extra stress:

  Den Mann **möchte ich kennen lernen.** *I would like to get to know that man.*

▶ Sometimes the direct object appears later in the sentence:

Ich bekam erst letzten *I did not get the letter until last*
Freitag den Brief. *Friday.*

▶ If there are two nouns after the verb (i.e. a direct object and an indirect object), the dative comes before the accusative:

Er schickte dem Direktor (dative) *He sent a long letter to the*
einen langen Brief (accusative). *head teacher.*

▶ If there is a pronoun and a noun, the pronoun comes before the noun:

Er schickte ihm (pronoun) **einen** *He sent him a letter.*
Brief (noun).

or:

Er schickte ihn (pronoun) **dem** *He sent it to the head*
Direktor (noun). *teacher.*

▶ If there are two or more pronouns after the verb, the order is

1 *nominative*, 2 *accusative*, 3 *dative*:

Ich (nom.) **gebe es** (acc.) **ihr** (dat.) **jetzt.** *I am giving it to her now.*

or:

Jetzt gebe ich (nom.) **es** (acc.) **ihr** (dat.). *Now I am giving it to her.*

14.3 THE POSITION OF OTHER ELEMENTS IN THE MAIN CLAUSE

Adverbs and adverbial phrases
When several adverbs or adverbial phrases are used after the finite verb the normal order for these is:

1 *time*, 2 *manner*, 3 *place* – i.e. answers to the questions **wann?** *when?*, **wie?** *how?*, **wo?/wohin?/woher?** *where?/where to?/where from?*:

Ich fahre (*wann?*) **nächste Woche** (*wie?*) *I am going to Geneva by*
   mit dem Zug (*wohin?*) **nach Genf.**   *train next week.*

Past participles
The normal position for the past participle is at the end of the main clause:

Ich habe ihn zwei Wochen lang   *I have not seen him for*
   nicht gesehen.   *two weeks.*

The infinitive after modal or auxiliary verbs
The normal position for the infinitive after a modal or auxiliary verb is at the end of the clause:

Er will nächsten Sommer nach   *He wants to travel/go to Australia*
   Australien *fahren.*   *next summer.*
Wir werden meinen Onkel in   *We will visit my uncle*
   Mexiko *besuchen.*   *in Mexico.*

The position of separable prefixes
The normal position for the separable prefix of a finite verb is at the end of the clause:

Er rief mich gestern Abend an.   *He telephoned me yesterday evening.*

---

15 Subordinate clauses *(Functional grammar Unit 10)*

A subordinate clause is an add-on element to a main clause. It does not make full sense in its own right. It can appear *either* before *or* after the main clause and always starts with a subordinating conjunction, which sends the verb to the end of the clause:

Ich bleibe heute im Bett (main clause),   *I am staying in bed today*
  weil ich krank bin (subordinate clause).   *because I am ill.*

If the subordinating conjunction begins the sentence, a verb–comma–verb construction appears in the middle, linking the two clauses:

Weil ich krank bin (subordinate   *Because I am ill, I am staying in*
clause), **bleibe ich heute im Bett.**   *bed today.*

When a separable verb is used in a subordinate clause, the verb goes to the end of the clause, complete with the prefix:

Ich warte auf dem Bahnsteig,   *I'll wait on the platform until the*
  bis der Zug ankommt.   *train arrives.*

The subordinating conjunctions are:

als	*when*	**bevor**	*before*
bis	*until*	**da**	*as, since, seeing that*
damit	*so that, in order that*	**dass**	*that*
ehe	*before* (cf. old-fashioned English 'ere')		

falls	*in case*	**indem**	*while, whilst*
nachdem	*after*	**ob**	*whether, if*
obgleich	*although*	**obschon**	*although*
obwohl	*although*	**seit/seitdem**	*since*
so dass	*so that*	**während**	*while, whereas*
weil	*because*	**wenn**	*if, whenever*

All of these send the verb to the end of the clause when used as a conjunction.

NB Beware! These subordinating conjunctions are easily confused with other word classes, for example with the prepositions **vor** *in front of*, **bis** *until*, **nach** *after*, **seit** *since, for*, **während** *during*, e.g.

Ich warte, *bis* **er kommt.**	*I am waiting until he comes.*
Seit **ich Deutsch lerne, bin ich sehr glücklich.**	*Since I have been learning German I have been very happy.*
Während **sie warteten, lasen sie die Zeitungen.**	*While they were waiting they read the newspapers.*

Prepositions do not, of course, send the verb to the end of the clause. The conjunction **als** (Als ich sie besuchte, ging es ihr viel besser. *When I visited her she was much better*), is also used in the comparative of adverbs and adjectives; and the conjunction damit (Er trinkt weniger Alkohol, **damit** er gesund wird. *He is drinking less alcohol in order to become healthy*), can be an adverbial preposition (see Unit 10).

When interrogatives (**wo? wann? warum?** etc.) are used at the beginning of subordinate clauses, they act like a conjunction and send the verb to the end of the clause:

Ich weiß nicht, *wo* **mein Hausschlüssel ist.**	*I don't know where my door key is.*
Können Sie bitte erklären, *warum* **er das macht?**	*Can you please explain why he does that?*

15.1 THE OCCASIONAL OMISSION OF CONJUNCTIONS

▶ In conditional clauses the subordinating conjunction **wenn** is sometimes omitted, and so the verb is not sent to the end of the clause. Compare:

Wenn **er das gesagt** *hätte,* **(so) wäre ich nicht gekommen.**	*If he had said that, I would not have come.*
Hätte **er das gesagt, (so) wäre ich nicht gekommen.**	*Had he said that, I would not have come.*

▶ In indirect (reported) speech the conjunction **dass** is sometimes omitted, with the result that the verb does not go to the end of the clause. Compare:

| Er sagte, *dass* er am Wochenende nach Hause *fahre*. | *He said that he was going home at the weekend.* |
| Er sagte, er *fahre* am Wochenende nach Hause. | *He said he was going home at the weekend.* |

▶ The expression **als ob** *as if* is normally followed by Subjunctive 2. **Ob** is sometimes omitted, in which case the verb is not sent to the end of the clause. Compare:

| Sie sah aus, *als ob* sie krank *wäre*. | *She looked as if she were ill.* |
| Sie sah aus, *als wäre* sie krank. · | |

15.2 RELATIVE CLAUSES *(SEE FUNCTIONAL GRAMMAR UNIT 5)*

Relative clauses are a sort of subordinate clause, and give us more information about the noun in the main clause. These clauses normally begin with a relative pronoun (occasionally with **welcher**). The relative pronoun must be preceded by a comma, and sends the verb to the end of the clause:

| Sie heiratet den Mann, der sie liebt. | *She is marrying the man who loves her.* |

Relative pronouns show the following changes of form:

	Singular masculine	feminine	neuter	Plural m, f, n
Nominative	der	die	das	die
Accusative	den	die	das	die
Dative	dem	der	dem	denen
Genitive	dessen	deren	dessen	deren

▶ The relative pronoun agrees in number and gender with the word it refers back to. In **Sie heiratet den Mann, der sie liebt,** the relative pronoun **der** is masculine singular because it refers to the noun **der Mann,** which is masculine singular.

▶ The case of the relative pronoun is determined by the role which it plays in the relative clause, e.g.

Sie heiratet den Mann, der die | *She is marrying the man*
Versicherungsgesellschaft | *who owns the insurance*
besitzt. | *company.*

The relative pronoun **der** is nominative because it is the subject of the relative clause. In the sentence **Sie heiratet den Mann, den sie liebt** *She is marrying the man (whom) she loves*, the relative pronoun **den** is accusative masculine because it is the direct object of the verb **liebt** in the relative clause. The subject of the relative clause is **sie**.

▶ If there is another verb in the sentence after the relative clause, a verb-comma-verb construction is required:

Der Mann, den sie | *The man (whom) she is*
heiratet, besitzt **die** | *marrying, owns the*
Versicherungsgesellschaft. | *insurance company.*

Key to exercises

Exercise A
1 D; 2 G; 3 J; 4 B; 5 F; 6 A; 7 I; 8 E; 9 H; 10 C

Exercise B
1 Wo? 2 Wie? 3 Woher? 4 Wohin? 5 Warum?

UNIT 2

Exercise A
1 I; 2 F; 3 E; 4 A; 5 H; 6 B; 7 J; 8 C; 9 G; 10 D

Exercise B
1 Ich bin die Frau von Karl. I am Karl's wife.
2 Mein Vorname ist Hans. My first name is Hans.
3 Ich kenne Dr. Schleiffenbaum gut. I know Dr Schleiffenbaum well.
4 Bist du Studentin, Christel? Are you a student, Christel?
5 Wissen Sie, wie er heißt? Do you know what he is called?
6 Kennen Sie einander? Do you know each other?
7 Wir kommen aus Wien. We are from Vienna.
8 Wie heißt du? What are you called?
9 Ich heiße Max Schulz. I'm called Max Schulz.
10 Dorothea und Waltraud sind Krankenschwestern. Dorothea and Waltraud are nurses.

Exercise C
1 Welcher Zahn tut weh? Dieser Zahn tut weh.
2 Welches Auto ist reduziert? Dieses Auto ist reduziert.
3 Welche Dame ist Doktor Brauns Sekretärin? Diese Dame ist Doktor Brauns Sekretärin.
4 Welche Maschine ist defekt? Diese Maschine ist defekt.
5 Welcher Student kommt aus Japan? Dieser Student kommt aus Japan.

UNIT 3

Exercise A

1 Haben Sie einen Bleistift da? 2 Gibt es einen Fön im Schlafzimmer? 3 Er hat ein Fahrrad parat. 4 Nürnberg hat ein Puppenhausmuseum. 5 Wir haben einen Tisch frei. 6 Jedes Zimmer hat ein Telefon. 7 Herr Meier hat eine neue Sekretärin. 8 Habt ihr einen Fahrplan zur Hand? 9 Das Schwimmbad steht Ihnen zur Verfügung. 10 Gibt es ein Kaffeehaus in der Nähe?

Exercise B

1 Am Dienstag spielen wir Tennis. 2 Immer fährt Otto mit dem Taxi. 3 Jeden Tag besucht Anita ihre Mutter. 4 Oft denken mein Mann und ich an Hans. 5 Nie essen sie Rindfleisch. 6 Jetzt muss ich gehen. 7 Meistens hat Inge keine Zeit zum Lesen. 8 Abends essen wir kalt. 9 Im Sommer fährt der frühere Bundeskanzler Kohl an den Wolfgangssee. 10 Dort macht er eine Kur.

UNIT 4

Exercise A

1 D; 2 H; 3 G; 4 B; 5 C; 6 A; 7 E; 8 F; 9 J; 10 I

Exercise B

1 Sie ist sehr krank. 2 Sie sind sehr faul. 3 Er arbeitet in einem Hotel. 4 Wir fahren mit ihnen nach Hamburg. 5 Frau Braun besucht ihn. 6 Heinrich wohnt bei ihr. 7 Sie hat am neunten Oktober Geburtstag. 8 Sie sind sehr nett. 9 Sie spielt Tennis mit ihm. 10 Der Brief ist für ihn.

UNIT 5

Exercise A

1 Inge fährt gerade nach Hannover. Inge is travelling to Hanover now.
2 Seit dem Unfall trinke ich keinen Alkohol mehr. Since the accident I no longer drink any alcohol.
3 Heute ist es schön. Die Sonne scheint. Today it's fine. The sun is shining.

4 Der Zug aus Köln kommt um 12 Uhr auf Gleis 2 an. The train from Cologne arrives at platform 2 at 12 p.m.

5 Das Baby schläft in dem Kinderwagen. The baby is sleeping in the pram.

6 Was lesen Sie da? Einen Roman? What are you reading there? A novel?

7 Am Samstagabend essen wir immer in einem Restaurant. On Saturday evening we always eat in a restaurant.

8 Spart ihr für die Englandreise, oder habt ihr schon genug Geld? Are you saving up for the trip to England, or do you already have enough money?

9 Fritz und Hanno studieren Jura an der Universität Marburg. Fritz and Hanno are studying law at the University of Marburg.

10 Was machst du jetzt? What are you doing now?

11 Der Schüler wartet schon zwanzig Minuten an der Bushaltestelle. The pupil has already waited twenty minutes at the bus stop.

12 Wie lange spielt Otto schon Klavier? How long has Otto been playing the piano?

Exercise B

1 Kommst du mit? 2 Mein Mann nimmt Zucker in den Tee. 3 Siehst du den Mann da? 4 Der Chef fährt oft nach Berlin. 5 Wir sehen abends fern. 6 Der Zug fährt um 12 Uhr ab. 7 Wir kaufen am liebsten bei Aldi ein. 8 Jakob kommt heute Nachmittag an. 9 Man gibt zu Weihnachten zu viel Geld aus. 10 Ich schlafe sofort ein.

UNIT 6

Exercise A

1 Ich mag gern Gulasch or Ich esse gern Gulasch.

2 Nein, ich schwimme nicht gern.

3 Ich finde Jazz nicht sehr interessant.

4 Ich höre die Musik von Strauß gern.

5 Die moderne Kunst gefällt mir gar nicht.

6 Die Kaffeehäuser von Wien gefallen mir besonders gut.

7 Ich besuche nicht gern Museen.

8 Der Prater gefällt mir gar nicht.

9 Ich finde die Oper nicht sehr interessant.

10 Die blaue Donau gefällt mir besonders gut.

Exercise B

1 Falsch. Sein Vorname ist Norbert. 2 Richtig. 3 Falsch. Er fährt leidenschaftlich gern Ski. 4 Falsch. Im Sommer wandert er gern im Berner Oberland. 5 Richtig. 6 Falsch. Er ist sehr sportlich. 7 Richtig. 8 Falsch. Abends spielen sie Elfer raus, Mensch ärgere dich nicht, Uno usw. 9 Richtig. 10 Falsch. Geschnetzeltes, Raclette und Fondue sind Schweizer Spezialitäten.

UNIT 7

Exercise A

Gut, und wie alt sind Sie, Herr Winkelmann? Ich bin dreißig Jahre alt.
Wo wohnen Sie? Ich wohne in Zürich in der Schweiz.
Sind Sie verheiratet? Nein, ich bin geschieden.
Haben Sie Haustiere? Ja, ich habe einen Hund.
Was machen Sie gern in Ihrer Freizeit? Ich spiele gern Gitarre.
Hören Sie gern Popmusik? Ich ziehe die klassische Musik der Popmusik vor.
Trinken Sie viel? Ich trinke gern Bier, aber ich mag keinen Wein.
Was ist Ihr Lieblingsessen? Mein Lieblingsessen ist Eisbein mit Sauerkraut.
Haben Sie irgendwelche Allergien? Ich bin allergisch gegen Fisch.
Übernachten Sie gern in Hotels? Nein, ich zelte lieber.
Wo zelten Sie am liebsten? In Griechenland und in Spanien.
Wie ist Ihre Traumfrau? Sie ist sympathisch, liebt Hunde und frische Luft, trinkt gern Bier, kurz gesagt, eine nette Blondine.

Exercise B

Anneliese wants to stay in England for a year. She doesn't like school and doesn't like studying. But her mother wants her to learn English. She would most of all like to live in a city like London or Manchester, and she would like to live with a family with toddlers. She enjoys listening to music and prefers English pop music to German pop music. She isn't a vegetarian but she prefers not to eat meat. She would like to have a single room and really doesn't want to do any housework.

UNIT 8

Exercise A
1 a watch television until 10 p.m. b use the washing machine until
8 p.m. c play the piano until 9 p.m. d make tea, coffee, etc. in the
small kitchen between 8 p.m. and 10 p.m. 2 use the large kitchen
3 to take their rucksacks to their rooms.

Exercise B

Anna	Dürfen wir die Tiere füttern?
Tante Inge	Ihr dürft sicher einige Tiere füttern, aber nicht alle.
Renate	Darf ich ein Eis haben, bitte?
Anna (aufgeregt)	Oh, ich kann einen Elefanten sehen! Kannst du ihn sehen, Renate?
Renate	Darf der Elefant unser Brot essen?
Tante Inge	Wie bitte? Ach, es ist hier so laut! Ich kann dich nicht hören, Renate! Ich frage den Zoowärter. Entschuldigen Sie, können Sie uns sagen, ob wir den Elefanten füttern dürfen?
Zoowärter	Selbstverständlich.
Renate	Tante Inge, darf ich bitte Mutti anrufen und ihr alles erzählen?

UNIT 9

Exercise A
1 Ich kann nicht gut sehen. 2 Ich kann nicht alleine stehen.
3 Ich muss im Bett bleiben. 4 Ich muss diese Tabletten dreimal am
Tag nehmen. 5 Ich darf nicht rauchen. 6 Ich darf keinen Alkohol
trinken. 7 Ich soll nicht so viel Schokolade essen. 8 Ich soll jeden
Tag Krankengymnastik machen. 9 Ich will sofort nach Hause
gehen. 10 Ich will jetzt schlafen.

Exercise B
1 Ich will im Freien arbeiten. I want to work in the open air.
2 Die Arbeit soll interessant sein. The work should be interesting.

3 Ich kann jeden Tag arbeiten. I can work every day.
4 Ich darf nichts Schweres heben. I am not allowed to lift anything
heavy.
5 Ich muss viel Geld verdienen. I must earn a lot of money.

UNIT 10

Exercise A
1 Er fährt immer damit. 2 Ich denke ungern daran. 3 Die Lampe
steht dicht daneben. 4 Der Kellner stellt das Glas Wasser darauf.
5 Meine Tante findet ihr Sparbuch darunter. 6 Die Mülltonne ist
dahinter. 7 Der Gärtner pflanzt Frühlingsblumen dazwischen.
8 Wir essen Pizza danach. 9 Er spricht gar nicht darüber. 10 Es ist
ein Fünfzigeuroschein darin.

Exercise B
1 Ich weiß, dass ich zu dick bin. 2 Ich weiß, dass meine ganze
Kleidung altmodisch ist. 3 Ich weiß, dass ich keine Hobbys habe.
4 Ich weiß, dass ich nichts Vernünftiges mache. 5 Ich weiß, dass du
mich sehr liebst!

UNIT 11

Exercise A
2 Um Viertel vor acht. 3 Um eine Minute nach elf. 4 Um zwölf
Uhr. 5 Um acht Uhr abends (zwanzig Uhr). 6 Um zehn nach elf
abends (dreiundzwanzig Uhr). 7 Um eine Minute nach Mitternacht.
8 Zwischen zwei und drei Uhr. 9 Um halb elf. 10 Von fünfzehn
bis siebzehn Uhr.

Exercise B
1 Hans duscht sich. 2 Ich wiege mich. 3 Lieselchen kämmt sich.
4 Karlchen zieht sich an. 5 Wir ziehen uns um. 6 Sie trocknen sich
ab. 7 Thomas rasiert sich. 8 Oma setzt sich. 9 Dr. Meyer putzt
sich die Zähne. 10 Sie wäscht sich das Haar.

UNIT 12

Exercise A

1 Wo ist meine Tasche? 2 Wie heißt sein Klassenlehrer? 3 Unser Auto hat eine Panne. 4 Ist das ihr Haus? 5 Wo sind unsere Koffer? 6 Seine Schwester heißt Silke. 7 Ihre Betten sind ungemacht. 8 Wohnt Ihr Sohn in Düsseldorf? 9 Hans, wo ist deine Kreditkarte? 10 Eure Rucksäcke stehen draußen vor der Tür.

Exercise B

1 Das Schlafzimmer des Kindes ist klein. 2 Das Auto des Pfarrers ist alt. 3 Die Freundin meines Bruders kommt aus Österreich. 4 Ich nehme immer zwei Tabletten am Anfang eines Migräneanfalls. 5 Das Sprechzimmer unseres Arztes ist immer kalt. 6 Die Nachbarin meiner Eltern ist verreist. 7 Der Direktor dieser Schule ist weltberühmt.

UNIT 13

Exercise A

1 R; 2 F; 3 R; 4 R; 5 R; 6 F; 7 F; 8 R; 9 F; 10 F

Exercise B

1 Schick mal ein Fax! 2 Rauch mal! 3 Bleibt bitte hier! 4 Wartet bitte hier! 5 Trinkt bitte eine Tasse Tee! 6 Beginnen Sie bitte! 7 Setzen Sie sich bitte hin! 8 Schenken Sie bitte noch ein Glas ein!

UNIT 14

Exercise A

1 Darf ich fernsehen? 2 Wann darf ich ein Glas Bier trinken? 3 Darf ich ein Stück Kuchen essen? 4 Darf ich morgen nach Hause gehen? 5 Was darf ich machen?

Exercise B

1 Er schenkt es ihm ein. 2 Er empfiehlt es ihm. 3 Jeden Tag zeigt er sie ihr. 4 Er gibt sie ihr. 5 Es liest sie ihm vor.

UNIT 15

Exercise A

1 In London regnet es. 2 In Madrid gibt es Gewitter. 3 In Oslo schneit es. 4 In Porto ist es bedeckt. 5 In Berlin gibt es Sprühregen. 6 In München ist es neblig. 7 In Wien ist es windig. 8 In Zürich hagelt es. 9 In Rom ist es sehr heiß. 10 In Athen blitzt und donnert es.

Exercise B
Der erste Verdächtige The first suspect

Er ist groß und dünn, und er trägt einen schwarzen Regenmantel, eine kleine Sonnenbrille und einen großen Hut. Er trägt auch eine alte, braune Aktentasche. Sein Haar ist lang und blond. Er sieht jung aus.

Die zweite Verdächtige The second suspect

Sie ist klein und dick. Sie trägt eine rote Bluse, einen grünen Rock, einen blauen Hut und eine große, weiße Handtasche. Ihr Haar ist dunkel und lockig. Sie sieht sehr alt und schmutzig aus.

UNIT 16

Exercise A

1 Ich werde öfter zu Fuß zur Arbeit gehen. I shall walk to work more often.
2 Ich werde nicht so viel Schokolade essen. I shall not eat so much chocolate.
3 Ich werde jeden Tag Gymnastik machen. I'll exercise every day.
4 Wir werden nicht so oft im Restaurant essen. We'll not eat out in a restaurant so often.
5 Ich werde immer früh ins Bett gehen. I shall always go to bed early.
6 Wir werden jeden Sonntag in die Kirche gehen. We'll go to church every Sunday.
7 Wir werden mehr Geld sparen. We'll save more money.

8 Wir werden jeden Samstagmorgen schwimmen. We'll go swimming every Saturday morning.

9 Ich werde fleißiger arbeiten. I shall work harder.

10 Wir werden Tante Gertrud regelmäßig besuchen. We'll visit Aunt Gertrud regularly.

Exercise B

Der Präsident und seine Berater werden um 20 Uhr in Hamburg ankommen und werden direkt zum Hotel Atlantik fahren. Sie werden sich schnell umziehen, und der deutsche Botschafter wird sie in den Speisesaal begleiten. Nach dem Essen wird der Präsident eine Rede über die Dritte Welt halten. Anschließend wird es einen Empfang im Goldenen Saal für alle Angestellten der Botschaft geben. Der Empfang wird um 24 Uhr zu Ende sein, und der Präsident und seine Gattin werden gleich danach zum Hotel zurückfahren. Eine weitere Pressemitteilung wird am Mittwoch erscheinen.

UNIT 17

Exercise A

1 In den sechziger Jahren wohnte ich in Paris, wo ich an einer Universität studierte. 2 Es gab oft Demonstrationen in der Stadtmitte. 3 Wir Studenten sangen Protestlieder, und wir trugen Transparente. 4 An jeder Straßenecke warteten Gruppen von Polizisten. Plötzlich liefen sie uns entgegen. 5 Ich hatte Glück. Ich kam, Gott sei Dank, unversehrt davon.

Exercise B

Dear Mrs Lane,

Many thanks for your letter. So, you wanted to know what it was like in the days of the GDR (German Democratic Republic). You know, it wasn't all bad before the Wall came down. We all had work and could take great holiday trips to the Baltic coast and to the mountains. Tickets for the opera and theatre were very cheap (as were tickets for public transport and books). Naturally we had to wait for years for our beloved Trabis (Trabant cars), but they were worth waiting for. And there were so many good opportunities for our children. We had enough kindergarten places, and there were wonderful opportunities for sport, and libraries for our young people. We got fresh vegetables from our allotment. In the summer we went on long cycle tours and swam in the beautiful lakes. In the evening we used to like to sit together and tell stories. And we weren't at all afraid of walking down dark streets at night. By the way, in those days the bread rolls tasted much better than today.

It is a pity that you did not have the opportunity to experience the GDR for yourself!

Yours sincerely,

Walter Trublich

UNIT 18

Exercise A
1 schreiben; 2 schlafen; 3 bekommen; 4 finden; 5 trinken; 6 an/fangen; 7 fliegen; 8 bleiben; 9 fahren; 10 verstehen.

Exercise B
1 Ilse hat Käsekuchen bestellt. 2 Du hast einen Fehler gemacht. 3 Der Zug ist um 12.15 abgefahren. 4 Wir haben sehr viel Deutsch gelernt. 5 Sie ist sehr müde geworden. 6 Habt ihr ein neues Auto gekauft? 7 Ich habe in Stuttgart ein Glas Wein getrunken. 8 Haben Sie Lotte im Krankenhaus besucht? 9 Hans ist so schnell gewachsen. 10 Sevim ist noch nie in der Schweiz gewesen.

UNIT 19

Exercise A
1 Nein, das Fax wird schon geschickt. 2 Nein, das Fenster wird schon zugemacht. 3 Nein, der Papierkorb wird schon geleert. 4 Nein, die Kaffeetassen werden schon abgewaschen. 5 Nein, die Briefe werden schon unterschrieben.

1 Nein, das Fax ist schon geschickt worden. 2 Nein, das Fenster ist schon zugemacht worden. 3 Nein, der Papierkorb ist schon geleert worden. 4 Nein, die Kaffeetassen sind schon abgewaschen worden. 5 Nein, die Briefe sind schon unterschrieben worden.

1 Das Fax war schon geschickt worden. 2 Das Fenster war schon zugemacht worden. 3 Der Papierkorb war schon geleert worden. 4 Die Kaffeetassen waren schon abgewaschen worden. 5 Die Briefe waren schon unterschrieben worden.

Exercise B
1 Man sagt oft, dass Zigaretten der Gesundheit schaden. 2 Auf Bierfesten trinkt man Bier oft aus Maßkrügen. 3 Zu Weihnachten isst man eine Gans nicht so oft wie früher. 4 Man erwartet zu viel von Kleinkindern. 5 Hier spricht man Deutsch. 6 Man prüft den Reifendruck kostenlos. 7 Man trennt den Müll in fast jeder deutschen Küche. 8 Man schneidet das Brot mit einer Schneidemaschine. 9 Man gibt immer mehr Geld bei den Sommerschlussverkäufen aus. 10 In dieser Schule lernt man nicht sehr viel.

UNIT 20

Exercise A
1 „Ich habe Hunger." 2 „Ich kann nichts mehr machen!" 3 „Haben Sie Tabletten?" 4 „Was läuft im Kino?" 5 „Darf ich deinen Ausweis sehen?"

Exercise B
Text der Studie: Die Deutschen schlafen jetzt weniger als vor zwanzig Jahren. Heutzutage braucht man eine halbe Stunde weniger Schlaf als damals, aber dafür nehmen mindestens 30% aller Erwachsenen Schlafmittel. Stress am Arbeitsplatz ist der Grund dafür.

Exercise A

1 C; 2 E; 3 B; 4 F; 5 G; 6 H; 7 D; 8 A; 9 J; 10 I

1 Wenn ich genug Geld habe, kaufe ich mir ein neues Auto.
If I have enough money I will buy myself a new car.

2 Wenn ich Millionär wäre, würde ich nicht mehr arbeiten.
If I were a millionaire I would no longer work.

3 Wenn ich von seiner Zuckerkrankheit gewusst hätte, hätte ich ihm keine Schokolade gegeben. If I had known he had diabetes I would not have given him chocolate.

4 Wenn wir mehr Platz hätten, würden wir euch alle zu Silvester einladen. If we had more room we would invite you all for New Year.

5 Ich wäre Ihnen sehr dankbar, wenn Sie das nicht weitersagen würden. I would be grateful to you if you did not pass it on.

6 Wenn du willst, besuche ich dich. If you wish I will visit you.

7 Wenn das Wetter morgen schön ist, können wir in den Bergen wandern. If the weather is good tomorrow we can walk in the mountains.

8 Wenn ich sie sehe, werde ich alles erklären. If I see her (them) I shall explain everything.

9 Wenn es weiter regnet, können wir nicht mehr im Garten arbeiten. If it continues to rain we cannot work in the garden any more.

10 Wenn ich Direktor dieser Schule wäre, würde ich die Samstagsschule abschaffen. If I were head of this school I would abolish Saturday school.

Exercise B

1 An deiner Stelle würde ich ein neues Hobby finden. 2 An deiner Stelle würde ich früher ins Bett gehen. 3 An deiner Stelle würde ich Diät machen. 4 An deiner Stelle würde ich nicht so viel Geld ausgeben. 5 An deiner Stelle würde ich nicht rauchen. 6 An deiner Stelle würde ich fleißiger arbeiten. 7 An deiner Stelle würde ich viel mehr lesen. 8 An deiner Stelle würde ich den Rasen öfter mähen.

9 An deiner Stelle würde ich eine Ferienreise buchen. 10 An deiner Stelle würde ich weniger Alkohol trinken.

Exercise C
Old Recipe for Happiness

Take: 12 months, clean them completely of bitterness, miserliness, pedantry and anxiety, and divide each month into 30 or 31 parts so that the supply lasts for exactly one year. Every day a portion of (the following) is served: 1 part work, 2 parts cheerfulness and humour. Add 3 heaped dessertspoonfuls of optimism, 1 teaspoon of tolerance, a grain of irony and a pinch of tact. Then love is poured very liberally over the mixture. Decorate the finished dish with bunches of attention and serve daily with merriment and with a good refreshing cup of tea ...

Glossary of terms

(items in **bold italics** have a separate entry in the glossary)

accusative is one of four *cases* in German. See also *nominative*, *dative* and *genitive*.

active voice – see voice

adjectival noun is a *noun* which changes its form like an *adjective*. See Reference grammar 5.2.

adjective is a word which gives us more information as to what a *noun* or *pronoun* is like. See Functional grammar Unit 15 and Reference grammar 5.1.

adverb is a word or group of unit words which tells us more about a *verb*, *adjective*, or another *adverb*. It often tells us how something is done and answers the questions how? when? where? why?: langsam (*slowly*), leicht (*easily*), sehr (*very*). In German there is no clear adverbial ending such as -ly in English.

agreement is when adjectives change their ending to reflect the nature of the noun or pronoun they describe.

article – see gender

auxiliary verb is a 'helping verb' which is used with another verb to form different *tenses* or the passive *voice*, e.g. haben, sein, werden.

cardinal number is a number used to show quantity, or when counting, e.g. fünf Tassen Tee (*five cups of tea*), eins, zwei, drei, vier (*one, two, three, four*). See also *ordinal numbers*.

case is when the form of the *definite* or *indefinite article* or other *determiner* changes according to context in a *sentence*. These changes are due to the fact that a so-called case system is still in use in German. It comprises four cases: *nominative*, *accusative*, *dative* and *genitive*. See Reference grammar 6.

clause is a group of words which contains a *subject* and a *verb*. A major or main clause can also form a sentence in its own right: Ich lachte laut (*I laughed loudly*). A minor or subordinate clause normally starts with a *subordinating conjunction*, e.g. weil (*because*), als (*when*), and cannot stand complete in its own right: als ich ihn sah (*when I saw him*). These two clauses can be combined to form a complex sentence: Ich lachte laut, als ich ihn sah (*I laughed loudly when I saw him*). A *coordinating conjunction*, e.g. und (*and*) and aber (*but*), can join two equal clauses: Ich sah ihn, und ich lachte laut (*I saw him and I laughed loudly*), Ich sah ihn, aber ich sprach nicht mit ihm (*I saw him, but I didn't speak to him*).

colloquial is a style of language suitable for familiar speech, but not for formal writing.

comparative is the form of the *adjective* or *adverb* which compares one thing or person with another, e.g. Er ist größer als ich (*he is taller than I am*). See Reference grammar 5.3. See also superlative.

complement is the part of a sentence you normally find after the verb, which is necessary to make a complete sentence.

compound noun is a word which is made up of two or more words, each of which could stand on its own. See Reference grammar 2.2.

compound tense is *a tense* which is formed using two verbal forms, e.g. ich habe geschlafen (*I have slept*) – see *perfect*, *pluperfect*, *future* and *future perfect*.

conditional is a *clause* normally starting with wenn (*if*). See Functional grammar Unit 21.

conjugation is the word used to describe the changes in a verb to denote a different *person*, *number* or *tense*.

conjunction is a word or group of words (apart from *relative pronouns*) used to join together two words, *phrases* or *clauses*, e.g. und (*and*), aber (*but*). If the conjunction joins two clauses which are of equal importance it is called a coordinating conjunction: und (*and*), aber (*but*), denn (for), oder (*or*), sondern (*but*, after a negative). These do not alter the word order in any way.

If a conjunction joins a major or main clause (which can stand alone and make sense) to a minor or subordinate clause, it is called a subordinating conjunction. In German the subordinating conjunction is preceded by a comma if it appears mid-sentence, and it sends the verb to the end of the clause: weil (*because*), so dass (*so that*), während (*while*), wenn (*if, whenever*), e.g. Ich komme heute nicht, weil es so stark regnet (*I'll not come today because it is raining so heavily*).

declension describes the way the *determiner* changes to show case: der Vater, den Vater, dem Vater, des Vaters.

definite article is the *determiner* der, die, das (*the*) which stands before the noun in the noun phrase, e.g. der Ingenieur (*the engineer*), die Kirche (*the church*), das Dorf (*the village*).

demonstratives are *adjectives* or *pronouns* which point something out: dieser (*this*), jener (*that*), diese (*these*), jene (*those*).

determiner is the name given to the word which precedes the *noun*, for example the *definite article* (der, etc.), the *indefinite article* (ein, etc.), the negative *indefinite article* (kein, etc.), *possessive adjectives* (mein, etc.), *demonstratives* (dieser, jener, etc.), and some numbers (zwei, etc.).

direct object refers to the person or thing which is directly affected by the action of the *verb*: der Mann erkennt *den Dieb* (*the man recognizes the thief*). See Functional grammar Unit 3. (Be careful! The direct object normally appears after the verb in English, but this is not always true in German.) See also *accusative case* and *indirect object*.

direct speech is the exact recording of words which someone has said or written. This is either preceded or followed by a reporting formula such as 'she said', 'he asked' and is enclosed in speech marks. In German the speech marks at the beginning of the quotation are often on the base writing line: „Hast du meine Uhr gesehen?" fragte er ('Have you seen my watch?', he asked).

feminine – see gender

finite verb is any part of the verb apart from the *infinitive* and *present* and *past participles*, i.e. it is the parts of the verb which change according to *person*, *number* and *tense*. The finite verb is usually preceded by a *subject noun* or *pronoun*: der Mann liest (*the man is reading*), wir kaufen (*we are buying*).

future perfect is a compound tense made up of the appropriate part of the present tense of the auxiliary verb werden plus a past participle plus the *infinitive* of either haben (*to have*) or sein (*to be*): Sie werden es schon gekauft haben (*they will already have bought it*).

future tense is the way of expressing something that is yet to happen, e.g. Die Hochzeit wird nächsten Juni stattfinden (*the wedding will take place next June*).

gender All German nouns are grouped according to whether they are *masculine* (der), *feminine* (die) or *neuter* (das). See Functional grammar Unit 1.

idiomatic is a particular usage of language which cannot necessarily be explained by grammar rules or translated directly into a foreign language, e.g. jemand auf den Arm nehmen (to pull someone's leg).

imperative is the *mood* of the *verb* used to give an order or command. See Functional grammar Unit 13. See also *indicative mood* and *subjunctive mood*.

imperfect tense – see preterite

impersonal verb is a *verb* which is normally used only in the es form: Wie geht es dir? (*how are you?*), es regnet (*it's raining*), es gefällt mir hier (*I like it here*).

indefinite article is the *determiner* ein (masculine), eine (feminine), ein (neuter) (*a, an*) which precedes a *noun*, e.g. ein Berg (*a mountain*), eine Stadt (*a town*), and ein Haus (*a house*).

indefinite pronoun 'man' is used irrespective of gender. It is translated into English as '*one*', '*you*', '*they*' or '*people*'. See Functional grammar Units 8 and 19.

indicative mood is the normal form of the *verb* used to make statements or ask questions. See also *subjunctive* and *imperative* moods.

indirect object is the recipient or beneficiary of the activity of the verb and the *direct object*. See Functional grammar Units 4 and 14.

indirect speech (also known as reported speech) is the reported account by a third party of what has been said or asked, recording the gist of what was meant rather than the exact words. Because there is some uncertainty as to the accuracy of indirect speech, the *subjunctive mood* is used to record it. Speech marks are obviously not needed for indirect speech. Er sagte, er sei krank (*he said he was ill*).

infinitive is the form of the *verb* you always find in the dictionary: schlafen (*to sleep*), sparen (*to save*). In German this form usually ends in -en, e.g. schlafen, sparen; or sometimes in -n, e.g. wandern (*to hike*), wechseln (*to change*).

inflection describes the changes of form which take place in *nouns*, *adjectives*, *determiners* and *verbs* to show number, *person*, *case*, *tense*, *mood* or *voice*.

inseparable verb is a verb preceded by a *prefix* which always remains in front of the verb: der Arzt verschrieb mir Schlaftabletten (*the doctor prescribed me sleeping pills*). See also *separable verbs*.

interrogative forms are used to ask a question or to seek information: wer? (*who?*), wen? (*who(m)?*), wessen? (*whose?*), welcher? (*which?*), was? (*what?*). Welcher? can also be an interrogative adjective. Wo? (*where?*), wohin? (*where to?*), woher? (*where from?*) are interrogative *adverbs*.

intransitive verb – see transitive verb

irregular verb is a *verb* whose forms cannot be predicted, and must therefore be checked in the verb lists and then learned. These verbs usually undergo a vowel change. See Reference grammar 10.7.

masculine noun – see gender

modal particle a modal particle is an uninflected word, usually an *adverb*, which is common in speech. It is not translated directly and does not change the overall meaning of the *sentence*, but it can show emphasis or reflect the attitude or mood of the speaker. Examples are: aber (*but, however* – literally 'but'), denn (*because, as*), doch (*but*), mal (just, e.g. Komm mal her! *Just come here!*), schon (*already, yet*).

modal verb is a *verb* which can be used in conjunction with another verb to reflect the mood of the speaker, i.e. to express a wish, sense of obligation, volition, liking, ability or possibility, etc. See Functional grammar Units 7, 8 and 9.

mood is used to express a factual meaning (see *indicative* mood), a non-factual meaning (see *subjunctive* mood) or a command (see *imperative* mood).

negative is the means of expressing the idea of 'not a', 'no' or 'nothing' (kein, nicht or nichts), e.g. Das ist keine Ausrede (*that's no excuse*), Das ist nicht richtig (*that's not right*).

neuter noun – see gender

noun is a word used for naming a person: der Mensch (*the person*); place: die Stadt (*the town*); thing: der Tisch (*the table*); or abstract idea: die Freiheit (*freedom*). See Functional grammar Unit 1.

noun phrase is a group of words which is equivalent to a noun, e.g. der junge Arzt (*the young doctor*), ein regnerischer Tag (*a rainy day*).

number shows whether a *noun, pronoun* or *verb* is singular (referring to only one) or plural (more than one). Some nouns which are *plural* in English are singular in German: die Schere (*scissors*), die Brille (*glasses*), die Hose (*trousers*).

object – see either *direct object* or *indirect object*

ordinal number is a number which shows a certain position within a sequence of numbers: *first, second, third*, etc. In German these inflect like ordinary adjectives, e.g. der dritte Versuch (*the third attempt*), am ersten Januar (*on the first of January*).

passive – see voice

past participle is the form of the verb which, together with an *auxiliary verb*, haben or sein, forms the *compound tenses* of the *perfect* and *pluperfect* or the *passive* voice. See Functional grammar Unit 18. It can also be used as an *adjective* with the appropriate adjectival ending: der gemähte Rasen (*the mown lawn*).

perfect tense is a *compound tense* made up of the *present* tense of either haben (*to have*) or sein (*to be*) plus a *past participle* at the end of the *clause* or *sentence*. See Functional grammar Unit 18.

person enables us to distinguish between the speaker (the first person), the person(s) being addressed (the second person) and someone or something else (the third person).

	Singular	Plural
1st person:	ich (I)	wir (we)
2nd person:	du (you, familiar)	ihr (you, familiar)
	Sie (you, polite)	Sie (you, polite)
3rd person:	er, sie, es (he, she, it)	sie (they)

personal pronouns – see pronouns

phrase is a group of words which does not contain a *finite verb* and is therefore not complete on its own, e.g. mein neuer Chef (*my new boss*).

pluperfect tense is a *compound tense* made of the simple past tense of either haben (*to have*) or sein (*to be*), plus a *past participle* at the end of the **sentence** or **clause**: See Functional grammar Unit 17.

plural – see number

possessive forms show ownership or possession.
See Functional grammar Unit 12.

prefix – see verbal prefix

preposition is a word (or words) showing the relationship in time or space between one thing or person and another. It often shows the position that a *noun* or *pronoun* is in. See Reference grammar 6.

present participle is the present form of the verb which in English ends in *-ing*: weinend (*crying*), schlafend (*sleeping*), sprechend (*talking*).

It is used less frequently in German than in English, but can be used as an adjective with the appropriate adjectival ending, e.g. das schlafende Kind (*the sleeping child*).

present tense – see tenses

preterite, also known as the *imperfect* or *simple past tense*. See Functional grammar Unit 17.

pronoun is a short word which stands instead of a *noun* or *noun phrase*. It is used to avoid repeating the noun, for example er replacing der Mann in Er kaufte ein Buch (*he bought a book*), sie instead of die Kinder in Sie spielten im Garten (*they played in the garden*). There are five main groups of pronoun:

1 *Personal pronouns:* ich (*I*), mich or mir (*me*), du, dich or dir (*you*), er (*he*), ihn, ihm (*him*), etc.
2 *Reflexive pronouns:* mich or mir (*myself*), dich or dir (*yourself*), sich (*himself*), (*herself*), etc.
3 *Possessive pronouns:* meiner, meine, meins (*mine*), etc.
4 *Relative pronouns:* der, die, das (*which, who, that*).
5 *Demonstrative pronouns:* dieser, jener (*this, that*).

pronoun of address is a *personal pronoun* used to address someone. Du (you) is used to address a person with whom one is on familiar terms, ihr for more than one. Sie is a polite form used to address one or more persons known less well.

question – see interrogative

reflexive verbs express an action which is both carried out and received by the subject, e.g. Ich wasche mich (*I wash myself*). See Functional grammar Unit 11.

relative clause normally starts with a *relative pronoun* der, die, das (*who, which, that*), e.g. Der Mann, der dieses Buch schrieb, ist Anthropologe (the man who wrote this book is an anthropologist). See Functional grammar Unit 5.

reported speech – see indirect speech

regular verbs have forms which follow a pattern and can be predicted by rules.

sentence is a group of words which makes full grammatical sense and contains at least a *subject* and a *finite verb*. In the written language it ends with either a full stop, exclamation mark or question mark.

separable verbs have an *infinitive* which begins with a *prefix*. This prefix moves to the end of the clause when the *verb* is used as a *finite verb*, e.g. an/kommen (*to arrive*): Der Zug kommt pünktlich an (*the train is arriving on time*). See Reference grammar 9.3.

simple past – see preterite

singular – see number

stem is the part of the *regular verb* to which endings are added to indicate change of person or tense. See Functional grammar Unit 5.

subject is the *noun* or *pronoun* which carries out or initiates the action of the *verb*, e.g. Der Arzt untersuchte meinen Onkel gestern (the doctor examined my uncle yesterday). To check whether someone or something is the *subject* of a *clause* or *sentence*, ask the question 'Who or what is doing the verb?' The answer (here: the doctor) is the subject and requires the *nominative* case. (Be careful! In English the subject normally appears immediately before the verb, but this does not always happen in German.)

subjunctive is the *mood* of the *verb* used when the content of the sentence is doubted or unlikely, as in indirect speech or when expressing unreal or hypothetical conditions, and often after the word wenn (*if*) in *conditional clauses*. See Reference grammar 11. See also *indicative* and *imperative moods*.

subordinating conjunction – see conjunctions

suffix is a part of a word which never occurs on its own, and is used to form new words. It is found at the end of the word, e.g. schön + heit → Schönheit (*beautiful* → *beauty*), Milch + ig → milchig (*milk* → *milky*).

superlative is the form of an *adjective* or *adverb* which denotes the very highest or lowest level of quality, for example 'the biggest and best'. See Reference grammar 5.3. See also *comparative*.

Syntax means the formal study of the grammatical arrangement of words or patterns of words in a phrase, clause or sentence. It comes from two Greek words, the first meaning together and the second meaning arrangement.

tag question is a short phrase such as nicht wahr?, gell?, nicht? or oder? (*isn't it?*, *aren't you?*, *don't we?*, etc.) which, added to a statement, changes it into a question.

tenses of the *finite verb* show you the time at which the action of the *verb* takes place. See Reference grammar 10.

transitive verb is a *verb* which needs a *direct object* to complete its meaning, e.g. Er kauft einen Hund (he is buying a dog). An *intransitive verb* needs only a subject to make sense, e.g. Der Lehrer kommt (*the teacher is coming*). (Be careful! Some verbs can be either *intransitive* or *transitive*, e.g. Ich fahre lieber (*I would prefer to drive*) and Ich fahre jetzt einen Mercedes (*I drive a Mercedes now*).)

umlaut is the name for the symbol (¨) which can be placed above the vowels a, o or u. The addition of the umlaut alters the pronunciation of the vowel, e.g. Vater → pl. Väter (*father(s)*), Bruder → pl. Brüder (*brother(s)*).

verbal prefix is a short element which can be attached to the infinitive, e.g. *be*suchen (*to visit*). See Reference grammar 9.3.

verb is a word or group of words which tells you what a person or thing (i.e. the subject of the sentence) is doing or being. Without a verb a *sentence* is incomplete. A verb can be used in various *tenses* e.g. I read, I was reading, I have read, I had read, I shall read, I shall have read.

Verb phrase is a verb plus its complement, which could be a direct object (e.g. 'reads a book'), a prepositional phrase (e.g. 'goes into the garden') or an adverbial phrase (e.g. 'comes next Saturday').

voice is a way of using a verb actively or passively. Both forms have the same meaning but a different emphasis. See Reference grammar 13. The passive voice is used much less frequently than the active voice.

vowels In addition to the five vowel signs a, e, i, o, u, German also has ä, ö, and ü. Occasionally y is used as a vowel, as in der Zylinder (*top hat*), das Asyl (*asylum*).

weak nouns a group of unusual **masculine nouns** to which -n or -en is added in every case apart from the **nominative singular**. See Reference grammar 2.4.

Taking it even further

A WORD OF ENCOURAGEMENT

Now that you have reached this stage, you will realize that a
detailed understanding of grammar gives you confidence in
handling the language. You will also realize that it is a long
process! But rest assured: even advanced students of the German
language still need to consult a grammar book from time to time.
The more you use it, the more confident you become. Remember
that even native speakers do not always use entirely correct
grammar but they are, nonetheless, understood perfectly.

A FEW HINTS

The most effective way to learn is little and often. Try to learn one
irregular verb in all its tenses every day for five days each week.
Write the verb down several times, chant it, ask someone else to
test you. Before long, you will find that you are developing a feel
for patterns of verb formation. Then the appropriate tense of the
verb will automatically come to mind whenever you want to use
it. If you find a particular point of grammar hard to master, write
it on a postcard and keep reading through it whenever you have a
spare moment.

Aim to spend fifteen minutes a day systematically learning a specific
point of grammar. Once you have learned it, try to use it yourself
as soon as possible, in speech or in an e-mail or letter. A German
penfriend is a great encouragement, even for adult learners.

Glance through the advertisements and short articles in a local
newspaper or magazine such as *Brigitte* or *Focus* and, using a
highlighter pen, mark all the examples you can find of the grammar
you have just learned. Once you have mastered the subjunctive,
look up the report of a speech in the Bundestag (Lower House

of Parliament) in the political pages of a German newspaper and highlight all the subjunctive forms. Then try to work out what the speaker would have said in the original speech, using the indicative form of each marked verb. A highlighter pen is a very good friend to the language learner, providing you are working from your own copy of the book or newspaper!

At the same time as firming up your grammar foundations, you will also want to extend your vocabulary. You can achieve this by reading widely, visiting websites, visiting a German-speaking country and watching German channels on satellite television. Vocabulary is best learned in context, rather than from long vocabulary lists. Each time you come across a new word, look it up in as big a dictionary as you can afford. Write it down immediately in a small vocabulary book. You should also write down the English meaning plus the gender and plural for nouns.

Aim to spend a quarter of an hour each day learning the new vocabulary you have come across. Take your book around with you and learn some vocabulary on the bus, or in the doctor's waiting room.

Be creative in the ways you learn. If you use different techniques you will keep it up for longer. Try recording the material you want to learn and listen to it in the car or in bed. Write out specific rules and stick them around your office or home. That should encourage your colleagues or family to test you and so make the whole process more fun. When you reach this point, you won't want to stop. Language learning is, after all, about communicating. *Viel Spaß!* Have fun!

Jenny Russ

Some useful websites

Some local newspapers (these often have shorter, simpler articles)
- *Kieler Nachrichten*   www.kn-online.de
- *Mittelbayerische Zeitung*   www.mittelbayerische.de
- *Rhein Neckar Zeitung*   www.rnz.de
- *Schwäbisches Tagblatt*   www.tagblatt.de

National newspapers
- *Die Welt*   www.welt.de
- *Frankfurter Allgemeine Zeitung*   www.faz.net
- *Süddeutsche Zeitung*   www.sueddeutschezeitung.de
- *Die Tageszeitung*   www.taz.de
- *Frankfurter Rundschau*   www.frankfurter-rundschau.de
- *Das Bild*   www.bild.de
- *Die Zeit*   www.diezeit.de
- *Neue Zürcher Zeitung (Switzerland)*   www.nzz.ch
- *Der Standard (Austria)*   www.derstandard.at
- *Die Presse (Austria)*   www.diepresse.com

Magazines
- *Focus*   www.focus.de
- *Der Spiegel*   www.spiegel.de
- *Brigitte*   www.brigitte.de
- *Stern*   www.stern.de
- *Profil (Austria)*   www.profil.at

TV channels
Why not watch a German games show, a soap or a short news bulletin? Try one of the following TV channels:

- *ZDF*   www.zdf.de
- *SAT.1*   www.sat1.de
- *3SAT*   www.3sat.de
- *ARD*   www.ARD.de
- *ProSieben*   www.proSieben.de
- *RTL*   www.rtl.de

Other useful resources

Goethe-Institut	www.goethe.de
Goethe-Institut London	www.goethe.de/gr/lon/enindex.htm
Deutschland im Internet	www.goethe.de/r/dservlis.htm
Tourism, etc.	www.deutschland.de
Institut für Deutsche Sprache	www.ids-mannheim.de
Duden	www.duden.de
Gesellschaft für deutsche Sprache	www.gfds.de
Langenscheidt	www.langenscheidt.de

AND FINALLY ...

If you would like to contact me, I'd be delighted to read your e-mail on tygg@gmx.net

Credits

Front cover: © Oxford Illustrators

Back cover and pack: © Jakub Semeniuk/iStockphoto.com, © Royalty-Free/Corbis, © agencyby/iStockphoto.com, © Andy Cook/iStockphoto.com, © Christopher Ewing/iStockphoto.com, © zebicho – Fotolia.com, © Geoffrey Holman/iStockphoto.com, © Photodisc/Getty Images, © James C. Pruitt/iStockphoto.com, © Mohamed Saber – Fotolia.com

Pack: © Stockbyte/Getty Images